DECISION SUPPORT SYSTEMS:
AN ORGANIZATIONAL PERSPECTIVE

ADDISON-WESLEY SERIES ON DECISION SUPPORT

Consulting Editors
Peter G. W. Keen
Charles B. Stabell

Decision Support Systems: An Organizational Perspective
Peter G. W. Keen and Michael S. Scott Morton

Electronic Meetings: Technical Alternatives and Social Choices
Robert Johansen, Jacques Valee, and Kathleen Spangler

DECISION SUPPORT SYSTEMS:

AN ORGANIZATIONAL PERSPECTIVE

Peter G. W. Keen
Graduate School of Business
Stanford University

Michael S. Scott Morton
Alfred P. Sloan School of Management
Massachusetts Institute of Technology

ADDISON-WESLEY PUBLISHING COMPANY
Reading, Massachusetts • Menlo Park, California
London • Amsterdam • Don Mills, Ontario • Sydney

ISBN 0-201-03667-3
ABCDEFGHIJK-MA-798

FOR ALICE AND MARY

SERIES FOREWORD

The Addison-Wesley series on Decision Support focuses on managers' decisionmaking activities and the use of computer-based technology to support them in complex and unstructured tasks. It explores systematic approaches to improving the effectiveness of decison processes. These approaches often imply the use of Decision Support Systems (DSS), computer systems designed to mesh with managers' existing activities and needs while extending their capabilities. This first book in the series discusses the concept of DSS—their design, implementation, and evaluation. However, its central concern and the overall theme of the series is the end to be achieved—Decision Support—which may require the exploitation of *many* technologies.

It has been recognized for some time that systems to assist managers in relatively complex and nonprogrammable activities are different from the structured decision systems that have been developed for the more operational tasks in the organization. There has been relatively little exploration of the implications of these differences. Most of the literature in the Management Information Systems field is technical and prescriptive. Decision Support requires a behavioral and descriptive grounding. A major aim in the series is, therefore, to provide a rich set of perspectives and methodologies for studying decisionmaking. The emphasis is on meshing description—how are decisions made?—and prescription—where can computer technology be applied to improve how they are made?

The concept of Decision Support has evolved from two main areas of research: the theoretical studies of organizational decisionmaking done at the Carnegie Institute of Technology during the late 1950s and early '60s and the technical work on interactive computer systems, mainly carried out at the Massachusetts Institute of Technology in the 1960s. The Carnegie school provided some key concepts for what H. A. Simon termed a "new science of management decision." It emphasized "bounded" rationality in the individual's decision processes, with the implication that extending the limits on the bounds could improve effectiveness.

Simon's distinction between "programmable" and "nonprogrammable" tasks is central to the argument that Decision Support provides a strategy for making the computer useful to managers, whose decision tasks are relatively nonstructured. Newell, Simon, and Shaw's early work on simulating human problem solving both presented a concept of heuristic analysis and helped establish an emphasis on the study of cognitive processes that has become the most well-established "behavioral" perspective in MIS and Management Science.

One interesting aspect of the work of Simon, Cyert, March, and their colleagues at Carnegie is that while it indicates a major role for computers as a tool for individual decisionmaking and for organizational communication and information processing, the technology it implies did not exist until much later, in the 1960s, when prototype interactive systems were developed that pointed toward the (admittedly far distant) man-machine symbiosis idealized by Licklider. Much of this work was purely technical; M.I.T.'s project MAC, for example, aimed at providing a powerful general-purpose time-shared system that could be applied in a variety of contexts and that would permit "machine-aided cognition," "multi-access computing," or "man-and-computer." In 1978, many of the interactive tools initiated by MAC are becoming commonplace. It is worth stressing, however, that most of these techniques were developed well before 1970 and that they were mainly the outcome of academic and technical research projects. Decision Support, as a concept of how computers could be used in complex decisionmaking, initially developed from a synthesis of the Carnegie and M.I.T. traditions. Scott Morton's *Management Decision Systems* (1971) is the first explicit meshing of the two streams. Although his book presented a major technical innovation in organizational use of computers, it differed strongly from ongoing work in computer science in its dominant focus on the issues raised by the Carnegie group: the dynamics of decisionmaking and the organizational implications of changes in information-processing technology.

Scott Morton's book provided a toehold for a behavioral perspective in what has always been a passionately technical field. Between 1971 and 1976, there grew up a fairly substantial body of work on Decision Support Systems, a term that some observers equated with interactive computer systems. Gerrity and Ness provided much of the momentum for the technical activity in this field, but at the same time a number of researchers focused on the behavioral issues their work raised. Although the specific theoretical models they used often differed from the Carnegie perspective, they shared its focus on the context of technical design: bounded rationality, unstructured tasks, organizational information processing, and the cognitive characteristics of decisionmakers.

Five years ago, this series would have been entitled *Interactive* Computer Systems and three years ago, Decision Support *Systems.* Its actual title reflects a maturation in computer technology; interactive systems are no longer new and do not need explicit justification and description. At the same time, the title points out that the issues raised by the Carnegie school remain critical ones. Regardless of the technology available at any one point in time, there is a need for a concept of decisionmaking that can define the criteria for exploiting it and for a detailed study of decisionmaking from a variety of perspectives, especially cognitive and organizational ones. In 1978, the time is ripe. There is now an established tradition of work on Decision Support Systems and widespread application of them in organizations. Now that the systems exist, we can address the main issue of Decision Support and begin to pull together the various practical, theoretical, behavioral and technical insights gained so far. We can be more confident in our claims that a clear understanding of decisionmaking can provide a framework for assessing and using *any* new technology. In short, we can claim that Decision Support is a distinctive concept and methodology for developing computer-based decision aids.

This series is intended as a practical, theoretical, behavioral, and technical forum. Keen and Scott Morton provide an overview of Decision Support. Subsequent books in the series will address some of the issues they discuss and raise new ones. In all cases they address two common themes: improving the decision process, and computer technology as a motivating force and reference point. Any single perspective on decisionmaking or on computer technology is inadequate.

A single perspective on Decision Support must similarly be incomplete. This series is an exploration of a complex and important topic. We feel that its meshing of the descriptive and prescriptive, and the technical and behavioral can substantially help researchers, managers, and students understand and make use of computer technology and indeed help build a real science of management decision.

May 1978

Peter G. W. Keen
Charles B. Stabell

ACKNOWLEDGMENTS

This book has evolved out of the efforts of many people, especially at the Sloan School of Management at the Massachusetts Institute of Technology, where much of the work that shaped our ideas began. In particular, Tom Gerrity developed a prototype computer system that established a methodology for Decision Support System design and then built a company, Index Systems, that helped move DSS from an academic concept to a practical and widespread tool. David Ness, now at Wharton, Larry Meador, Eric Carlsen and his colleagues at the IBM Research Laboratory in San Jose, California, and John Donovan and Stuart Madnick similarly developed a range of computer systems that were major technical innovations while at the same time addressing the needs of decisionmakers. Charles Stabell, Michael Ginzberg, and Steven Alter carried out many field studies and built, through their doctoral dissertations, a detailed and broad conceptual base for DSS. All these individuals are friends and colleagues. In this book we are as much spokesmen for them as authors, and we acknowledge their direct and individual help with gratitude, and hope that we have not stolen too many of their ideas.

M.I.T. and Stanford University have given us much appreciated time and resources to work on this book. We are also grateful to many organizations, especially the First National Banks of Chicago and Boston, who supported student research on DSS. Their willingness to sponsor joint exploration of a new and risky field provided an invaluable meshing of the "real world" and the academic. Without this, both this book and the whole DSS field would be narrower and less developed.

Jim McKenney of Harvard University was the chairman of both our dissertation committees. Although he has played no direct role in the writing of this book, he has been and will always be a strong influence on us. He encouraged us to explore new and often wild ideas and has been a good friend and a generous mentor.

When we were able at last to say, "we've finished The Book," all we really meant was that we had a four-pound manuscript. Turning this into a physically elegant, edited, and indexed product required far more effort than mere writing, and we had many helpers. Bennett Wiseman typed the initial version, Sarah Fitzgerald produced the final preliminary draft (tentative), soothed egos, and acted as a communication link between Cambridge and Stanford. Jointly and individually we owe her many thanks for her help, initiative, and coordination over the last few years, not just in relation to this book. Suzanne Harris provided expert assistance in correcting galleys, and Ken Burke coordinated the production of the book and should take credit for its technical design. Throughout the process, Charles Stabell has worried with us and provided valuable criticism.

Without the support of our families, this book would be even more delayed, our neuroses more acute, and the product less satisfying.

May 1978

Peter G. W. Keen
Michael S. Scott Morton

CONTENTS

DECISION SUPPORT SYSTEMS: SOME PRELIMINARY DEFINITIONS

ONE

INTRODUCTION

Decision Support Systems (DSS) represent a point of view on the role of the computer in the management decisionmaking process. Decision support implies the use of computers to:

1. Assist managers in their decision processes in semistructured tasks.

2. Support, rather than replace, managerial judgment.

3. Improve the effectiveness of decisionmaking rather than its efficiency.

These aims have been made increasingly practicable by rapid changes in computer technology that now permit low-cost access to models, systems, and data bases through the use of "interactive" terminals. As these facilities become cheaper, more flexible, and more powerful, they open up new opportunities for managers to draw on computer support in making key decisions.

There have been many efforts to exploit this new technology. However, it is apparent from the successes and failures of these attempts that very different design and implementation strategies are needed to support decisionmaking than to develop data processing systems. This book is concerned with addressing these differences and presenting a comprehensive overview of DSS, from both the perspective of the system user and the system builder. A main argument of the DSS approach is that effective design depends on the technician's detailed understanding of management decision processes and the manager's clear recognition of the criteria for developing useful computer-based decision aids.

The concept of DSS overlaps with other commentators' views on Management Information Systems (MIS) and on the broad field of Operations Research/ Management Science (OR/MS). This relationship is discussed in the next three chapters. At this point we merely assert that the DSS approach merits a distinctive label and that it differs from MIS and OR/MS in terms of its area of impact on and payoff to the organization and its relevance for managers.

1. *Management Information Systems:*

   a. The main impact has been on *structured* tasks where standard operating procedures, decision rules, and information flows can be reliably predefined.

1

b.   The main payoff has been in improving *efficiency* by reducing costs, turnaround time, and so on, and by *replacing* clerical personnel.

c.   The relevance for managers' decisionmaking has mainly been indirect, for example, by providing reports and access to data.

2.   *Operations Research/Management Science:*

a.   The impact has mostly been on *structured* problems (rather than tasks) where the objective, data, and constraints can be prespecified.

b.   The payoff has been in generating better *solutions* for given types of problems.

c.   The relevance for managers has been the provision of detailed *recommendations* and new methodologies for handling complex problems.

3.   *Decision Support Systems* (these are claims as much as accomplishments):

a.   The impact is on *decisions* in which there is sufficient structure for computer and analytic aids to be of value but where managers' judgment is essential.

b.   The payoff is in extending the range and capability of managers' decision processes to help them improve their *effectiveness*.

c.   The relevance for managers is the creation of a *supportive tool,* under *their own control,* which does not attempt to automate the decision process, predefine objectives, or impose solutions.

To a large extent, DSS represent a natural evolution in computer applications. Within the past 5 years the use of computers in organizations has reached a degree of maturation. Before that, technical problems were dominant and qualified system builders—and systems users—were hard to find. The triumphs of the 1960s were no more or less striking than the fiascos. Even in 1970, companies still experienced problems in using computers in routine operations such as accounts receivable. In the second half of the 1970s many problems still remain, but we clearly have more understanding of the nature and limits of technology. Qualified technical personnel are far more available and managers have, if they wish to obtain it, better access to information about computer applications.

Electronic data processing (EDP) in the 1960s was thus faced with a mass of opportunities and problems. It concentrated on getting under control the class of applications that was most prominent and that provided immediate payoff. These were the large-scale, "paper-pushing" operations of payroll, invoicing, inventory, record keeping, etc. Automation of these was relatively easy to cost justify. Thus the focus in the EDP field was on replacement, routinization, and, above all, on data. This did not lead to an emphasis on management decisionmaking.[1] The early

---

[1]This emphasis on automating data flows and procedures generated several counterattacks based on the argument that the lack of attention to managerial rather than

efforts to provide true management information systems, for corporate planning or for strategic intelligence, floundered quickly; the available software was insufficient and there was no clear understanding among technicians of the use of information by decisionmakers. Managers tended to "need" information that was not available and that often could not even be collected. Their jobs involved more exceptions than rules and resisted systematization.

The most obvious feature of computer technology during the last half of the 1960s was the drift toward centralization and size.[2] The third-generation machines, led by the IBM/360 series, almost all emphasized economies of scale: more core storage, higher-level languages, operating systems, mass storage devices, and so on. During this period the utopian dream (in retrospect, perhaps demonic would be the better term) of the total integrated data base emerged.[3] For example, some organizations aimed at storing *all* the company's data in a huge set of files that could be accessed through the computer. This "data-centered" approach, carried to such an extreme, was neither useful nor feasible. Other organizations moved more slowly and with a clearer focus on what was possible and desirable. They evolved a set of specific data bases which became basic components of the company's information resources, and on which a range of MIS and DSS can draw.

These developments reinforced the tendency for the computer to be used for processing data rather than for decisionmaking. Of course, "better" data could be expected to improve the quality of decisions; that is the assumption behind the phrase management information system. However, data processing in general had little impact on the decisionmaking *process* of managers. It did not map into their problem-solving activities and frequently the rigidly structured corporate MIS, built around the financial accounting system, was inflexible and unresponsive to their needs.

The development of time-sharing in the late 1960s began a parallel movement that is still accelerating—toward personalized systems, direct access to and interaction with models and data, decentralization of the computer resource, and increased differentiation of applications.

With the present availability of mini- and even micro-computers, desk top machines, time-shared general purpose systems, and data communication networks, managers now have access to powerful systems for relatively little cost.

---

technical issues meant that "MIS Is a Mirage" (Dearden, 1972). Ackoff (1967), Hall (1973), Diebold (1969), and Soden (1973) all similarly address the need for MIS and OR/MS to broaden their focus.

[2]Withington's "Five Generations of Computer Use" (1972) provides a simple historical classification of trends in computer technology. Nolan and Gibson (1974) provide an insightful summary of the dilemmas brought about by the expansion of the computer resource in organizations. Virtually every recent commentator on the history of the MIS field accepts that the emphasis on "big is beautiful" in the 1960s severely damaged the effectiveness and credibility of EDP (see, for example, Kanter, 1977).

[3]Dearden (1966) scathingly dissects technicians' myopic fantasies that a company can be run from a terminal accessing up-to-the-minute data on operations. A main point in the responses to Dearden has been that, if technical design is sensibly matched to managers' tasks and needs, real-time systems can be very useful; the approach he attacks reflects some EDP specialists' naive misunderstanding of decisionmaking rather than a fundamental flaw in the technology.

Software tools include generalized data management systems, a wide range of languages, and specialized packages. Any decisionmaker who is willing to commit time and a few thousand dollars can hire a summer graduate student to build a cash management simulation, a credit scoring model, or a variance analysis reporting system. The company's main computer does not have to be used since time can be rented on an outside time-sharing system. The system can be designed for the manager's own direct use or for a staff assistant to operate.

These technological changes that permitted the decentralization of the software and hardware, and hence of applications, have caused a major shift in the use of computers in some organizations. For the first time, it is feasible to build systems for managers rather than for functional applications. The fixed cost of developing systems and the elapsed time involved are much smaller than before. Most important of all, the user of the system can be an individual or group of individuals whose needs can be made clearly visible. The sales accounting reports generated by a company's EDP unit must accommodate the requirements of the controller's department, marketing staff, sales staff, and customer accounting functions and link in with the accounts receivable system. By contrast, the production-planning system used by both the manufacturing and marketing departments to schedule operations (this is a real life example, discussed at the end of this chapter; see pages 16 to 32) can be built around these decisionmakers and this decision process. Because of the rapid turnaround and the accessibility provided by the new interactive technology, computer systems can also be designed to be problem-solving aids very much like scientific calculators or even staff assistants.

As the technology advanced and understanding of how to exploit computers for classical MIS applications improved, many organizations had also to adjust to an increasingly unpredictable environment. The favorable business conditions and expansion of the 1960s were suddenly replaced by a period of economic swings, shortages, inflation, and increasing governmental regulation. The 1973 oil embargo dramatically altered expectations and constraints; organizations now found themselves in a new environment with little experience to help them revise their plans. The computer became an increasingly necessary tool, if only for record keeping and data access. Some organizations began, in a piecemeal fashion, to exploit the opportunities the new technology provided and built small interactive systems and models to help them in their planning.[4] These were generally commissioned by individual managers and tailored to their needs. Many of the efforts were experimental and built outside the companies' centralized computer departments by consultants, summer graduate students, and academics armed with research grants and bright ideas. M. S. Scott Morton's "Management Decision Systems" (1971)

---

[4]It is worth contrasting these systems, represented by Meador and Ness's Projector (a DSS described in Chapter 5) with those strongly espoused by the proponents of total systems in the 1960s. Gershefski, for example, described the Sun Oil planning model (1969), which contained over a hundred forecasting equations derived from regression analysis, generated detailed *pro forma* financial statements, and required 4 months' preparation of input data for a single run to be made. Gershefski's article reads like a striking proof of the effectiveness of centralized systems and attracted much attention. In fact, the Sun Oil model was a fiasco—monolithic, divorced from the planning process, and of no relevance to managers (see Hall, 1973, for a discussion of this and similar models).

describes a DSS used by marketing and production managers to coordinate production planning for laundry equipment. The study focuses on changes in the decision process and in its effectiveness stimulated by the system. T. P. Gerrity's "Design of Man-Machine Decision Systems" (1972) builds on this work and defines an explicit methodology for "decision-centered" design of a DSS. In both these cases, the main focus is explicitly on improving the decisionmaking of managers.[5] The brief list below of some sample DSS developed in the past 6 years suggests the common assumptions and aims that underlie their differing applications and technical characteristics:

1. Portfolio Management System (T. P. Gerrity, 1971): this system supports investment managers in their day-to-day decisions in administering clients' portfolios. The system includes a range of functions to analyze stocks, portfolio performance and characteristics, and so on. Some of the facilities are mainly clerical in nature (records of account reviews and summary of historical activity, for example) and others are highly technical (regression analysis). The system has been installed in several major banks. Usage by managers is very personalized, and has required a lengthy adjustment period for them to come to terms with this new form of support.

2. Brandaid (J. D. C. Little, 1975): this is a marketing-mix model for product promotion, pricing, and advertising decisions. It is based on Little's definition of a decision calculus: criteria for designing models that managers will use in preference to or in conjunction with other sources of information. The criteria include robustness, ease of control, simplicity, and completeness in relevant detail. Brandaid provides a structure for relating brand sales and profit to a manager's actions so that manager and staff can quickly and easily analyze strategies.

3. Projector (C. L. Meador and D. N. Ness, 1974): this is an interactive DSS for support of corporate short-term planning. It includes a range of functions designed to help the manager structure problems and explore possible lines of analysis. A distinctive feature of Projector, which justifies the phrase decision *support* system, is its emphasis on the explicit value of this exploration—the system in no way provides "solutions," but helps decisionmakers develop their own analytic approaches.

4. Geodata Analysis and Display System (GADS): this experimental system developed by the IBM Research Division constructs and displays computerized maps. It has been used to help design police beats, to plan urban growth, and to assign school district boundaries. Sub-

---

[5]The DSS developed by Gerrity has been studied over a 6-year period by several researchers (Stabell, 1974a; Alter, 1975; and Andreoli and Steadman, 1975). The evaluation of a complex DSS requires a long time frame for observation; PMS evolved and was adapted by its users, so that predictions about the fate of the system made in 1972 turned out to be incorrect (and overpessimistic). Meshing a DSS into its organizational context is a *dynamic* process.

stantial attention has been given to the training of nontechnical users (see J. Bennett, 1975; B. Grace, 1975; and C. A. Holloway and P. E. Mantey, 1976, for a discussion of training in the context of GADS).

5.   Capacity Information System (CIS): this system is used by the planning department of a large truck manufacturing company. It allows rapid development and modification of product plans that involve scheduling many plants, components, and end products and that are highly complex. It does not provide detailed solutions and addresses only part of the planning decision. However, the designers' emphasis on simplicity has provided a flexible and powerful tool for pinpointing potential bottlenecks and ensuring that plans are feasible.

6.   Generalized Management Information System (GMIS): this system represents a different approach. It aims at integrating existing tools; the manager can use languages and data management systems with which she or he is already familiar, even though some of these may even be mutually incompatible. The "virtual machine," a combination of hardware and software, makes any translations required. This system has mainly been used to provide an ad hoc DSS for dealing with energy planning problems.[6]

All these systems are described in more detail in Chapter 5. They are by no means typical—the emphasis in the DSS approach on building systems for specific types of problems, tailored to specific decision situations and decisionmakers, means that there is no "typical" design. The examples do indicate the range of technical choices and applications successfully addressed by DSS and the extent to which the computer can be made relevant to managerial decisionmaking.

Over the past few years, we have built several DSS and observed the progress of many others. Some were failures. Some were developed by computer professionals and management scientists to be innovative applications within their own technical discipline of MIS or OR/MS. Others, though, were initiated and implemented by managers, drawing on consultants for technical assistance. These systems are growing in number and variety. They represent a very different trend from that in mainstream MIS and OR/MS. In particular, they demonstrate a concept of the role of a computer system within the management decision process that has not been shared by many MIS and OR/MS professionals.

The aim of this book is to formalize the DSS approach. We define a strategy for meshing the analytic power and data processing capabilities of the computer with managers' problem-solving processes and needs. But this is a book about decisionmaking rather than computer systems. We subordinate technical issues to the goal of improving managers' *effectiveness*. A main stimulus to the development of the concepts underlying DSS has been the recognition of many managers' frustration with computer technology in general and with their own organization's techni-

---

[6]*Ad hoc* is here contrasted with institutional DSS built to support an ongoing task. Virtually all the DSS discussed in this book are institutional. New tools, such as GMIS and the APL language, now make it much easier to develop systems *quickly*; it seems likely that more ad hoc systems will therefore be built in the future. See Keen (1976), *EDP Analyzer* (1976), and Berry (1977) for discussions of the use of APL, and Donovan (1976) for details of GMIS.

cal staff; the tools available have not been matched to the managers' reality, and the computer remains, at best, of indirect assistance and, more generally, an irrelevant nuisance. The missionary aim of this book is to provide a common ground and joint strategy for the suppliers of computer products and their users.

EFFECTIVE DECISIONMAKING

The distinction between effectiveness and efficiency in decisionmaking is central to the argument of this book. Efficiency is performing a given task as well as possible in relation to some predefined performance criterion. Effectiveness involves identifying what should be done and ensuring that the chosen criterion is the relevant one. The implications of the distinction can be illustrated by the hypothetical example of a company's computer center that proudly boasts of its efficiency: it generates more output—management reports—than almost any other center in the country. The computer downtime is low and the machine is fully utilized, with minimal idle time. Inputs are quickly processed and outputs are delivered promptly. Unfortunately, the reports produced are not seen as useful by their recipients. Managers instruct their secretaries either to file the hundred-page summary of last month's operations unread or to throw it into the waste basket. The center is efficient in its pursuit of an ineffective goal.

There is often a conflict between efficiency and effectiveness. Effectiveness requires adaptation and learning, at the risk of redundancy and false starts. Research and development can be thought of as an "inefficient" investment of resources to provide for future effectiveness; actually, R & D is not needed to carry out existing tasks and could be eliminated, with favorable impact on this year's profits.[7] Efficiency involves a narrowing of focus and minimization of the time, cost, and/or effort required to carry out a given activity. It is essentially programmatic.

Obviously, every organization needs a balance between maintenance and adaptation, between carrying out its existing activities as well as it can and redefining those activities. In general, the more unstable the environment, the greater the need to focus on effectiveness.[8] In stable situations, next year's operations can be reliably predicted from this year's, and precise rules defined for carrying them out. Efficiency is then the central aim. In uncertain environments, however, *change* is the main issue. Efficient performance of last year's tasks is much less relevant than responsive adjustment to environmental shifts. The practical implications of this relationship are that in stable contexts management focuses mostly on operations and management control, but in unstable ones its main concern is with planning and strategic analysis.

As we suggested earlier, there are now few stable environments. The expansive economic growth of the 1960s seems unlikely to be repeated in the next few years. During that period, it was often easy to be effective, in that growth creates

---

[7]Hirschman (Hirschman and Lindblom, 1961) in his argument in favor of unbalanced economic growth and Klein and Meckling's (1958) strategies for deliberately uncoordinated management of R & D make a convincing case that inefficient approaches are often far more effective in that they stimulate new opportunities and generate constructive tensions. See also Keen (1977) "The Evolving Concept of Optimality."

[8]This issue is discussed in Keen (1975) "Managing Organizational Change." The broader relationship between organization and environment has been widely studied, notably by Lawrence and Lorsch (1968) and Katz and Kahn (1966).

opportunities for all, with relatively few risks. Of course, there was still the need for a balance; the organization had to develop efficient control over its expanding operations to avoid being swamped by its work load. Nonetheless, in a period of favorable instability, efficiency is a secondary concern, but in a time of largely unfavorable uncertainty, effectiveness is vital.

The traditional cost replacement applications of EDP mainly affected efficiency, and the standard linear programming and critical path scheduling techniques of management science are similarly concerned with efficient allocation of resources. During the 1960s, these tools provided valuable support to organizations' growing operations. They were often essential in making it possible to manage the mass of clerical and administrative activities that grew each year. They were not concerned with effectiveness; this was the province of managers, relying mainly on their judgment and experience. Of course, the computer was used, mainly through simulation models, to assist in this planning, but overall it was primarily a tool for efficiency. (It may well have reached a point of diminishing marginal returns in this respect.) Senior decisionmakers, especially in the largely hostile business environment of the late 1970s, are most concerned with effectiveness; efficiency can be programmed and delegated. This suggests both that the DSS approach to the use of computers will be immensely relevant for managers, and that without some such focus computer professionals will find that they have a more limited and lower-level role in the organization than they might aspire to.

EFFICIENCY AND EFFECTIVENESS IN COMPUTER APPLICATIONS: AN EXAMPLE

The following example is based on an actual company, one of the nation's leading banks. It is given here to provide a specific illustration of the implications for computer development of these differences between efficiency and effectiveness.

The Megabuck Trust Department in the early 1960s consisted of 10 investment managers and 40 clerical workers. As the volume of stock and bond market activities expanded, at an almost exponential rate, the need for better record keeping became critical. Megabuck spent substantial money on building applications to extend its punched card computer systems. These included: (1) trust accounting, (2) customer reporting, (3) portfolio performance analysis, and (4) profitability accounting. The aim was to reduce clerical cost, speed up the recording and reporting process, and provide more accuracy. Collectively, these applications were referred to in the department as "the MIS" (though clearly they do not provide management information).

In the early 1970s, the Trust Department's research staff began to build small time-shared models and systems for (1) risk analysis, (2) portfolio growth/income analysis, and (3) stock performance forecasting. These varied in complexity, but several drew on formal statistical techniques such as linear regression and on financial portfolio theory.

By 1972, there were a number of computer systems, designed and maintained by the EDP department, in use in Megabuck, together with the analytic models mainly employed by the research staff. The department now consisted of 25 investment managers and 4 clerical personnel. The managers made little direct use of the computer output, except to check it against their own records of customer activity. (Due to the general "back-office" chaos in Wall Street brokers' offices, many stock certificates were not transferred from seller to buyer for weeks, even months, after the trade. In 1973, the New York Stock Exchange had to close one afternoon a week to allow firms to catch up on the paperwork. This is a perfect instance of a situation where computerization was needed—and lacking—to provide efficiency.) The managers did not use the mathematical models at all since the theory underlying them represented a complex and normative viewpoint they did not regard as relevant to their own decisionmaking, except in very general terms. They considered MIS necessary and beneficial for the organization as a whole, and believed the systems saved substantial time and effort but that they were, at most, an indirect influence on their decisions.

After 1972, there were a number of developments in the investment industry that led Megabuck to reevaluate the objectives, operations, organization, and strategy of the Trust Department. Its environment had become highly competitive, with large pension groups shifting from one bank to another and rewarding the best performer with an increased allocation of their funds. Mutual funds, specialized professional analysis, investment management groups, and the expected abolition of fixed commissions all contributed to a need for a much more aggressive strategy. Megabuck placed a high emphasis on marketing and attracting new customers, as well as on outperforming its rivals (in terms of increasing the asset value of its portfolios). The need for more *effective* decisionmaking was clear; the department had to respond to these environmental shifts, rather than simply reduce administrative costs and delays.

Later in this book we discuss more completely the Portfolio Management System (PMS), a DSS built for a bank whose experience paralleled Megabuck's, but we will take a brief look at it here. This system was initiated by this bank's Trust Department to improve the investment managers' decisionmaking. It was apparent, from a number of earlier efforts, that:

1. The company's EDP systems (their MIS) were irrelevant here.

2. The investment process is such a complex mix of marketing, analysis, judgment, and experience, that no formal rules could be provided; analytic models could help in econometric forecasting or in defining broad strategies for balancing growth and income, risk and return, but most portfolios had exceptions that made general rules inapplicable.

3. The investment managers were very competent, and compared well to those in competing banks.

4. There were important organizational constraints and pressures, especially in terms of performance appraisal and management control, and of the relationships among the research, accounting, trust, and marketing units.

The portfolio management system was built with explicit attention to these four points:

1. The designers did not assume that more information or more timely information was needed, but that each manager, as a problem solver, required varying types of information, in varying format and detail. The system was thus intended to m⟨ ⟩h with individual information-processing needs and behavior.

2. The system in no way provided "answers" or rules. It was recognized that managers must be in control of the decisionmaking process and

that they simply would not use a system that imposed structure, solutions, or mode of analysis.

3.   The system was intended to help managers exploit their own specialized abilities and to extend them by providing analytic support and opportunities to test new concepts and explore potential scenarios.

4.   The designers also recognized that the system would be ineffectual if it did not mesh with the wider organizational constraints. At the same time they were aware that the DSS could be a major initiator of organizational change.

The philosophy represented by such a DSS is different from that underlying traditional systems associated with MIS and management science. A DSS emphasizes the decision *process,* and thus requires a very descriptive understanding of the investment activity, and subordinates design to context. On the whole, analytic and computer-based techniques have been introduced into organizations from a *prescriptive* definition of how tasks should be performed. Very little attention has been paid to contextual issues, especially the managers' modes of operation.

"IMPROVING" DECISIONMAKING

In the Megabuck example, the decision process in 1960 was fairly effective and very inefficient. In the succeeding 10 years, it was made far more efficient. But by 1972 there was little additional payoff from any further effort in this direction. However, a small increase in effectiveness could provide substantial benefit: for example, an improvement in return on capital of only 0.25 percent amounts to $500,000 for a portfolio of $200,000,000—which is not an unusually large one. Similarly, for a consumer goods company, a more effective allocation, in terms of timing and media chosen, of an advertising campaign could provide an increase in profit that far exceeds the cost of the DSS that contributed to the improvement (increased efficiency would be obtained by, for example, using analytic models to allocate advertising funds to obtain financial discounts or economies of scale). We do not suggest that the DSS *causes* the improvement; managers do that, with the support and perhaps the stimulus of the DSS.

For Megabuck, as for almost all organizations, it is difficult to identify what is meant by "improving" effectiveness. Efficiency can usually be measured in terms of cost and time. Defining effectiveness requires a detailed understanding of the variables that affect performance. We have little understanding of this issue in relation to the stock market. The "chartists" argue, at one extreme, that there are some clear analytic rules that, if followed, remove much of the need for judgment. The "intuitive" school of thought rejects this and regards "playing the market" as an art that cannot be taught. The "efficient market" theorists regard the market as amenable to neither art nor science; for them it is a random walk in which the interactions of investors quickly bid up undervalued securities and discount overvalued ones so that there is no long-term difference between them in terms of return on investment.[9] Which of these viewpoints one adopts determines one's definition of improved effectiveness. The chartist claims that there are common trends and pat-

---

[9]Markowitz (1959) and Sharpe (1963) are the classic presentations of this theory which has attracted increasing, if reluctant, support from most commentators on the stock

terns and that providing analytic facilities will extend the decisionmaker's ability to search out and evaluate information. The artists stress finding and rewarding the individuals who have the best sense of the market and freeing them from distracting and time-consuming administration and reporting. The believers in the efficient market recommend an emphasis on portfolio considerations rather than a fruitless search among individual securities.

STRUCTURED VERSUS UNSTRUCTURED TASKS

The DSS approach cannot resolve these conflicting viewpoints. Instead, it recommends that we examine a task, for example, investment management, define the key decisions it involves, and identify which parts of the decision process seem—given our knowledge of the task and the criteria for improving effectiveness—*structured* and which *judgmental* (see Chapters 3 and 4).[10] The former can to some degree be automated but the nonstructured components need to be left to the manager. While there is a "best" way to carry out the structured subtasks, the others require each manager to make situational value judgments from a personal frame of reference. Obviously, it is not always easy to analyze a complex decision process in these terms. The artists deny that the important components are in any way structured and the chartists insist that they all are. The methodology used to develop a DSS is to work mainly from the manager's perspective and accept his or her implicit definition of which components must be left to personal judgment. Frequently, of course, a manager's perceptions will shift over time; the DSS, which automates certain parts of his or her existing process, may later help to identify other potentially structural subtasks. The designer should thus look for "semistructured" tasks. Where a decision process is fully structured, automation is feasible (at a price) and the traditional techniques of EDP and OR/MS are practicable. Where it is unstructured, from the perspective of either the decisionmaker or the main body of theory relevant to understanding the task, the DSS philosophy argues that computer tools are inapplicable. In the Megabuck example, the investment process is semistructured in that it requires substantial systematic search through data on portfolios and securities and thus can be improved by the provision of retrieval, reporting, and display routines and simple analytic techniques. At the same time, the criteria for making specific investments for a portfolio need to be left to the manager's judgment. The concept of decision *support* is based on this balance between human judgment and computer replacement. A DSS provides a coherent strategy for going beyond the traditional use of computers in structured situations while avoiding ineffectual efforts to automate inherently unstructured ones.

---

market. Index funds, investments in a cross section of stocks rather than the traditional selection of a portfolio of potential "winners," reflects this support and the acceptance that it is impossible in the long term to beat the market.

[10]Simon (1965) used the terms *programmed* and *nonprogrammed* tasks and predicted that by 1975 most management tasks would be programmed. This clearly has not occurred, perhaps because such tasks are performed in an organizational context that is political and resistant to being programmed (see Keen and Gerson, 1977). Simon's "New Science of Management Decision" (in *The Shape of Automation for Men and Management*, 1965) was a key influence on the theory of decisionmaking underlying MIS, OR/MS, and DSS in the late 1960s.

The issue of task structure is discussed in detail in Chapter 4. It is obviously central to the concepts and practical methodologies of DSS. It is important to emphasize that structure often reflects knowledge. For example, well-qualified managers were at one time responsible for reordering parts for inventory in most companies. They needed to balance inventory costs and stockouts for high-volume components. They generally operated from experience and relied on their own judgment. As operations researchers examined this task, its underlying structure became apparent. Simple models and algorithms were developed, based, for example, on the Economic Order Quantity formula (EOQ).[11] These enabled organizations to replace this aspect of a manager's tasks by a computer system. The extent to which *all* managerial tasks can be structured is a question underlying the debates between artists and chartists in all fields. Management science, for example, generally assumes that problems can eventually be structured.[12]

Decision Support Systems focus on semistructured tasks. The criteria for systems development are, then, very different than for structured situations. Key words are *learning, interaction, support,* and *evolution* rather than *replacement, solutions, procedures,* and *automation.* Perhaps the key difference, however, is that for structured problems effectiveness and efficiency are almost equivalent. Thus a DSS cannot rely on the criteria and methods of MIS and OR/MS since *effectiveness* is its main concern.

THE TECHNOLOGICAL DIMENSION

This is not a book on technology. Our emphasis is on decisionmaking, rather than on technical design, and we strongly argue that the technological perspective is a secondary one.

There have been several developments that have made the DSS approach practicable. The most obvious of these is time-sharing. By the mid-1970s general purpose computers used operating systems that permitted nontechnical users to work at a terminal without needing specialized skills and knowledge. The machines have become increasingly reliable, and "user-oriented" languages are widely available. More recently, versatile video display devices have replaced the slower and noisy teletype. Systems designers have also paid more attention to issues of human engineering, so that working directly with a computer is more comfortable. The development of such flexible, robust, and inexpensive tools has made possible "interactive" computer systems.

Computer technology is an immensely varied and complex topic, and the advances described above have not meant that systems development has become an easy exercise. However, it now seems more useful to think of technology as a set of building blocks that can be combined to provide a particular system. Advanced de-

---

[11]This formula can be found in the first chapter of most Operations Research textbooks. It is an excellent indicator of the power of the analytic approach in structured situations; the formula is simple, precise, and *counterintuitive.*

[12]Simon's 1965 argument reflects this assumption. The DSS approach implicitly rejects it, if only on the practical grounds that we lack the necessary knowledge to identify the underlying structure of most complex problems. Braybrooke and Lindblom (1970) attack Simon's "synoptic" conception and claim that such problems are *inherently* unstructurable and can be resolved only by a nonanalytic strategy of "muddling through" (see also Lindblom, 1959). Chapter 3 expands on this important debate.

sign concepts require the most complex blocks, and in specialized applications the designer may have to struggle through the long manic-depressive cycle programmers have always experienced as they tried to invent new systems. The more important aspect, from the viewpoint of the user, is that we now have a tremendous variety of building blocks and that managers who have a *clear* idea of what they wish a DSS to do and how they will make use of it can generally obtain a system that accomplishes most of their aims.

Table 1-1 lists building blocks and some of their applications. The table is by no means exhaustive but it indicates fairly clearly that managers now have many tools to draw on that make the resulting system theirs, under their own control, and tailored to their needs and convenience. This contrasts completely with the late 1960s when the tools were clumsy, monolithic, expensive, and accessible only through centralized EDP units. A DSS can be *assembled* selectively, drawing on those building blocks that offer the best combination of power, cost, turnaround time, and suitability to the problem statement—that is, the best mix of efficiency and effectiveness. Note that we include, only half-frivolously, human building blocks. As we discuss in Chapters 6 through 9, effective implementation of a DSS requires a real dialogue between user and system-builder.

DECISION SUPPORT SYSTEMS— WHO IS THE "DESIGNER"?

Decentralization of the technology and the evolving shift of attention from technique to application has meant a potential decentralization of the design process. In the classical MIS area, computer systems are designed by technical professionals and managers play a passive role, at best. They have been consumers in an industry in which overselling has been too common. Perhaps the most practical aspect of the DSS approach is that it allows managers to initiate, design, and control the implementation of a system. That is, a DSS is built around a decisionmaking task and while the technical issues may be extremely complex, the main focus is managerial. One main stumbling block to the diffusion of computer-based methods in organizations has been the dominance of the technical role. Managers have often had trouble in developing the computer resource in relation to their business and decisionmaking needs. They have often been passive, wary consumers, not initiators and innovators.[13]

The intended audience for this book is the manager as much as the technical professional. We hope that the latter will get a richer insight into the organizational reality and, more especially, into the manager's perspective, so that technical skills can be applied in more depth and across a broader range of applications. For managers, we offer guidelines for exploiting the very real potential support that com-

---

[13]Nolan and Gibson (1974) and Morgan and Soden (1973) suggest that substantial maturation in an organization's use of computers is essential before managers can be brought into the initiation process. The introduction of the computer (the "missionary" and "contagion" stages in the life cycle described in Chapter 9) generally involves the computer specialist "selling" products; the emphasis on management control that occurs once the computer has become accepted also results in blockages to communication and innovation. In both situations, the computer personnel seem to be seen as, and often act as, high priests guarding a Delphic mystery.

TABLE 1-1 Some Technological Building Blocks

Building Blocks	Relevance for the Manager
Hardware	
General purpose time-sharing systems	Permit easy access to substantial computer power; allow faster development of systems, with closer involvement between technical specialist and manager.
Graphic terminals	Provide effective means for presenting large volumes of data in a meaningful format.
Desk-top or micro-computers	Provide (potentially—innovation too recent for any trends to become apparent) personalized, cheap, and easily transported tools that may become as indispensable as pocket calculators.
Telecommunication networks	Extend the computer from "number-crunching" and data processing to message sending and data sharing; provide mutual access to information among decentralized organizational units.
Software	
Data-base management systems	Extend range of information that can be collected; allow better access to existing data files; allow answers to relatively complex questions.
Specialized simulation and application languages	Reduce development time, especially for complex models and decision problems.
Application "packages"	Permit "off-the-shelf" installation of systems specially designed for particular types of application and thus fitting users' needs, background, and skills.
Human	
Technical intermediaries	Help involvement with design process, formalizing of ideas and needs, and evolving personalized system.
Staff intermediaries	Can act as the interface between the manager and the system, translating questions, operating the system, and providing analyses.

puter techniques provide, without needing to be knowledgeable about hardware and software. We assume that our readers have the following interests and characteristics, which we view as integral aspects of DSS development:

1.   Exposure to the complexity of real world decisionmaking, with empathy for managers' pressures and constraints, together with a recognition of the value of the analytic approach.

2.   A broad familiarity with the main functional areas of accounting, production, finance, and marketing, plus some overview of disciplines relevant to them, such as OR/MS, MIS, and/or organizational behavior.

OVERVIEW

In an emergent field such as DSS, any initial book has a difficult task. It is tempting to make large claims and to argue that its ideas are *new*. Our *synthesis* is, we believe, new, and we do have some very definite claims to make. However, we build on previous work: our concepts stress the links with MIS, OR/MS, and organizational behavior, and we view DSS as part of an evolution and maturation within the computer and management fields. Much of what we say should be obvious, and much will appear the opposite. In the next chapter we review the perspectives of the specialized disciplines that have contributed to the computer and business fields; they all tend to assume that what is obvious to them must be so in general, and that this piece of the elephant is the whole beast (we allude here to the hoary parable of the blind men touching an elephant and identifying what the beast must be, based on what part of the animal they touched). This is a book about the whole elephant.

In this book we have tried to compromise. We make no secret of others' work on which DSS ideas build. The book comes from ten years of practical work, at times more vigorous than at others, and from actively watching the use of DSS in real settings. We believe we have developed enough perspective to start making general observations.

The book has four major themes interwoven in the nine chapters. The first is one of perspective. We try to give a flavor of what we perceive DSS to be, and how they fit in with other analytical approaches to improving management problem solving.

The second is a discussion of the decisionmaking process and the dynamics of individual problem solving. This new and poorly understood area actually deserves several books. A serious weakness of the whole study of management has been ignorance of, and lack of interest in, how decisions really are made. A descriptive understanding of the problem-solving process is absolutely essential for decision support.[14]

The third theme is the design, implementation, and evaluation of interactive computer-based DSS. This material relies heavily on examples drawn from working systems to make its points. In DSS, design, implementation, and evaluation are tightly interwoven and cannot readily be separated. The evolutionary nature of a

---

[14]Stabell (1975) discusses the need for decision research, that is, specific methodologies for describing decision processes and identifying criteria for improving them.

DSS, or, more accurately, the evolving characteristics of the decision being supported, precludes such separation. Nonetheless, we can define specific strategies, many of which apply to computer systems and models in general, for the delivery of a DSS.

The final component consists of examples from working systems. We present fairly detailed descriptions of several DSS to give a more technical and complete picture of how the concepts and strategies we present are translated into a real, working, useful system.

The sequence of the following chapters can best be summarized in terms of the key questions we raise and, we hope, answer:

Chapter 2: What have we learned about management, information, and systems from the 20 years of research and application? What is the base on which DSS can build?

Chapter 3: What do we know about decisionmaking? How *are* decisions made? Where are the leverage points for improving decisionmaking?

Chapter 4: What is a DSS? Why? What problems and tasks can it support?

Chapter 5: Are there any real world DSS that have improved the effectiveness of the decision process?

Chapter 6, Chapter 7, and *Chapter 8:* How do we design, implement, and evaluate DSS?

Chapter 9: OK, if we believe the arguments so far, what can we do to apply them?

These questions define the elephant.

EXAMPLE: THE LAUNDRY EQUIPMENT CASE

Introduction

This description of a DSS built for the laundry equipment division of one of the largest corporations in the United States is taken from "Management Decision Systems" (Morton, 1971). This DSS was one of the earliest attempts to use interactive computer technology to support a management decision process. The project was a successful experiment, and many of the principles presented in this book rose out of this first effort. Since 1968, the technology for building such systems has become cheaper, more powerful, and more reliable, and this DSS could now be replicated with ease and at a fraction of the original cost. However, the case is still of more than historical interest in that it highlights the issue of decision *support* rather than the use of computer technology. Morton comments (1971) that the project group involved in the laundry equipment DSS "almost fell into [the] trap of letting the task of building become an end in itself"; this is an ever-present, too rarely resisted temptation for true believers in the value of computers. Morton's study allowed him to step back from the manic-depressive activity of trying to integrate an overloaded second-generation computer with an $80,000 terminal[15] (comparable

---

[15]The computer was not designed for time-sharing applications. The terminal had to be specially built and was extremely expensive to operate.

devices 2 years later cost $15,000, and now are well under $2,000) and examine in detail the *impact* of the system on a complex management task. His findings stimulated a number of follow-up efforts, several of which are presented in Chapter 5 of this book (Gerrity's Portfolio Management System and the Geodata Analysis and Display System developed by IBM's Research Laboratory). All involved significant and laborious extensions of the technical state of the art, but in each case the technology was only a means to an end—the end was the support of a decision process in a semistructured task. Successful implementation of the laundry equipment system required the following new skills:

1. An ability to characterize and analyze the users' problem-solving processes and tasks.

2. A definition of criteria for matching the formal design of the system to the context.

3. An evolutionary approach to DSS development.

These, and not computer technology for its own sake, were the central issues to be studied and resolved; this still remains true, though the technology has advanced immensely. The main reason for selecting the laundry equipment case as the first example of a DSS given in this book is *because* it is technically out of date and thus reinforces our main argument—that the *objective* is decision support and the *vehicle* is whatever interactive computer technology is suitable and exploitable.

The Laundry Equipment Division

The laundry equipment division is one of 70 decentralized units, organized by product group, in one of the largest American corporations. The marketing and manufacturing operations are separate profit centers. The marketing division buys its consumer products from a number of factories that also maintain warehouses; the units are "sold" to marketing at a transfer price. The division, at the time of the study, was organized by specific products or groups of products, which were assigned to particular managers. Three individuals—the marketing-planning, marketing (sales), and production managers—jointly developed the production and sales plans. Every month they defined plans for the next 12 months. These were used by manufacturing personnel to establish work force levels, schedule production, and manage inventory. Marketing also consulted them when defining their pricing and merchandising strategies. The production and sales plans formed the operational goals for the coming months.

Marketing began its planning from a computer-based sales forecast that would be modified by the marketing manager to take into account special circumstances or objectives. Similarly, production began with a forecast of manufacturing and inventory requirements, adjusted to provide an efficient schedule (where efficiency essentially meant least cost and lowest levels of disruption). Obviously, the two sets of plans would often conflict. Marketing required availability of ample products and flexible response to sudden shifts in demand; production aimed at minimizing inventory and manufacturing costs. Because profit margins were low, excess inventory costs would substantially affect profitability. At the same time, stockouts quickly eroded the company's market position, and demand was seasonal, so that a lost sale was hard to make up.

The marketing-planning manager's main task was to combine the sales and production plans into specific production targets for the products for which he was responsible. The manager had to balance expected demand, which was partially influenced by merchandising plans, with production capacity, inventory, and work in process. Expected demand was the most difficult element to assess. Aggregate forecasts were available, though of limited reliability. Sales levels were strongly affected by a range of factors and could be fairly volatile in the short term. If the sales staff were encouraged to sell a particular product model, for example, aggregate demand for that product *type* might remain roughly the same but sales for the *model* could be increased for the duration of the merchandising campaign. The products would need to be in the right place at the right time (marketing would therefore obviously prefer that substantial buffer stocks were available at the warehouses). After much experimentation, the division had decided to use a statistical model to forecast "latent" or basic demand; this was then subjectively adjusted. The forecast was mailed to the managers since the computer on which it was generated was located far from division headquarters. There was no opportunity to suggest changes or test out possible variations on the basic forecast.

The marketing manager for a product had sole responsibility for merchandising strategy. He had annual sales and profit targets and used merchandising campaigns as short-term marketing tools. These obviously depended on the availability of the product at the warehouse. Timing was important. The marketing-planning manager needed to translate the merchandising plans into a concrete projection of units required in each local area; a heavy advertising campaign in the Midwest for the Christmas season, for example, had to be projected in terms of expected sales by month by area by model.

Data on product inventories were available from routine computer-generated reports. However, these were almost 3 inches thick and broken down to the lowest level of detail so that combining them was time consuming. Scheduling production was complex, particularly since capacity considerations placed major constraints on short-term operations. If a factory were operating either under or over capacity, the optimal manufacturing schedule and product mix, from the company's perspective, might be very different from that required by the marketing manager's plans and also would be unlikely to match actual demand in any given period. If the plant were over capacity, the marketing-planning manager would need to choose which products to make and which to cut back on; customer goodwill, promised delivery dates, and so on would have to be taken into account.

Over some years, the laundry equipment managers had evolved a decision process to handle the balancing of the sales and production plans and the trade-offs among conflicting goals. Even though more and more up-to-date information was now available from the computer, this process was still lengthy, fragmented, performed under substantial time pressure and essentially manual. Figure 1-1 is a flowchart of the distinct activities required. The marketing-planning manager (MPM) first worked with the forecasts and preliminary objectives and schedules (steps 1 and 2). Spread sheets which combined and organized all this data (see Figure 1-2) were developed. The computer-generated forecast was generally modified to take into account the manager's own knowledge and expectations (step 3 in Figure 1-1). At this stage, the marketing-planning manager met with the marketing manager (MM) to agree on an aggregate figure (step 4). The process was then repeated (steps 5 and 6) at the next level of detail, the individual product models; these forecasts

Figure 1-1   Flowchart of Decision Process Prior to Introduction
of DSS

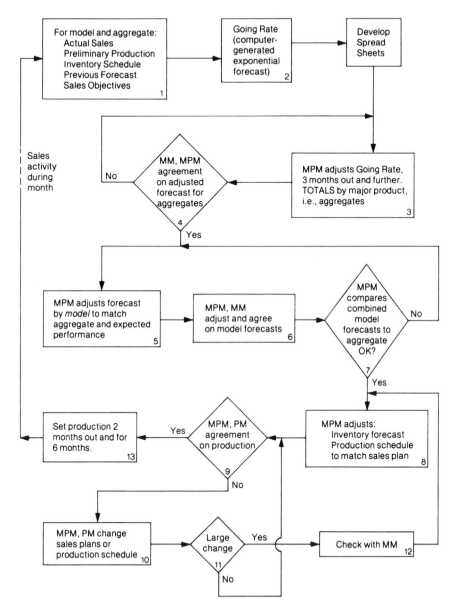

were reconciled with aggregate estimates. Obviously, there was substantial clerical
work involved in all these stages.

Only after this point, when the forecasts were complete and the impact on
production and inventory apparent (step 8), were the production manager (PM) and
staff brought into the planning process. The marketing-planning manager negoti-

Figure 1-2   Sample Spread Sheet Data (Partial Only)

TUMBLER	JAN	FEB	MAR	APR	MAY	JUNE	JULY	Total (12 mos)
1967 Actual	1635	2004	2654	2150	2400	2600		
1968 Actual	1820	2430	2300					
Going Rate				2100	2200	2400	2400	
Previous Fcst			2800	2300	2600	2600		
Current Fcst				2200	2300	2600		
1968 Objectives	1700	2100	2500	2700	2600	2700		
Production:								
Actual		2000	1500					
Planned				2500	2000	2200		
Inventory—Factory	1000	800	900	1200	1500	1000		
Total	3000	2600	1800	2200	2000	1800		
Objective	4000	4100	4200	4200	4400	4800	4800	

ated changes in the proposed schedule with them. The forecast and sales plans might need modification to take into account production constraints (steps 10 and 11).

This process required 20 days of elapsed time, largely because of the clerical effort required. Any change involved reworking the spread sheets, which took from 2 to 10 hours. The managers operated intuitively with few rules and no systematic methodology. The process relied on negotiation. The difficulties of fitting meetings in with the three managers' other responsibilities meant substantial fragmentation. Bottlenecks were frequent. Also, 16,000 manual calculations were made each month, and 8,000 numbers, from a data base of 75,000 elements, were transcribed. The elements were derived from three different computer reports. The numbers used gave few clues as to likely problem areas in a particular month, and there were no predefined guidelines for selecting data, alternatives, and criteria for analysis. The cost of calculating the detailed figures for a single alternative meant that the managers avoided innovation and tried to limit examination to one or two plans. They "satisficed" (found "good enough" solutions rather than optimizing) and accepted the first acceptable alternative.

The inadequacies in the existing process were not caused by lack of competence. Many efforts had been made to streamline it, but technical constraints and cognitive limitations, particularly in terms of a lack of capacity to manage large computations and alternatives simultaneously, had resulted in this inefficient sequence of steps. The process was even more ineffective, in that extremely few alternatives were ever assessed, and those that were had been consciously picked out because they involved only small deviations from the status quo.

Obviously, this decision process has many structured elements (this was not so obvious at the time to many of the personnel involved). Morton analyzed the process in terms of Simon's model of decisionmaking, which identified three distinct stages: Intelligence, Design, and Choice. Morton broke each of these down into subphases: (1) *generation* of input data, (2) *manipulation* of the data, and (3) *selection* for the following phase. The resulting classification was used to identify the bottlenecks in the existing decision process (see Table 1-2).

The DSS developed to support this decision drew on a relatively new technology. The incentive for the experimental study had been the feeling that an interactive system that provided *graphical* output would permit far more rapid presentation and assimilation of data by managers, and that reports would be more conceptually meaningful with graphs, trend lines, and plots substituted for inert masses of unorganized numbers. It was decided to use exactly the same input data that the

*TABLE 1-2 Bottlenecks in the Previous
Decisionmaking Process*

	Intelligence	**Design**	**Choice**
Generation	1. Large data base.	4. a. Implementation of a strategy. b. Conceptualization of strategy.	7. Solution space not explored.
Manipulation	2. a. Large quantity of computation. b. Low information content. c. Variable operations required.	5. a. Large quantity of computation. b. Variable operations required.	8. Multiple criteria for comparing solutions.
Selection	3. a. Different criteria over time. b. Time requirements. c. Cognitive limitations.	6. Implications of the solution for other variables.	9. Comparison of multidimensional alternatives.

managers currently had available. In many respects the DSS was an improved methodology for handling the manual spread sheets; it eliminated bottlenecks that prevented the following type of dialogue in the managers' meetings:

"Why don't we take a quick look at what the inventory will look like 7 months out?"

"I don't like that. Let's try it with 3 months' supply for July through October."

"No, go back and adjust June and see if we increase production and get those inventories back in balance."

Such dialogue was impossible before the DSS. More importantly, because of the bottlenecks, the managers' interactions were mutually defensive, even hostile. With the DSS, this changed to an atmosphere of joint *exploration*. The managers saw the graphical displays as a communication device. They explained ideas, pointed to supporting data, focused on details, looked ahead rather than concentrating on next month's plan, and made comparisons—and, of course, explored far, far more alternatives. Whereas with the manual system there was a large cost to considering even one more alternative, the DSS reduced marginal effort almost to zero. The result was that the 6 days of managers' time spread over 20 days was reduced to a half-day spread over 2 working days.

In itself, this reduction in time is an improvement in efficiency, but it is less relevant than the change in effectiveness implied by the new decision process.[16] Morton assessed this change by flowcharting the decisionmaking cycle using the DSS (see Figure 1-3) and comparing it with the original one (Figure 1-2). A major change was that while the aggregates (product types such as washers and tumblers) were forecast first and later broken down by model, with the DSS the managers worked from the model upward:

> The significance of this is that attaching too much importance to the aggregates can lead to errors. The whole is only the sum of the *parts* that are under the managers' control. If a certain forecast is made for agitators (aggregate), it can only be achieved by selling specific models. . . . It is reasonable to consider most closely those variables that are under managerial control. . . . Under the new system the structure of the decisionmaking process is not distorted by the requirements of the data-manipulation process (Morton, 1971, pp. 112–114).

Liberated from the bottlenecks imposed by time, technology, and cognitive limitations, the managers quickly adapted to the new system. The DSS faith assumes that managers are, in general, competent[17] and that an inadequate decision process generally reflects some external constraints; if these can be removed, the decisionmaker learns and adjusts.

The original process had been very sequential with few feedback loops. The managers exploited the flexibility the DSS allowed them and moved back and forth among subphases; they were able to follow their train of thought through to an answer. The difference is represented in Figure 1-4 in terms of the three phases and three subphases in the full decision cycle.

The dashed area in Figure 1-3, which shows the new decision process, represents steps included in the original cycle but now speeded up because of the DSS (and dealt with by model and not aggregate). The boxes enclosed in solid lines (boxes 2 and 8) are new activities. With the time constraints of the manual process, there could be no joint review; the marketing-planning manager made his own (cursory) assessments.

Table 1-3 summarizes the impact of the system on other aspects of the overall planning activity. Figures 1-5 through 1-13, with annotations from Morton, show a sequence of displays from the DSS. The terminal used was an advanced and expensive device that used a light-pen to eliminate the need for typing.[18] The terminal was

---

[16]The improved efficiency allows managers to shift their efforts toward other tasks, but in itself it has no real impact on the quality of the production-sales plan. Of course, the dollar savings in such situations may in themselves cover the cost of the DSS.

[17]OR/MS and, to a lesser extent, MIS too often imply that any manager who is not "rational" and fully computerized is incompetent. This prescriptive viewpoint assumes that there is a right way to make decisions and that the analyst should therefore act as a missionary converting the ignorant and heathen. The DSS approach begins from a descriptive perspective and has the additional merit of humility and curiosity about how and why managers behave.

[18]Apart from being more convenient and reducing time and errors, the light-pen sidesteps many managers' reluctance to use a computer if it requires them to type (Carter, 1974, comments that typing conflicts with their self-image).

linked to a pair of Univac 494 computers, which were not time-shared but were made to provide interactive capability with a response time of under 10 seconds, through imaginative and complicated programming. The managers found the interactive system easy to use.

Figure 1-3   New Process of the Decisionmaking Cycle

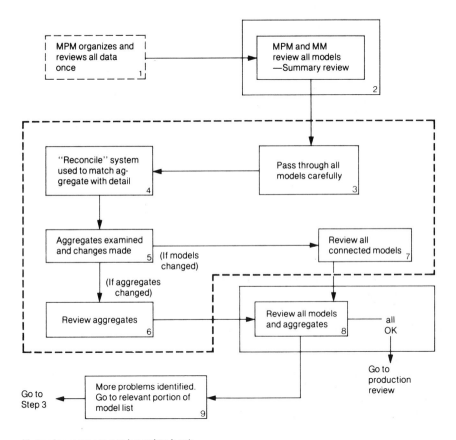

Notes (comments are keyed to box):

1. This process was employed by the MPM in sessions 1 and 2 but not thereafter. The manager indicated after the third session that he would no longer do this. Box 2 now became the first step.

2. No models are changed. This is a once-over-lightly review to find potential problems.

3. Each of the models is taken in turn and examined.

4. When the last model is finished, all models are compared with the relevant aggregate. No changes are made until step 7 is finished.

5. Step 3 is repeated for aggregate.

6. 7. Depending on results of steps 4 and 5, one or both of the aggregates and various models are changed.

8. Models are then reviewed as in step 2.

9. If any problems are seen from step 8, the process is iterated from step 3.

Figure 1-4   Comparison of Problem-Solving Phases Before and with the DSS. (a) Former Decision Process. (b) Decision Process with the DSS.

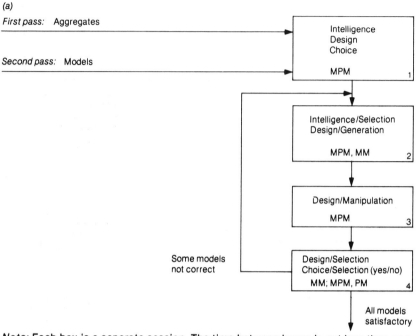

(a)

First pass: Aggregates

Second pass: Models

Intelligence
Design
Choice

MPM   1

Intelligence/Selection
Design/Generation

MPM, MM   2

Design/Manipulation

MPM   3

Some models
not correct

Design/Selection
Choice/Selection (yes/no)
MM; MPM, PM   4

All models
satisfactory

Note: Each box is a separate session. The time between boxes is not less than one-half day.

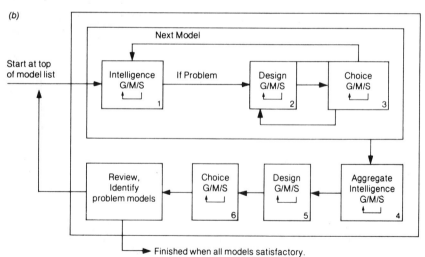

(b)

Next Model

Start at top
of model list

Intelligence
G/M/S   1

If Problem

Design
G/M/S   2

Choice
G/M/S   3

Review,
Identify
problem models

Choice
G/M/S   6

Design
G/M/S   5

Aggregate
Intelligence
G/M/S   4

Finished when all models satisfactory.

Note: This is one session with no break. Small arrows with the G/M/S (Generation/Manipulation/Selection) indicate cycling through these subphases several times.

TABLE 1-3   Other Changes in the Overall Decision Process

	Old Cycle	**New Cycle**
Time Horizon	*Managers focused on next 4 months.*	*Plans adjusted for all months in the 12-month rolling horizon.*
Communication	*Marketing-planning manager often required to act as arrbitrator and mediator between production and marketing.*	*Substantially more lateral communication; reduced conflict.*
Presentation of Information	*Little exploration of data base, no highlighting of key information; computations required substantial lead time and clerical effort.*	*Graphs immensely compress data, make numbers meaningful, and increase volume of data that can be assimilated; "instant" computations.*
Planning	*Highly constrained by time pressure and data presentation and manipulation.*	*More exploration of planning issues, in terms of detail and scope.*

Figure 1-5   Sample Performance Data—Graphical

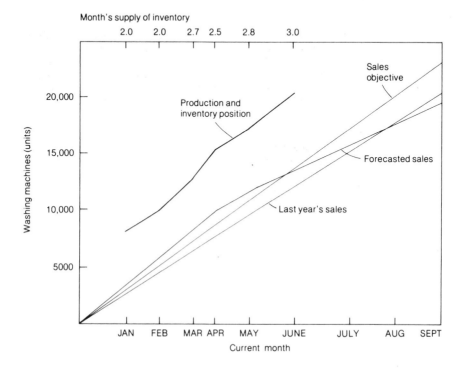

Figure 1-6   End-Point Project

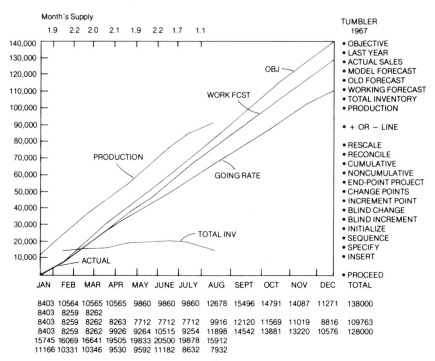

Note: Having looked at Figure 1-6, perhaps the user does not like the working forecast (present sales plan) for the tumblers, presently set for 128,000 units by December 31. Instead he decides to expand merchandising in the last half of the year and feels he can meet his objective of 138,000 by December 31. He wants to expand his sales rate, starting in JULY, in order to meet his objective by year end. This is done by hitting the following control points in any sequence:

1. WORKING FORECAST and END-POINT PROJECT (to indicate which manipulation is to be carried out on which variable).
2. JULY (to indicate the starting month of the projection).
3. An ending value to project to, in this case 138,000. This is typed on the keyboard.
4. PROCEED (this results in the next picture).

Figure 1-7   Change Points

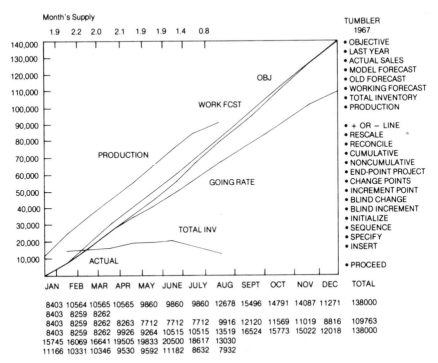

Month's Supply

| 1.9 | 2.2 | 2.0 | 2.1 | 1.9 | 1.9 | 1.4 | 0.8 |

TUMBLER
1967

* OBJECTIVE
* LAST YEAR
* ACTUAL SALES
* MODEL FORECAST
* OLD FORECAST
* WORKING FORECAST
* TOTAL INVENTORY
* PRODUCTION

* + OR − LINE
* RESCALE
* RECONCILE
* CUMULATIVE
* NONCUMULATIVE
* END-POINT PROJECT
* CHANGE POINTS
* INCREMENT POINT
* BLIND CHANGE
* BLIND INCREMENT
* INITIALIZE
* SEQUENCE
* SPECIFY
* INSERT

* PROCEED

JAN	FEB	MAR	APR	MAY	JUNE	JULY	AUG	SEPT	OCT	NOV	DEC	TOTAL
8403	10564	10565	10565	9860	9860	9860	12678	15496	14791	14087	11271	138000
8403	8259	8262										
8403	8259	8262	8263	7712	7712	7712	9916	12120	11569	11019	8816	109763
8403	8259	8262	9926	9264	10515	10515	13519	16524	15773	15022	12018	138000
15745	16069	16641	19505	19833	20500	18617	13030					
11166	10331	10346	9530	9592	11182	8632	7932					

Note: The display in Figure 1-7 shows that there was only 0.8 month's supply of inventory on August 31 (small number at top of graph). If the manager regarded this as unsatisfactory, he might change his production plan. In this example, the following control points were hit to generate the next picture:

1.   PRODUCTION; CHANGE POINTS (to identify the variable and the manipulation).
2.   AUG (to identify month).
3.   Type in new value (for example, 18,000 for August).
4.   PROCEED
5.   Repeat for September and October.

If INCR. PT. (add or subtract an increment to a point) had been used, then the difference of 10,068 (18,000 − 7,932) would be typed.

Figure 1-8   Reconcile

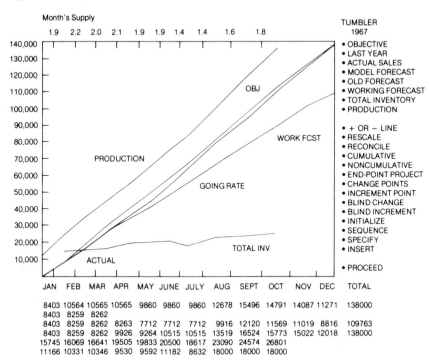

	JAN	FEB	MAR	APR	MAY	JUNE	JULY	AUG	SEPT	OCT	NOV	DEC	TOTAL
	8403	10564	10565	10565	9860	9860	9860	12678	15496	14791	14087	11271	138000
	8403	8259	8262										
	8403	8259	8262	8263	7712	7712	7712	9916	12120	11569	11019	8816	109763
	8403	8259	8262	9926	9264	10515	10515	13519	16524	15773	15022	12018	138000
	15745	16069	16641	19505	19833	20500	18617	23090	24574	26801			
	11166	10331	10346	9530	9592	11182	8632	18000	18000	18000			

Note: The new picture generated in Figure 1-8 has, obviously, a new production line. In addition, the month's supply has been recalculated and a new Total Inventory line plotted (bottom of screen).

If the manager now wanted to check this with last year's sales, he could bring those data on the screen by hitting the following control points:

1. Data-control point LAST YEAR.
2. Manipulation point + or − LINE.
3. PROCEED.

Figure 1-9   Last Year's Sales

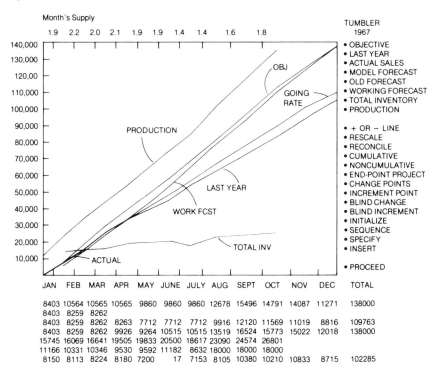

Month's Supply

| | 1.9 | 2.2 | 2.0 | 2.1 | 1.9 | 1.9 | 1.4 | 1.4 | 1.6 | 1.8 |

TUMBLER
1967

• OBJECTIVE
• LAST YEAR
• ACTUAL SALES
• MODEL FORECAST
• OLD FORECAST
• WORKING FORECAST
• TOTAL INVENTORY
• PRODUCTION

• + OR − LINE
• RESCALE
• RECONCILE
• CUMULATIVE
• NONCUMULATIVE
• END-POINT PROJECT
• CHANGE POINTS
• INCREMENT POINT
• BLIND CHANGE
• BLIND INCREMENT
• INITIALIZE
• SEQUENCE
• SPECIFY
• INSERT

• PROCEED

JAN	FEB	MAR	APR	MAY	JUNE	JULY	AUG	SEPT	OCT	NOV	DEC	TOTAL
8403	10564	10565	10565	9860	9860	9860	12678	15496	14791	14087	11271	138000
8403	8259	8262										
8403	8259	8262	8263	7712	7712	7712	9916	12120	11569	11019	8816	109763
8403	8259	8262	9926	9264	10515	10515	13519	16524	15773	15022	12018	138000
15745	16069	16641	19505	19833	20500	18617	23090	24574	26801			
11166	10331	10346	9530	9592	11182	8632	18000	18000	18000			
8150	8113	8224	8180	7200	17	7153	8105	10380	10210	10833	8715	102285

Note: If the Tumbler is now regarded as satisfactory, the manager might want to see how he stands in relation to the Tumbler models. He then hits the RECONCILE and PROCEED control points. (See Figure 1-10 for the display results.)

Figure 1-10   Reconcile Specifications

	FROM		TO	
WASHER: TO: TUMBLER, AGITATOR	JAN		JAN	
	FEB		FEB	
TUMBLER: TO: MODELS	MAR	1966	MAR	1966
	APR	1967	APR	1967
AGITATOR: TO: MODELS	MAY	1968	MAY	1968
	JUNE	1969	JUNE	1969
	JULY		JULY	
	AUG		AUG	
	SEPT		SEPT	
	OCT		OCT	
	NOV		NOV	
	DEC		DEC	

SALES   PRODUCTION

PROCEED

Note: In Figure 1-10, one item from each column is selected with the light-pen. A choice is then made between sales and production. If the following were hit, the next picture would appear: TUMBLER: MODELS; JAN; 1967; DEC; 1967; SALES; PROCEED.

Figure 1-11   Sales Reconciliation

1967   TUMBLER   :   MODELS

	JAN	FEB	MAR	APR	MAY	JUNE	JULY	AUG	SEPT	OCT	NOV	DEC	TOTAL
T-1	2764	3126	2896	3702	3084	3643	4279	5117	6032	7258	6973	5441	54315
T-2	2574	2664	2646	2686	2700	3140	2925	2064	1053	309	207	207	23175
T-3	2763	2323	2584	3116	2661	3352	2686	2049	1147	382	114	207	23384
T-4	0	0	0	0	0	0	328	2405	5131	5297	6032	4288	23481
T-5	0	0	0	0	0	0	0	0	0	0	0	0	0
T-6	0	0	0	0	0	0	437	1440	2601	2405	2265	2405	11553
T-7	302	146	136	422	110	154	64	30	85	54	33	12	1548
TOTAL	8403	8259	8262	9926	8555	10289	10719	13105	16049	15705	15624	12560	137456
TUMBLERS	8403	8259	8262	9926	9264	10515	10515	13519	16524	15773	15022	12018	138000
DIFFERENCE	0	0	0	0	709	226	204	414	475	68	602	542	544

•PROCEED	•INITIALIZE	•SPECIFY	•FINISH	•REFRESH
•INSERT	•RATIO	•RETURN	•FREEZE	•GRAPH
•CHANGE-PTS				

Note: If the user wishes to reconcile the discrepancies between the sales plan for the tumblers, aggregate, and the plan for the models, he or she may take the difference in May of 709 units and spread it through all the models proportionately, by using the light-pen to select MAY; RATIO; PROCEED. The May column of the display will then look like that in Figure 1-12.

Figure 1-12   Reconcile

1967   TUMBLER   :   MODELS

	JAN	FEB	MAR	APR	MAY	JUNE	JULY	AUG	SEPT	OCT	NOV	DEC	TOTAL
T-1	2764	3126	2896	3702	3343	3643	4279	5117	6032	7258	6973	5441	54574
T-2	2574	2664	2646	2686	2927	3249	2925	2064	1053	309	207	207	23511
T-3	2763	2323	2584	3116	2884	3466	2686	2049	1147	382	114	207	23721
T-4	0	0	0	0	0	0	328	2405	5131	5297	6032	4288	23481
T-5	0	0	0	0	0	0	0	0	0	0	0	0	0
T-6	0	0	0	0	0	0	437	1440	2601	2405	2265	2405	11553
T-7	302	146	136	422	110	157	64	30	85	54	33	12	1551
TOTAL	8403	8259	8262	9926	9264	10515	10719	13105	16049	15705	15624	12560	138391
TUMBLERS	8403	8259	8262	9926	9264	10515	10719	13105	16049	15705	15624	12560	138391
DIFFERENCE	0	0	0	0	0	0	0	0	0	0	0	0	0

•PROCEED	•INITIALIZE	•SPECIFY	•FINISH	•REFRESH
•INSERT	•RATIO	•RETURN	•FREEZE	•GRAPH
•CHANGE-PTS				

Note: When all differences are zero, the data are entirely reconciled. The user can then select graphs for display. For example, the following selection will generate the graph shown in Figure 1-13: GRAPH-NONCUM; TUMBLER; NORMAL; JAN; 1967; JULY; 1967; PROCEED.

Figure 1-13   Noncumulative Graph

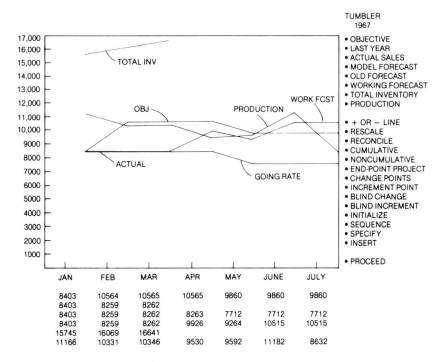

Note: This is simply an example of a noncumulative graph for a 6-month time span. It is possible to display the cumulative version by selecting the CUMULATIVE control point and the PROCEED. All control points listed in a display are legitimate options.

The aim of this brief discussion has been to provide an orienting example. We will explore in detail issues of design, methodology, and concept in the rest of this book. The following comments draw attention to issues that are central to DSS, whether the technology is that of 1966, when the laundry equipment DSS was initiated, or that of 1978, or, we firmly believe, that of 1982. (Beyond that horizon we are less certain.)

1. The situation involved, that of managers operating under pressure in a complex task, is not one where a computer-based aid can be easily or quickly defined—there is no optimization model, data retrieval system, or MIS that can be specified. It is essential to have a detailed methodology for making sense of the situation, by defining and assessing the *process* by which the managers arrive at a decision.

2. The decision process in a multidimensional, multiobjective, and only partially defined task cannot be automated. However, computer support that takes over some of the subprocesses that can be programmed—data manipulation, retrieval, and display, for example—can have a remarkable impact on how the managers operate. Managers exploit the facilities of such a decision aid in innovative and effective ways.

3. The technology used must provide managers with access to computer power, give fast response, and be easy to use.

4. The design and implementation strategy requires awareness of managers' processes and needs and an avoidance of a narrowly technical perspective.

5. Computer support, carefully matched to the decision problem, decisionmakers, and decision context, can *substantially* help the manager. Decision support seems a sensible goal for the computer professional who wishes to make a clear contribution to the organization and a valuable service to the manager concerned with improving personal effectiveness.

PERSPECTIVES ON MANAGEMENT, INFORMATION, SYSTEMS, AND MIS

TWO

INTRODUCTION

Management Information Systems (MIS) is a prime example of a "content-free" expression. It means different things to different people, and there is no generally accepted definition recognized by those working in the field. As a practical matter, MIS implies computers, and the phrase Computer-Based Information Systems (CBIS) has been used by some researchers as being more precise. This difficulty in applying an exact meaning to MIS has been complicated by the fads that have swept the field at recurrent intervals. Since the early 1960s we have seen successively: Integrated Information Systems, Total Systems, On-Line Real-Time Systems, Data-Base Systems, and Distributed Processing Systems. None of these have been particularly well defined, and all of them have been oversold. Collectively they have made it hard to build on experience.

Most frequently, the interpretation of MIS depends on the profession from which it is approached. The educational background or the current occupation of the person interested in the MIS field tends to determine the way in which she or he will define it. There are two obvious professional groups, with different biases and priorities: management and data processing. Most other practicioners and researchers in the computer field have been trained in one of the following four academic disciplines: computer science, information economics, management science, and behavioral science. The interpretation of what MIS means is very different for each of these; and sometimes the definitions are incompatible. Each has a built-in set of attitudes and axioms that leads its proponents to preface their statements with "of course, . . ." It is rare that an individual has been trained in more than one of the four fields, so that most commentators look at the broad area of information systems from a single—and too often a single-minded—perspective. A main theme of this book is that we now need to integrate these highly differentiated viewpoints, each of which is insightful but incomplete.

The major point to be made in this chapter is that the definition of a Management Information System shifts as one includes consideration of contextual issues. The physical technology and formal design are central features of the "system" but are constrained by the organizational setting, the specific task for which it is designed, the dynamics of the development process, and the nature of its intended usage. All these influence how the technology can and should be used. Each of the disciplines we identified regards particular aspects of the context or the computer as

33

the critical component of the system. Computer science, for example, largely ignores nontechnical concerns, and behavioral science in turn has little to say about technology.

In this chapter we give our own, idiosyncratic perspective on MIS. Our survey is not "objective"; we try to sort out, from the viewpoint of DSS design, what technical, academic, and organizational areas are of most relevance and which particular aspects of them we should select in our synthesis of the concept of decision support. This review may also give readers a clearer idea of where the DSS movement has come from, its implicit biases, its academic home, and its selective focus. Our discussion of, for example, computer science is extremely narrow; the reader should not assume it gives an accurate summary of the field as a whole, but only a brief description of how computer science looks from the applied perspective of DSS. The world of computers has become far too broad and technically specialized for *any* compact summary to be possible. Some organizing framework, inevitably simplistic, is needed for one to come to grips with it.

We do not yet have a mature academic MIS field of study which would stand as a "discipline" in its own right. At the moment any serious information systems work (in universities) is an outgrowth of either management science or computer science.[1] This is not to downgrade those active in the information systems area, it is simply a comment on the immaturity of the discipline and the level of understanding with which we are still struggling. These realities about the extent of our formal knowledge are particularly aggravating for managers who are looking for solutions to real problems. They are often not trained in any one of the academic fields. They may have a master of business administration or a liberal arts degree and only a cursory knowledge of any of the four fields. Inability of the MIS-related disciplines to communicate what MIS is all about from their own viewpoint has resulted in a serious lack of mutual understanding between those in the academic information systems field and the managers they are trying to serve. This is unfortunate, at the very least, since *managers* are ultimately responsible for the success of information systems (especially since they hold the purse strings). It seems fair to say that they have not been, on the whole, well served by academicians in this area, who have made an insufficient effort to understand (and more importantly empathize with) *managers'* needs and dilemmas.

It is equally unfortunate that data processing professionals often do not seem to have a clear perspective on what a MIS is or should be. They tend to view it in terms of programs or functions. Their view is largely a reactive one. They see their job as exploiting newly available technology in terms of the application needs of their organizations. Since this technology is constantly changing, they are not really able to fix on central, clarifying concepts. For example, in the mid-1960s they had, very quickly, to come to terms with third-generation technology, then switch focus to large-scale data bases, and then remote job-entry, time-sharing, and minicomputers. They face a constant struggle in trying to keep up-to-date with new developments while handling the day-to-day crises of their job.

The MIS profession as a whole has, perhaps, too often tried to divorce the computer from its context, causing many of the problems we have had in making ef-

---

[1]There are, for example, no academic journals of any stature that specifically concentrate on MIS, although the recent introduction of *MIS Quarterly* may change this situation.

fective use of computers. In many ways, the traditions we discuss differ mainly in the degree to which they include this context (and which parts of it— organizational, psychological, mathematical, and so on—they stress). We maintain that to gain a robust perspective on what an information system is, it is essential to examine *all* these aspects, each of which is covered by the six viewpoints mentioned above. After reviewing them we add our own integrating perspective. Our contribution is not a better one than the other six, but it highlights some areas that they either ignore or downplay, and in particular it shifts the emphasis from the computer to management and managerial problems.

COMPUTER SCIENCE

Many of those interested in Management Information Systems have been formally trained in computer science. This broad field involves a wide spectrum of interests we subdivide into three major areas. This is an arbitrary breakdown and is made from the perspective of our focus on MIS and not in terms of the development of the computer science field in and of itself.[2]

Computer Hardware and Software

One main effort in applied computer science is to develop better technology. The hardware and software available at any moment in time have been a limiting factor on the design of computer-based information systems. It always seems that with a more powerful machine or a slightly better set of languages a task that is proving difficult or impossible in the implementation of a particular information system will become more tractable. A review of just the developments in primary storage over the past 15 years indicates the continuing changes in hardware and the degree to which these have shifted problems of implementation. In the early days, storage was always in short supply, but with different software addressing schemes and new hardware technology storage is now available in sizes that no longer make it a serious limitation for most business programs. So, for example, in 1958, 10,000 positions of core memory on an IBM 650 seemed generous, yet 20 years later the availability of half a million positions of core memory is regarded by many programmers as rather limiting. The development of virtual memory[3] has in many

---

[2]The computer science field is most concerned with developing a formal theory of computing. Knuth's monumental *Art of Computer Programming* (1968) focuses on algorithms, key issues in the design of compilers and languages, and central problems in ensuring efficient and reliable performance of programs. Minsky (1967) similarly discusses computer hardware from an idealized perspective that obviously does not relate to the practical needs of computer specialists but is essential for the development of a computer *science*. Our book is concerned with practicalities; our review of computer science is thus unfairly narrow—we comb it only for outputs useful for DSS.

[3]This allows a program to use more memory than is actually available on the computer; the software operating system effectively divides the program into segments brought into memory as needed. In the days when an IBM/1401 machine had only 4,000 positions of core available for a program to run, considerable ingenuity and knowledge of the hardware was essential. Virtual memory is only one of the tools that now makes the physical computer "transparent" to the programmer.

respects removed the problem altogether from the set of issues an ordinary programmer must deal with.

This story of constant change and improvement in hardware is matched, though less dramatically and at a slower overall pace, by developments in software. The evolution from machine language to assemblers to higher level languages like FORTRAN and COBOL has been consistent and impressive. There is also a wide range of more specialized languages—so many in fact that J. Sammet's 1969 survey of them shows the Tower of Babel on the book's cover. The list of software tools now widely available reads like an incantation: GPSS, APL, TROLL, MARK IV, IMS, DYNAMO, and so on.[4] Some of these are general purpose languages and some are designed for particular applications. All in all, there has, over a relatively short period of time, been considerable improvement in software aids, for both the professional programmer and the nontechnical user.[5] These innovations have often caused trauma and turmoil when first introduced; new operating systems, database management techniques, and so on required organizations to learn additional skills, redefine existing operations and programs, and, at the same time, wrestle with the inevitable glitches in the advanced software.

It is obvious that the relative ease with which simulation models, data retrieval systems, and statistical analysis packages can now be developed and used is the outcome of the immense intellectual efforts of the computer science field. It is also obvious that there are still many new tools needed; one major current area of research, for example, is in developing theories and practical techniques for proving that a program is "debugged," that is, that it will work for all combinations of input and that its internal logic is correct. A generation of angry managers, MIS directors with ulcers, and crestfallen programmers will attest to the value of this work—if it can succeed.[6]

A good sense of the flavor of the computer science approach can be found in such journals as *Communications of the ACM* and *IBM Systems Journal.* On the whole, work in this area quickly becomes obsolete: for example, in the early 1960s

---

[4]GPSS stands for General Purpose Simulation System, which allows complex simulations to be built and run relatively simply. APL is a mathematical interactive programming language (see Berry, 1977) that has become increasingly popular for building models. TROLL is an econometric modeling language. MARK IV is a commercially available "package" that simplifies the process of writing standardized data processing programs. IMS (Information Management System) is IBM's widely used generalized data management software system. DYNAMO is a simple simulation language based on feedback loops (DYNAMO has been used in the Systems Dynamics models developed by Forrester and his colleagues, including the famous Club of Rome world simulation summarized in Meadows et al., *Limits to Growth,* 1972).

[5]Most students now enter graduate school with exposure to a higher level language such as FORTRAN or BASIC. Relatively few professional programmers now have detailed familiarity with machine language. The recent explosive growth in home computers that use BASIC suggests that nontechnical users will quickly be able to work with this simple but fairly powerful language (see Terrell, 1977).

[6]The problem is, of course, that a complex computer program involves literally millions of possible combinations. Testing a program generally involves creating data inputs that cover as many of the processing alternatives as possible. *Proving* that a program is fully debugged requires a formal theory, based on either mathematical logic or statistics, together with specialized languages.

there was substantial discussion of sorting algorithms and paging systems that was of great impact but now seems dull and even trivial. As we are all aware, keeping up-to-date in the computer field is difficult, but in computer science it seems close to impossible. Because of this, the general reader has difficulty locating relevant literature. Many technical books are obsolescent when published.[7]

The literature on Management Information Systems written by individuals involved in hardware and software development indicates two principal points of view. Their focus is not so much on a Management Information System (MIS) but rather on an Information Management System (IMS). This distinction is much more than just a play on words—it reflects a fundamental difference in perspective. Hardware and software developments have tended to be concerned with the management of large data bases or with improvements in operating systems. (This is due in part to the fact that many of the computer manufacturers' best customers, banking, insurance, military, and bureaucratic organizations, have large clerical data-handling tasks which they put on the computer and for which they are always in need of better, bigger, or cheaper facilities.)

This managing of data, viewed as synonymous with information, is a difficult task that has stimulated the development of new physical devices and software languages. Virtually all organizations with computer-based MIS now have permanent data bases, frequently very large, which need to be created and maintained and from which data need to be retrieved when required. To manage these processes in the face of organizational and technical change and uncertainty of use is a major endeavor in itself and a crucial aspect of Management Information Systems. However, the focus on Information Management ignores the decisions about what data should be put in in the first place, the "models" that are needed for the data to be useful, and the *organizational* difficulties of building a data base and maintaining it over time. These latter issues are more naturally dealt with by the management scientist and the organizational theorist.

It is important to recognize that when computer scientists talk of a Management Information System they may in reality have Information Management in mind. Certainly their literature tends to use these terms interchangeably despite the fact that from a *management* perspective their view looks excessively technical and ignores the "real" issues. At the same time, this narrow focus is often the key first step toward making possible new uses of the computer. The Information Management approach has generated the criteria for effective software and applications, but its technical emphasis and intellectual complexity has often made it difficult to translate from Information Management to Management Information; that is, the techniques provide criteria but not guidelines for application.

The second major thrust discernible in the computer science literature relevant to the MIS area deals with the development of more *efficient* computer systems. Workers in this field essentially argue that if a certain job has to be done (for example, providing information to management or accessing a data base), a key need is to define the technological changes needed to reduce the cost or effort of doing it. For example, the development of disk files for random access retrieval

---

[7]The National Computer Conference, sponsored by AFIPS (American Federation of Information Processing Societies), is probably the most accessible source of knowledge on *applied* developments in computer science. ACM (Association for Computing Machinery) is similarly the major society in this area; its periodic *Computing Surveys*, which discuss some aspect of computer science in great detail, are particularly useful.

clearly had an enormous impact in many data processing applications, and time-sharing opened up access to computer power for a whole new class of users.

This second group of computer science professionals defines information system as almost synonymous with the computer that drives the system. In some sense it views that system as the engine of a car, which needs to be refined and improved for its own sake. The use to which the car is put is examined only to the extent that it implies new design changes. This approach leads to important improvements in the efficiency (and thus potential effectiveness) of the hardware and software available to MIS users. Clearly, from our perspective, it is a necessary but not sufficient view. For example, computer users have not yet assimilated the recent revolution in mini-computers, which is a typical contribution of this group. The mini provides tremendous potential improvements in applications and efficiency; however, the provision of the necessary hardware and software is obviously vital but does not guarantee the exploitation of this potential.

Once again it should be stressed that this is an oversimplified view of computer science professionals. However, it highlights two important tendencies of those trained in this discipline: to focus on managing information for its own sake and to give priority of attention to further development of more efficient hardware and software systems. Of course, without their considerable creativity and innovation, many of the applications we see in business today would be close to impossible.

Information Theory

A second subset of computer science is based on the concepts of information theory, which was initially developed by R. E. Shannon, who first defined information in quantifiable terms and opened up new fields in engineering, communications, and control theory. Those who have built on his work have analyzed information systems in terms of channel capacity, transmission rates, storage capacity, and so on.[8] This theoretical level of analysis has been extended to include both cost and cost per bit of information transmitted. (The term *bit* as the basic unit of information came from Shannon.)

It is worth stressing how recent the technical term *information* is. Shannon's work is less than 30 years old; he provided key terms in our current vocabulary: *noise, channel,* and so on, and focused our attention on information as a literal commodity, a quantifiable flow of bits. He helped us see the difference between information and data. This rigorous viewpoint was of critical importance in the early development of hardware systems. Even now, however, we have comparatively little insight into what "information" really is. Information theory may be the least directly useful contribution to MIS; nonetheless the major conceptual problems that

---

[8]Bello (1953) enthusiastically hails information theory as giving electrical engineers, "For the first time, a comprehensive understanding of their trade. It tells them how to measure the commodity they are called upon to transmit—the commodity called 'information'—and how to measure the efficiency of their machinery for transmitting it." As this quote implies, information theory is more in the domain of electrical engineering than computer science; we group it under the latter heading because it played a major role in shaping the early ideas of workers in the computer field before it split into neat categories such as computer science, artificial intelligence, computer architecture, and so on.

still remain are likely to require its formal, theoretical analysis for solution. Colin Cherry's *On Human Communication* (1957) provides an excellent summary of information theory and related topics in cybernetics, which similarly stresses communication, control, and feedback processes in the operation of a system.[9]

The most practical impact of information theory can be seen in computer manufacturers' proud boasts that the cost per bit of storage has declined precipitously over the past 20 years and that the new Super-Zoom VI can perform x million operations per second. More recently, the growth of data communication networks to link remote users to a central computer or to allow communication among many machines has made the concepts and techniques of information theory of immense importance. These networks require that data be encoded as compactly as possible and that messages be sent over telephone or microwave links in such a way that the expensive transmission lines are efficiently employed and errors are identified. Until very recently, remote access to computer power was mainly through voice-grade telephone lines, which could transmit 300 or 600 bits per second (bps) (a single number or alphabetic character generally requires 8 bits to encode it). Speeds of 9600 bps are now common and conservative forecasts assume transmission rates of 50,000 bps will be available by 1985. There are several commercial networks now in use that allow a user in California to communicate with one in Boston with a transmission delay of 1 second.[10]

These developments in data communications are a recent part of the decentralization of the computer resource. The work on DSS discussed in this book mostly draws on a more standard technology, where the user communicates with a central time-shared computer. However, the data communications facilities now available open up many potential applications, although here again, the technical, context-free focus of computer science provides tools whose *exploitation* requires a different and broader conceptual approach.

Artificial Intelligence

Artificial intelligence (AI) is a more recently recognized subfield within computer science and has perhaps the greatest potential with respect to decisionmaking. Artificial intelligence researchers have drawn on and contributed to cognitive psychology, linguistics, and philosophy. As P. H. Winston (1977) points out, understanding computer intelligence is a useful way to study general intelligence. E. H. Shortliffe's summary of the four core topics in AI (1976) similarly suggests

---

[9]Wiener, whose name is often linked with Shannon's as the founders of information theory, presented a cybernetic theory that "any organism is held together by the possession of means for the acquisition, use, retention, and transmission of information" (1948). Beer's *Platform for Change* (1975) provides a rich application of cybernetics to social and organizational decisionmaking and information systems. The major practical impact of this intersection between information theory and cybernetics has been in mathematical control theory; this allows computers to control complex processes in manufacturing, petrochemicals processing, and navigation while monitoring their own performance, detecting errors, and responding to changes in their physical environment.

[10]The packet switching network now being built by Nippon Telegraph and Telephone and due to be operational in 1979 has a target transmission time of 150 milliseconds (see Takatsuki et al., 1977).

that this field's eclectic, abstract research, involving "toy" problems such as chess, blocks, theorems, and robots can play a central role in the practical development of "intelligent" information systems and problem-solving aids:

1. Modeling and representing knowledge: Minsky's theory of frames is perhaps the most influential paradigm in this area of study, although a wide range of approaches has been used to represent knowledge (which is, of course, far more complex than storing *data*) in a computer.

2. Reasoning, deduction, and problem solving: much early AI research simulated human reasoning processes [E. A. Feigenbaum and J. Feldman's excellent book *Computers and Thought* (1963) summarizes both the content of this work and its overoptimistic expectations about future progress].

3. Heuristic search: Simon, whose ideas on problem solving have been a major influence on work on management decisionmaking (see Chapter 3), helped direct AI toward basing computer intelligence on human strategies rather than trying the British Museum algorithm—the old parable of a million or so monkeys hammering away at typewriters in the museum until eventually one of them writes *War and Peace*. Such exhaustive enumeration is theoretically possible but in practice not feasible. "Despite the computer's speed and computational powers, many human problems . . . are so complex that thorough evaluation of each possible move can be shown to require a near-infinite amount of time! . . . researchers attempt to identify good strategies that absolutely limit the number of alternatives that must be studied" (Shortliffe, 1976, p. 19).

4. AI systems and languages: AI programs require extremely powerful languages, especially for processing "strings" such as English sentences. Developing these capabilities has been an essential activity in AI and is obviously within the mainstream of computer science.

The first three of these four themes are directly relevant to decision support in its broadest sense. However, the claims of AI are generally far larger than its accomplishments, and its work has made only exploratory incursions into the difficult philosophic field of epistemology. It has often been said that AI involves clumsy, expensive programs that try to perform something a four-year-old child does naturally. That said, given that computer systems in organizations lack any sense of "intelligence" and dumbly carry out simple orders to add, search, write, and report, even this represents a substantial advance.

Much of AI is concerned with replacing human reasoning. The focus of attention is on the capabilities and behavior of the computer program that attempts the problem-solving task. The descriptive theory of human decisionmaking underlying the design of the program generally draws more on mathematics, linguistics, and logic than on empirical psychology. The early work of A. Newell, J. C. Shaw, and H. A. Simon (1958, 1962) on heuristic problem solving is based on observation of human subjects, but most extensions of it pay little attention to the issues of real behavior. At times, it seems that researchers and readers of AI work miss useful opportunities to synthesize each other's work. T. Winograd (1972) has begun to argue in this vein. He feels that AI lacks an adequate psychological base; however, many AI students of "human" intelligence reject this viewpoint.[11]

One AI project that seems especially relevant to decision support, and that may even be a prototype for an effective man-machine problem-solving system is MYCIN, developed by Shortliffe and his colleagues. MYCIN helps physicians diagnose and treat particular bacterial infections. It can defend its own behavior by explaining the rules and assumptions it used to arrive at a conclusion; it essentially provides the physician with good advice (see Winston, 1977). Interestingly, Shortliffe specifically describes MYCIN as a decision support system, although since it is a prototype he does not discuss implementation issues in any detail.

Physicians usually must treat bacterial blood infections without knowing what organism is responsible. Processing cultures in a microbiology laboratory may provide information, but requires several days. The physician thus often prescribes broad-spectrum drugs that cover all possibilities rather than more effective disease-specific treatments. Sometimes, "nonexperts" prescribe drug regimens where an expert would not recommend any antimicrobial therapy. One aim in the design of MYCIN was to narrow the gap between the practicing physician and experts in infectious diseases. MYCIN consists of three subprograms:

1.   The consultation system: this uses information about the patient and MYCIN's own knowledge to decide if the patient needs treatment, what microorganisms are likely to be causing the infection, possible drugs for dealing with it, and specific drugs suitable for this patient. MYCIN elicits information from the physician and applies its "knowledge" of 200 stored decision rules as it makes sense of this data.

2.   The explanation system: this answers questions from the user both during and after the consultation session. It tries to convince the physician and permits her or him to ask how MYCIN reached its decision or even why it has asked a particular question. MYCIN has a (limited) ability to understand English.

3.   The rule-acquisition system: this is currently incomplete but is intended to allow an expert to teach MYCIN new rules and update its knowledge base.

Figure 2-1 (from Winston) shows excerpts from a sample session. Much of MYCIN's knowledge is derived from experts' informal judgments and even intuitions. It is able to reach conclusions based on whatever information is available at the time. It interacts with the users in their own terminology and conceptual framework. It advises and does not usurp the physician's decisionmaking role or reasoning process. "MYCIN has also been developed with more attention to human engineering than is typical of much of the AI field. The goal has been to develop mechanisms for interacting with medical professionals who . . . have often never used computers before." (Winston, 1977, p. 244).

---

[11]Feigenbaum and Feldman (1963) offer an excellent introduction to the early claims and accomplishments of AI. Dutton and Starbuck (1971) provide a comprehensive update. Winston's *Artificial Intelligence* (1977) seems likely to become a standard textbook, which indicates the maturation of what has been up to now an extremely specialized field.

Figure 2-1 Sample MYCIN Session

■ What is the patient's name?

John Doe

■ Male or Female?

Male.

■ Age?

He is 55.

■ Have you obtained positive cultures indicating general type?

Yes.

■ What type of infection is it?

Primary bacteremia.

■ When did symptoms first appear?

May 5, 1975.

■ Let's call the most recent positive culture CULTURE-1. From what site was CULTURE-1 taken?

From the blood.

■ When?

May 9, 1975.

■ Let's call the first significant organism from this blood culture ORGANISM-1. Do you know the identity of ORGANISM-1?

No.

■ Is ORGANISM-1 a rod or a coccus or something else?

Rod.

■ What is the gram stain of ORGANISM-1?

Gramnegative.

■ Have there been positive cultures from sites which are not associated with infections about which you are seeking advice?

No.

■ Did ORGANISM-1 grow aerobically?

Yes.

■ Did ORGANISM-1 grow anaerobically?

Yes.

■ What is the suspected portal of entry of ORGANISM-1?

The gastrointestinal tract.

.

.

.

When satisfied that it has a reasonably good feel for the situation, MYCIN starts a short line of questions in preparation for recommending a course of treatment:

■ My recommendation will be based on the opinion that the identity of ORGANISM-1 may be 1 Pseudomonas aeruginosa, 2 Klebsiella pneumoniae, 3 E. coli, 4 Bacteroides fragilis, 5 Enterobacter, or 6 Proteus nonmirabilis. On a scale of 0 to 4, where higher numbers indicate greater severity, how would you rate the patient's degree of sickness?

3.

■ Does the patient have a clinically significant allergic reaction to any antimicrobial agent?

No.

■ How much does the patient weigh?

70 kilograms.

■ My first recommendation is as follows: In order to cover for items 1, 2, 3, 5, and 6, give Gentamycin using a dose of 119 mg (1.7 mg/kg) q8h IV [or IM] for 10 days. Modify dose in renal failure. And in order to cover for item 4, give Clindamycin using a dose of 595 mg (8.5 mg/kg) q6h IV [or IM] for 14 days. If diarrhea or other gastrointestinal symptoms develop, check for pseudomembranous colitis.

■ Do you wish to see the second choice?

.

.

.

MYCIN is by no means typical of AI products and is experimental. Nonetheless, this example suggests that AI may eventually be of direct value to MIS professionals trying to build tools that handle complex problems, that respond intelligently, and that permit the use of natural language.

INFORMATION ECONOMICS

The second academic field we identified as relevant to MIS, information economics, is a small and ill-defined one. In the 1960s a number of researchers applied microeconomic theory and methods to the issue of computers. W. F. Sharpe (1963), for example, examined the trade-offs relevant to the development of hardware.[12] (This work has had little follow-up.) A. M. McDonough (1963) defined a frame-

---

[12]Sharpe relies on standard microeconomic techniques. Cotton (1975) summarizes this and related work, which he views as mainly valuable in providing a "sound framework for the pricing of computer services." The force of the analysis is weakened by the lack of empirical data and a complete absence of emphasis on *information* as opposed to "basic computer services."

work for assessing the worth of information and A. E. Amstutz (1966) similarly classified the dimensions of information. R. R. Andrus (1971) synthesized much of this work and presents propositions such as: "The value of information increases as (1) the format, language, and degree of detail approach the desire of the user; (2) the ease and right of access increases; and (3) the time of acquisition approaches the time of use" (p. 43).

The whole issue of what is information *worth* is obviously a key one. It is difficult to discuss economic trade-offs between hardware or software components, and at present it is virtually impossible to evaluate the "worth" of information systems. None of the work on information economics in relation to MIS is widely read and there is no critical mass in the research field. We include this discipline in our list for two main reasons. First, the questions it raises are among the most important of all for the practical development of an information *science*. Second, there is a substantial amount of work in this field in disciplines tangential to MIS. Decision analysis, increasingly a standard part of the curriculum in business schools, applies Bayesian techniques to place a value on information that reduces uncertainty.[13] In accounting research, information economics is a well-established discipline that should eventually generalize to MIS (see Demski, 1972).

Sharpe's work was intended to outline a general methodology for comparing computer systems (and components). His approach is tentative and lacks a definition of "cost" and "benefit." (These definitions are still lacking.) Generally, hardware effectiveness has been described in terms of "instructions per dollar" or "cost per bit"; these are not very meaningful for comparing an IBM 1401, which had virtually no operating system and used machine language, with an IBM 370 used under MVT or VS (advanced operating systems) with COBOL as the main language. Comparing data management software systems with all their myriad schemes for leasing, maintenance, core requirements, and so on is still more difficult. Even such tentative approaches as Sharpe's are valuable and it seems important for MIS that the information economics perspective becomes more influential. We can assume, because the issues are so important, that there will be cross-hybridization among researchers in this area, in the fields of accounting, decision analysis, technology transfer, microeconomics, and so on. This book would be far stronger if we had an operational set of concepts and techniques for discussing the value of information. The evaluation of DSS, the comparison of particular design approaches and the definition of the organization's data bases, to list a few examples, requires concept of "worth." At present, we can only fall back on intuitive definitions and trade-offs.

MANAGEMENT SCIENCE

To the extent that MIS has a single academic home, it is in management science. University departments, professional journals, conferences, and textbooks are predominantly organized around management science, and the information generated by those in this area is easy to obtain and quickly disseminated. Although

---

[13]Bayesian techniques provide formal methodologies for analyzing the implications of a decisionmaker's subjective judgments of probabilities, updating these assessments as new evidence is obtained. They have become the most accepted framework for resolving problems involving uncertainty. See Howard (1968).

many computer scientists and data processing professionals are unfamiliar with this well-organized effort, management science has made major contributions to the MIS field. There is no MIS journal comparable in academic prestige to *Management Science*.[14]

From an information system standpoint, we can divide the management science field into major subareas, all concerned with models and model building: optimization, simulation, and heuristic models. While operations research has mainly focused on theoretical aspects of mathematical programming and on methodological issues, the business of applied management science has been model building. In terms of MIS, this means that the "system" is a combination of computer routines applied to a particular problem or class of problems. Some management scientists are interested in models for their own sake and take for granted the organizational context in which they are embedded, but many others are more broadly concerned with the procedures and decisionmaking processes needed to use the model.

The most prominent work in management science has obviously been the development of optimization models, especially linear programming and related techniques. While many of the algorithms are still fairly esoteric (there are probably more articles on integer programming than there are real world uses of it), this effort has had a substantial impact on many large organizations. It is commonplace, for example, in the oil industry to schedule daily refinery operations through linear programming. Large-scale manufacturing activities frequently are planned on the basis of a formal optimization model, and there is increasing use of linear programming in banks, the transportation industry, and utilities. For problems that are well understood and that involve a large number of interacting variables, these techniques have proved to be powerful aids to decisionmaking for particular subunits of organizations. Many of the models link in to the company's computer-based information system. For example, the refinery optimization model may obtain cost coefficients or demand forecasts from disk files and also provide data for regular manufacturing and distribution reports. For workers in this subfield of management science, MIS is synonymous with the use of optimization techniques to *replace* the decisionmaker in the control of some function or decision.[15]

Other model builders have focused on simulation rather than optimization. They tend to be more directly concerned with the wider organizational system. Thus, while the *algorithm* may be the central interest in an article on dynamic programming, the researcher's focus will be on the *decision* in a similar paper on, say, simulation techniques for evaluating alternative distribution systems or investment opportunities.

It seems fair to say that simulation is the most widely used managerial computer-based technique in both government and industrial decisionmaking.

[14]*Management Science* has published several major articles on MIS (for example, Ackoff, 1967; Argyris, 1971; and Mason and Mitroff, 1973). At the same time, such articles are infrequent, and the topic of MIS fits in awkwardly with the themes and publishing procedures of the journal.

[15]They also focus on decision *problems*; individual workers in this field generally become experts in either a technique (such as dynamic programming) they apply to several types of problems or on specific decision tasks (such as inventory lot size choice, capital investment, or project management).

While much work on optimization tends to focus on powerful abstract models and methodologies that managers find unrealistic and hard to follow, the simulation approach generally draws on more accessible methods. The value of a simulation is that it often replicates a manager's environment in his or her own terms and makes it possible to test alternative decisions. Moreover, there is a wide body of software support for simulation, ranging from FORTRAN, the lingua franca of the computer world, through special-purpose languages such as GPSS (General Purpose Simulation System) or DYNAMO (the language used in the well-known *Limits of Growth* study for the Club of Rome), right up through complex econometric forecasting aids such as TROLL (see Emshoff and Sisson, 1970, for a useful overview of simulation languages and techniques).

Simulation is a powerful decisionmaking aid. Once again, for its supporters the term Management Information System implies model-based decision aids, with the simulation routine drawing on stored data files and generating management reports.

There is a wealth of literature on management science models, with new textbooks appearing literally every month (reflecting the growth of courses on the topic at the undergraduate level). H. M. Wagner's *Principles of Operations Research* (1975) is perhaps the classic text now in use.[16]

A smaller, less developed subfield within management science is *heuristic* modeling. This is related to simulation and involves descriptive models of a decision process, built up from observations of human problem solvers. The models are generally fairly crude and are intended as a means of analyzing the decision process in order to improve it, rather than of optimizing the solution. G. P. E. Clarkson's (1962) simulation of a portfolio manager's investment decisions in a large bank was the earliest and most visible use of a heuristic model. (The term *heuristic* relates to rules of thumb and standard operating procedures of a decisionmaker; it comes from Newell, Shaw, and Simon, whose theories of human problem solving focus on these heuristics.) Clarkson's striking results have since been challenged (see J. M. Dutton and W. H. Starbuck, 1971) but the concept of modeling a management decision process was an invaluable insight. T. P. Gerrity, Jr., among others, adapted it as the basis for designing Decision Support Systems; his decision-centered analysis involves *describing* the decision process as the first step toward improving the decision.

Heuristic models have not had the impact Simon forecast in 1965 when he proclaimed heuristic programming as the next breakthrough for OR/MIS.[17] A major bank attempted, with expensive and embarrassing results, to directly imple-

---

[16]There has been a refreshing increase in the number of textbooks that focus on applications rather than just techniques. Even so, there are still extremely few books that provide surveys, illustrations in complex settings, or case studies. G. Hoffman (see Halbrecht, 1972) claims that over 60 percent of materials in a broad sample of OR textbooks relates to mathematics and less than 10 percent to real world decisionmaking.

[17]Wiest (1966) defines heuristic programming as "a set of instructions for directing the computer to solve a problem—the way a manager might do it if he had enough time." He suggests that this methodology is extremely useful in such problems as assembly line balancing, job shop scheduling, and portfolio selection. Winston (1977) emphasizes that heuristic search methods are a central topic in AI.

ment Clarkson's model to actually make investment decisions. The heuristic models developed by Simon and his colleagues for chess playing and logic problems were highly influential in AI in the early 1960s but work on them has since come to a standstill (see Feigenbaum and Feldman, 1963, for several stimulating discussions of these models). Nonetheless, heuristic model building still seems to have considerable potential for decision support and underlies many of our recommendations for designing systems (see Chapter 6).

Classifying management science model building in organizations in terms of the three subfields of optimization, simulation, and heuristic decision models is obviously arbitrary and incomplete. Nonetheless, most management scientists would define themselves as working mainly in one of these areas; they also interpret information systems in terms of their own focus.

An alternative approach to discussing model building in management science is to classify the field by application area rather than methodology. For example, some modelers are mainly interested in production, marketing, or finance; this functional perspective is apparent in the frequent references to marketing information systems, accounting information systems, and so on. Most work in the information systems/management science area has focused on particular applications: production and distribution are especially suited to optimization techniques, while marketing has made heavy use of data banks and statistical models. Simulation models have been widely used in finance, especially for capital investment projects.

The major contribution of management science to MIS has been to emphasize the need for and value of *models* as an integral part of an information system. In the early stages of computer use, from 1955 to 1965, this need was clearly not recognized, as the term data processing implies. Electronic data processing was dominated by accounting *data* but not supported by accounting *models*. D. B. Montgomery and G. L. Urban's (1969) definition of a marketing decision system clarifies the importance of models within an information system. As Figure 2-2 shows, the model is generally the analytic aid that *integrates* stored data.

A small but growing number of management scientists have increasingly emphasized the actual process of building models. They criticize OR/MS professionals for their frequent disinterest in the *use* of the models they build; many articles present theoretical applications and treat the model almost as a theorem, ending their discussion with a perfunctory Q.E.D. with no examination of the model's relevance for a real manager with a real problem in a real organization. J. C. D. Little (1970) states that very few models are in fact ever used and defines criteria for model design, such as robustness, ease of control and understanding by the manager, and completeness in relevant detail. (This, and such work as Urban's "Building Models for Managers" [1974] are discussed in Chapter 7 on the implementation of DSS.) M. Zeleny (1974) has more recently spearheaded the development of new approaches to model building under the label multicriteria decisionmaking (MCDM). He argues that the traditional concepts of optimization, requiring prior definition of a simple objective function, are inapplicable in situations involving multiple, conflicting objectives (profit versus market share versus customer goodwill), and incomparable attributes. J. S. Dyer (1973) and S. Zionts and J. Wallenius (1976), among others, have developed interactive computer systems that allow the decisionmaker *situationally* to determine trade-offs and objectives. This work on MCDM has several parallels with that on DSS, especially in its emphasis on support rather than replacement and its reliance on the decisionmaker's judgment. Zeleny

*Figure 2-2   Decision-Information System Structure
(from Montgomery and Urban, 1969)*

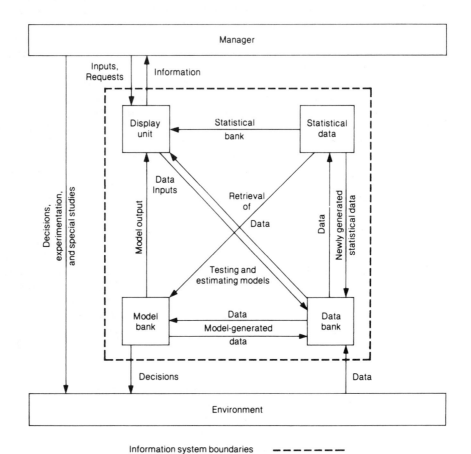

Information system boundaries   — — — — — —

has edited several collections of papers on MCDM, which promises to extend both the concepts and applications of management science model building.[18]

The overall contributions of management science, both in themselves and in relation to MIS, are considerable. It has developed models that work, that are used, and that help the organization. At the same time, there has been considerable overselling and force fitting of inappropriate models onto unwilling organizations. Nonetheless, the overall impact has been beneficial. It should be recognized, however, that those engaged in this model-building activity are quite clear in their own minds that a MIS must contain, at its center, a model. There are even those who

---

[18]See, especially, Cochrane and Zeleney (1973), Zeleny (1974), and Starr and Zeleny (1977). Many MCDM models lack a humanized person-machine interface. Dyer's methodology, for example, is clumsy and difficult to use. The MCDM technique requires the skills of interactive systems design found in the MIS field. A marriage between MCDM and DSS promises to be practically and intellectually fruitful.

consider that if the model is to be of any use at all it must be of the optimization type. In that sense the management scientist is similar to the computer scientist; each believes that the computer or the model itself is the key ingredient. However, neither of these views seems to be shared widely by the manager or the EDP professional.

A further fundamental contribution of management science has been to show how information systems development can benefit from the application of analytic thinking (the "systems" point of view) to an organization's very often ill-defined problems. The use of systematic analysis in what appear to be fuzzy decision situations is in some cases indistinguishable from logic or common sense, but there is an analytic methodology and discipline that can be taught and used quite apart from specific applications and models. This perspective provides a strategy for problem solving and a formal approach to structuring problems (C. W. Churchman's *The Systems Approach* [1968] and Simon's *The New Science of Management Decision* [1960] describe its spirit well).

BEHAVIORAL SCIENCE

Behavioral research on computers and analytic methods has been fairly fragmented. Behavioral science is concerned with people—in organizations and small groups, and as individuals. Some of the earliest applications of the behavioral perspective were E. Mumford and T. B. Ward (1968) and T. I. Whisler's (1970) studies of the impact of introducing computers into organizations. Mumford and Ward examined this from the perspective of clerical workers, while Whisler focused on middle management. Their work has some useful insights but has not been followed up in any significant way by other researchers.[19] A. Pettigrew's (1976) study of political aspects of computers is, similarly, a fascinating and detailed study, unfortunately read more by behavioral scientists than MIS specialists. The lack of follow-up may partly reflect a general sense that the central issues for MIS are technical and that the introduction of the computer into organizations' operations is beneficial and inevitable. There has been little incentive for MIS professionals to absorb the largely negative arguments of behavioral science in the 1960s.

Argyris' (1970, 1971) attacks are typical of this negative stance. Argyris has been a constant and influential critic of the MIS profession. He argues that the rationalization and systematization of MIS threatens the individual and inhibits the openness and adaptiveness essential for a healthy organizational climate, that MIS reinforces the status quo and generates forces that impede effectiveness (partly through an overemphasis on efficiency). Argyris' attack is easy to shrug off and hard to counter. In the past few years, it has been followed up from a more positive perspective, and the work of such independent researchers as I. I. Mitroff, J. Weizenbaum, I. Vertinsky, and A. Moshowitz reflects a much more humanistic attitude toward the wonders of technology than was generally found in discussions in the 1960s. This work has been written by insiders—Argyris was an outsider and

---

[19]Whisler's prediction that computer systems would lead to centralization and substantial replacement of middle management has been partially supported, but as Hunt and Newell (1971, p. 42) suggest: "Rather than leading to centralization, the computer appears to be a neutral element which will be fitted into the basic managerial philosophy of the organization." In general, computer prophets have underestimated the speed of technological change and overestimated the rate of social and organizational change.

hence both more easily ignored and less insightful as to the legitimate (from the perspective of behavioral scientists concerned with its social impact) uses of the computer. The early behavioral research on MIS forced attention to the fact that information systems are not abstract artifacts but are built and run by *people* in the context of a *social* system in the organization. The word forced was chosen carefully; on the whole there has been little explicit recognition of even the relevance of behavioral issues by the technical tradition.[20]

Much of the more recent behavioral research within MIS and OR/MS has focused on the implementation process (in contrast to technical design). In particular, a number of academics and practitioners have described implementation as the management of social change, emphasizing the dynamics of the process, resistance to change and the need to institutionalize a change program.[21] This work, discussed in Chapter 7, also emphasizes that the failure of a system or model is now rarely due to technical inadequacies.

A third growing body of behavioral research on information systems is psychological in focus. It examines cognitive processes in problem solving and in the use of information. It studies the different cognitive "styles" and cognitive structures of managers and system builders and points out that information is not an objective commodity but a personalized response to one's environment. This cognitive research (C. B. Stabell, 1974; J. L. McKenney and P. G. W. Keen, 1974; and J. H. B. M. Huysmans, 1970, 1973) is discussed in Chapter 3; it provides a descriptive perspective on the decision process and emphasizes the need to match system design to the individual needs, processes, and capacities of the user.

The behavioral work in MIS has shown quite clearly that paying attention only to "computer" issues is not nearly enough for consistent success in developing information systems in an organization. In the very early days of EDP, the information systems that were developed were small and localized and generated curiosity because of their technical novelty. The wider "people" considerations were often less important, or at least less apparent. Computer systems have become far more widespread and larger in scope and impact, so that it is essential to consider human aspects very carefully, both in terms of the effect of computerization on the work force and on the nature of work and of the process by which large-scale systems are introduced into the organization. It must be admitted that, on the whole, the importance of these behavioral aspects was made apparent by the many failures that resulted from their being dismissed as irrelevant.[22]

The impact of the computer on the work force is of increasing concern as automation takes over more of a company's operations. For example, the use of computers for order entry is now a fairly common application (whether is deserves

---

[20]Urban (1974) points out that over an 18-month period, only 5 out of 150 (3 percent) articles in *Management Science* (Applications section) discussed systems that had ever been implemented in real organizations. The mainstream of OR/MS and, to a lesser extent, MIS involves theorems, hypotheses, conceptual models, and algorithms, but rarely people.

[21]See, for example, Urban (1974), Ginzberg (1975), Keen (1974, 1975, 1976, 1977), Vertinsky et al. (1975), Lucas and Plimpton (1972), and Sorenson and Zand (1973).

[22]See Keen's *Implementation Research* (1977), which identifies a distinct category, the failure study, which largely aims at drawing technicians' attention to the consequences of elegant designs matched to the wrong context or ineffectually implemented.

the label MIS may be questionable, but it is described as such in the literature). Regardless of its label, it is clearly a computer function at the operational center of activities in the organization. A customer cannot order the company's product without going through this order entry process. If the clerical work force finds such a system awkward to use, or if the system is implemented without adequate consideration of the impact of such a drastic innovation on motivation, morale, and job characteristics, it may easily fail and bring the operations of the company close to a halt. This is perhaps an extreme example, but with growing unionization and an increasing concern about the quality of work and the job environment, these considerations may dominate technical computer-related questions. Technical analysts are ill equipped in terms of knowledge and attitude to deal with them.[23]

There are many documented cases where complex, innovative systems failed because of a lack of attention to human engineering. Over the past 3 years, for example, it has become apparent that the Universal Product Code, intended to automate supermarket operations, would require far more time to implement than was anticipated; the "user" of this computer system is the supermarket customer who, regardless of cost savings or convenience, simply wants to have the price of an item printed on it. To the customer this is "obvious." Behavioral scientists constantly stress that what is trivial from the viewpoint of the designer may be a critical feature of a person's or a group's psychology and behavior. For behavioral scientists, of course, these questions are the most important and they tend to view information systems not from a technical standpoint, but in terms of their impact on people.

As long as behavioral researchers were mainly pointing to inadequacies in the technical tradition, they had little impact. More recently, though, a number of important themes have become well established in behavioral research in MIS and OR/MS. A group at Northwestern University has made several large-scale longitudinal studies of the organizational factors that influence the effectiveness of systems and modeling efforts. In particular they have identified a "life cycle" effect. If the OR group is relatively new to the organization, for example, at the "missionary" stage, it needs a personalized style of leadership, and should choose only very visible and short-term projects to work on; it must aim at effectiveness and credibility rather than at efficiency. As the group's position matures and it becomes institutionalized, it must develop more control systems, including charge-out methods, and choose very different types of application. This type of research substantially adds to our knowledge but requires a lengthy time frame for study and patient, widespread surveys across a large number of organizations. We discuss some of its implications in Chapter 9.[24]

The phrase *resistance to change* is a common theme in management literature. By looking in detail at computer innovations as an organizational and social change process, behavioral research has highlighted the fact that resistance may not be pathological but a very reasonable response, that the technical change the computer represents is not necessarily desirable simply because it is change. Similarly, re-

---

[23]Woolsey (1972, 1975) has provided innumerable witty examples of the extent to which most technical specialists are innocents abroad in the real world and of the damage their innocence can cause.

[24]See, in particular, Radnor et al. (1968, 1970), Rubenstein et al. (1967), and Bean et al. (1973). The et al. is obligatory since this research is marked by teamwork and hence lengthy lists of coauthors.

search on the differences in attitude, training, and personality of managers and technical specialists has led to a much clearer awareness of the importance of the user in systems development: personal needs, involvement, and "style" are all now recognized as major constraints on systems design.[25]

Early behavioral research lacked any real knowledge of the computer world. Within the past few years we have seen the emergence of a group of behavioral researchers who have substantial experience in programming, model building, AI, and so on. For this reason alone we can expect an increased emphasis on behavioral issues in MIS, to the point perhaps that management science and behavioral science will become more fused, to reflect the fusion between the technical and the behavioral in real life.

DATA PROCESSING PROFESSIONALS

The four academic disciplines discussed above each have their own view of what a Management Information System is and ought to be, but among them they have contributed most of our basic knowledge. Without computer science we would not have the hardware and software advances that have allowed us to build the kinds of systems that are in place today. Management science has developed the models that are often a central component of an information system. The behavioral scientist has helped us understand the nontechnical causes of success and failure of MIS. All of this work has resulted in a substantial body of knowledge on which data processing professionals can draw.

Data processing professionals have to carry on the job of building, maintaining, and operating information systems in organizations, and they often have neither the inclination nor the perspective for academic contemplation. At most, there has been 20 years of usage of computer-based information systems in organizations. Many vice-presidents for the MIS function in companies gained their early experience in the "unit record" field. Even for those whose training is more recent, the bewildering rate of technological change, moving from the tape-based to disk-based systems, to virtual memory, multiprogramming, and time-sharing, has been sufficiently rapid to cause even the most adaptive manager many difficulties. Their relatively outdated early training, plus this pace of technological change, puts pressure on many heads of data processing to concentrate on the computer in and of itself, at the expense of focusing on the company's business needs. The increasing degree of technical professionalization of those entering the information systems field is partly influenced by professional societies; for example, the Association of Computing Machinery proposed a curriculum for a bachelor's and master's degree that attempts to pull together all the technical and systems-related material into a comprehensive 2-year program. This curriculum contains comparatively little material on managerial and behavioral topics. As a technical curriculum it is intimidating even for an incoming student let alone for a busy manager who can update her or his knowledge only casually (see J. D. Couger et al., 1973).

---

[25]There is a clear category of research on implementation that adopts this perspective, defined by Keen in *Implementation Research* (1977) as one of mutual understanding. See also Mason and Mitroff (1973), Churchman and Schainblatt (1965), Doktor and Hamilton (1973), McKenney and Keen (1974), and Huysmans (1970).

At the same time there appears to be a trend in organizations to put a non-technical individual, frequently a former line manager, in charge of the information systems and data processing activities of the firm. A recent informal survey of one major hardware manufacturer's principal customers shows that 22 out of 45 major accounts had appointed a new head of the MIS function within the past 12 months. This reflects, in part, the organization's attempts to get computer-related activities focused on real business problems. It suggests a recognition of the need for the individual in charge of data processing to be a real manager; technical competence is less important than ability to supervise personnel, plan, and maintain a business perspective.

For many data processing professionals, MIS are defined as computer programs in application areas maintained on the computer. This oversimplified view does not do justice to the achievements of the profession in constructing useful systems under conditions of pressure, change, and technological uncertainty. Many of the best EDP managers have little time for writing about their experiences because they are far too busy working on building new systems in their organization, while those who have time to do the writing very often have not been particularly successful, and the writing serves as some form of advertisement and is either self-serving or trivial. The best professionals in a way have the least to say. The problem they all face is that of obsolescence and sheer time pressure, and their experience does not generalize well. Outstanding EDP professionals seem to be individuals who devote effort to keeping up-to-date, reacting quickly to new technology without naively swallowing all the seller's claims, and who build a good track record within their organization. The dilemma for such individuals is that they can easily reach a well-paid dead end. As senior EDP professionals, they have had little lateral or upward mobility; their computer expertise, which led to their current position, needs to be backed by management skill or knowledge of a functional area. In a fast-moving and complex technical field, senior EDP professionals are in an extremely difficult position, hectically running to keep in the same place. R. L. Nolan summarizes their problems with sympathy and insight in "Plight of the EDP Manager" (1973).

Data processing professionals in organizations have wrestled with a complex technology and gradually got it under control. They have three distinctive achievements to their credit:

1. First and foremost, they now have an enviable record of developing *products*. The profession has built a substantial knowledge of families of applications, software packages, and programming languages. It has developed expertise in given functional areas that can be transferred to new companies and new situations; the pains and mistakes of its early efforts were necessary and have now led to an increasing competence and assurance.

2. They have provided a methodology for building systems. Systems development is often examined from an academic standpoint that underestimates its difficulties and limits; many organizations have, however, evolved effective and practical strategies for managing large-scale development projects. These methodologies tend to assume the problem is already defined and worries about implementation only from that point forward; nevertheless we now have a firm grasp on

how a system should be built, given the knowledge of its main technical characteristics.

3.   There is *implicit* recognition that the computer is less relevant than the rethinking and analysis that goes on before the computer programming is done. The work of the best data processing professionals emphasizes the immense payoff from reexamining and resystematizing tasks and functions as the organization and its environment change (see Churchman's *The Systems Approach,* 1968, for a rich discussion of this approach).

In many instances, data processing professionals view an information system as a set of computer programs that largely replace clerical operations. Thus payroll and accounts receivable programs and other clerical data processing activities are labeled as Management Information Systems in the professional literature, for example, in *Datamation.* These systems are designed to be cheaper than the clerical work force they replace (and if not cheaper they will certainly be more consistently adequate and often remove the need for an expensive clerical staff, which is also increasingly hard to recruit). The efficiency such automation facilitates, plus the added ability of a computer system to handle expansion and growth, have given the data processing fraternity some substantial successes.[26] The momentum built up through a series of successful applications too often, however, results in a continuation of the kind of systems developed in the past. There is a built-in bias for the data processing professional to continue with what has been successful and to view MIS in terms of "cost replacement." This also too easily leads them to a particular perspective on the use of the computer that may not be shared by the managers for whom they work. However, they are responsible for most of the progress we have made to date. Many of them are able to absorb the lessons of technological development and realize the *new* directions it makes possible while continuing to deliver systems of immediate value to their companies. Others are either prone to the "bandwagon" effect—jumping on new concepts too quickly—or have the narrow emphasis on clerical data processing we have described. But there is every reason to expect the profession to shift into its new, wider role, although it is likely to be the management-oriented members who lead the way, and the technical specialists who become conceptually and organizationally redundant.

MANAGEMENT

The term MIS implies that the information system is for managers. From experience many practicing managers argue that this is not so. They claim to be uninfluenced by computer-based information systems although they willingly grant that the organization under them has been considerably affected. The arguments we have used so far in this chapter would tend to support their view. There *has* been a shift in attitude; in the 1960s, as computer applications became widespread, managers tended

---

[26]Such successes tend to be taken for granted after awhile. We suggest our readers pause and reflect, the next time they catch a plane, on just what an incredible achievement airline reservation systems are—intellectually, organizationally, psychologically, and technically. A few years from now, automated supermarkets may similarly be taken for granted as one of the conveniences of life.

to polarize their viewpoints, with some strongly in favor of computers and others totally opposed to them. This polarization has now balanced out somewhere in the middle, and it is clear to almost all managers that computers can be very useful *under some conditions,* but most managers today distinguish between the use of computers in their organization and the information systems that are of direct help to them. They argue that the information they need as decisionmakers is not provided by most MIS.

Managers' perspectives on information systems have been influenced heavily by the bandwagon effect of "buzz" words and the jargon of the new technology. The few managers who get directly involved in the implementation process of an MIS have heard a series of rallying cries developed by the computer fraternity over the past decade. In rather a crude way they can be listed as follows:

1. "Computerize and save money." This early argument aimed at encouraging management attention and investment and claimed that the computer would dramatically reduce costs. In many instances, of course, there were savings, but in far too many cases the effort and time involved to bring in the computer were badly estimated. The oil company that wrote off a clerical expense accounting system in which it had invested $4 million is merely one of a number of examples of computerization for its own sake, which did not save money but accumulated horrendous costs.

2. "Scientific decisionmaking." There was a brief period when visionaries in OR/MS pushed hard to establish the idea that models could replace decisionmakers and take over many of the routine activities of the firm.[27] There *has* been considerable success in this respect in some areas, such as distribution and production scheduling, but the enthusiasts of automated decisionmaking were forced to recognize the limitations inherent in computers and computer models, and their claims shrunk to a more reasonable scale.

3. "On-line real-time systems." This rallying cry was mostly developed by hardware manufacturers. It assumed that decisionmakers need instant information, which would be generated by data collection terminals

---

[27]Weizenbaum (1976) speaks of his immense shock at finding that several influential commentators believed that his entertaining ELIZA system, which can play—"I should really say parody"—the role of a psychotherapist could *replace* psychiatrists. He quotes Colby, Watt, and Gilbert (1966): "Further work must be done before the program will be ready for clinical use. If the method proves beneficial, then it would provide a therapeutic tool which can be made widely available to mental hospitals and psychiatric centers suffering a shortage of therapists. Because of the time-sharing capabilities of modern and future computers, several hundred patients an hour could be handled by a computer system designed for this purpose. The human therapist, involved in the design and operation of this system, would not be replaced, but would become a much more efficient man since his efforts would no longer be limited to the one-to-one patient-therapist ratio as now exists." This example is not especially farfetched. The 1960s saw many glowing prophecies such as Dantzig's (1965, p. 26): "We are witnessing a computer revolution in which nearly all tasks of man—be it manual labor or complex higher ones such as decision making—all are being reduced to mathematical terms and their solutions delegated to computers."

and an on-line data base available to any manager in the organization. Among some managers, struggling with decisionmaking under uncertainty, the prospect of more and more current information generated an enthusiastic response and led to some useful real-time applications. However, the tasks that really require completely current information are few, far between, and very specialized.[28] The vice-president of operations of an airline might well find such information about aircraft availability and loadings useful, but no marketing manager would prefer daily sales figures to weekly except in special situations.

4. "Total systems" (integrated systems). This concept of a tightly linked set of computer applications covering *all* the information needs of management was extremely popular in the literature between 1968 to 1972. Frequently, it implied a hierarchical set of systems, each one building on the one below and incorporating the majority of the company's information needs. Apart from the conceptual difficulties (discussed in Chapter 4), the practical problems involved in building a "complete" set of applications with the resources normally available to an organization make this vision close to infeasible. Worse than infeasible, it was to some extent dangerous because it hid from managers the need to make decisions about which application areas to work on *next*. The few systems built were only as strong as their weakest links, were difficult to maintain and update, and, in fact, were not used by the managers they were designed to assist.

5. "Global data base." Growing out of the total system concept came the ideal of a global data base, containing all the data gathered and generated by the company, accessible to anyone who might need it in the future. There are two fallacies in this idea. One is the failure to distinguish between information and data, data being facts and information being facts that are necessary for some purpose and that have meaning and significance. If an organization collects *information*, someone has taken the trouble to decide which *data* are necessary. Some data are very much more relevant than others and can be organized and categorized in terms of need and use. But data cannot be assembled in a disaggregated format to be used for any purpose (using current technology, at least) so that the concept of homogeneous, global data bases is invalid. The second difficulty is the practical one involved in maintaining such a data base. Not only are there very large costs in building it initially, but the maintenance of the data at a level of quality and accuracy adequate for the decisions at hand is extremely expensive.

These five rallying cries were generated by the alliance of the computer industry, data processing professionals, and, occasionally, academics. For them to

---

[28]Dearden's (1966) attack on real-time information systems relies on the assumption that MIS aims only at giving chief executives access to "instant" operational data, which is, of course, useless for strategic planning. The distinction between "data" and "information"—meaningful data—is crucial here. Managers want information; more data are of no value to them.

become an active crusade, however, someone in management had to become a believer. The list of corporations who did so for at least one of these five covers the majority of the *Fortune* 500. In many cases a slogan substituted for a thought-out plan, and with company profits at an adequate level much money was spent with almost no careful examination of the ideas. In all of these instances, after the first burst of enthusiasm peaked, few results were forthcoming; managers' common sense reasserted itself and they stepped back more actively into the picture.

There is no question that the recession that began in 1973 and the uncertain economic climate of the 1970s has encouraged managers to spend much more time evaluating alternatives for computer-based applications. They are now more skeptical and more forthright in their definition of what is indeed useful to them and the organization, and what is not. These judgments are rarely collected or written up for outside consumption, but as far as MIS is concerned, managers are the final arbitrator of what is worthwhile. They can identify which applications are working in the organization rather than just being technically successful. On the whole they are by now skeptical of new claims for MIS, having been burnt so often before. On balance, this seems to us to be a healthy state of affairs.

Of course, the arguments above apply only if managers accept their responsibility and commit adequate effort to the planning and analysis required. Data processing professionals often complain that managers are reluctant to get involved and provide them with operational goals for systems development. A major aim of this book is to provide the information base for managers to exploit the opportunities of DSS. We certainly feel that it is not the technical specialist's task to define the organization's strategy for DSS, anymore than the team that designs a corporate planning model should decide the corporate plan. It is clear that many of the fiascoes of the 1960s in overambitious information systems development efforts were partly caused by senior executives delegating managerial decisions to EDP personnel.

As managers have come to terms with the computer revolution, they have also helped expand the horizons of technical professionals. As long as computers were guarded by a high priesthood who used a strange vocabulary and made the laity fearful of asking questions, the similarity between managing data processing and managing other areas of business, such as R & D, was obscured. Many commentators now stress that information systems require good management, just as production or marketing does (see, for example, *Unlocking the Computer's Potential* by Ewing). The gradual recognition of this need for a management perspective is the driving force behind the appointment of nondata processing people to head the MIS activity and is a welcome challenge to the overspecialized view of data processing and management science professionals. Many managers view MIS as a piece—and a small piece—of the set of tools needed to run an organization. MIS is not of primary concern or value to most top managers. It tends to be most relevant for the operational tasks that are of minor importance for them. That is, information systems are helpful to management but rarely is a computer-based system fundamental to their decisionmaking.

DECISION SUPPORT SYSTEMS

The additional view that we have labeled Decision Support Systems (DSS) is not intended to replace the others but to extend them. It focuses on supporting decision-making and shifts attention from the level of operations (an information system for job order status or accounts receivable) toward the issues of managerial problem solving. It adds an additional class of problems and opportunities to the management information systems field. The key question for anyone working on a DSS is: *"What specific decision or decision process are we trying to support?"* The decision may be repetitive and ongoing or a one-shot situation. The decision support focus assumes that the problem the manager is facing is not trivial and that it cannot, at this moment, be automated. This perspective requires the development of methodological tools to examine the key decisions of managers and to define the information that can or should be made available to them. It suggests that for a *manager's* information system, one should start from his or her decisionmaking activities and mesh the system into the user's problems and needs.

The second term in the phrase is *support*: a DSS supports and does not *replace* the manager. This emphasis on enhancement of decisionmaking exploits those aspects of computers and analytical techniques that are appropriate for the problem and leaves the remainder to the manager. Most, if not all, of managers' key decisions tend to be fuzzy problems, not well understood by them or the organization, and their personal judgment is essential. It is not possible to think of a computer system replacing managers or most of their decisions. Of course, over time, as our level of understanding increases, it may be possible to take some problems that we now consider fuzzy and systematize them so that they can be delegated to a computer or a clerk. An obvious example of this process is credit scoring. Most banks and loan companies now have simple procedures, based on actuarial data and supported by credit bureau reports (which, of course, rely on on-line computer systems) that replace the prior judgment of a senior loan officer.

The key point for a DSS is to support or enhance the manager's decisionmaking ability. The payoff from this can be great. Many problems have components that can be structured and others that require subjective assessments. In pricing some consumer products, for example, management intuition alone is inadequate, a computer model alone is inadequate, but the two together may be most effective.

The third term in the expression is *system*—here we imply both the manager and the machine. The system considerations include the wider context in which the manager is operating. The focus on managers, their decision setting, and the organization raises a host of new problems for the "system" designer because a model or program cannot be built in isolation from that wider context. In a strict sense, the phrase Decision Support Systems does not necessarily imply a computer at all. Clearly, a clerical system may support a manager in decisionmaking. For our purposes, we use Decision Support Systems to imply a conversational, interactive computer system with access through some form of terminal to the analytic power, models, and data base held in the machine. The computer, however, is subordinate to the context.

The final aspect of the concept of DSS that we stress centers on the fundamental characteristics of the system to be delivered. Many classical data processing systems were built with the goal of delivering a *product* to the organization. Hence such terms as "signing off" on "final" designs and taking delivery of the "finished" system are commonplace in the data processing vocabulary. A DSS is more a service than a product. Since the problem can only partially be structured, and since managers grow in their understanding and needs over time, a DSS must constantly grow and evolve as the user adapts and learns. This is its very nature and implies much for the construction of such a system, the kind of software used, and, more importantly, the way it is implemented and maintained in the organization itself.

Our definition of a DSS is both old and new. It is fully compatible with the other perspectives we described but it is also very different from each of them, especially in its emphases. Computer scientists would agree that it is the relatively recent development of time-sharing and interactive terminals and software that makes DSS feasible; however, they would be at best uninterested in the in-depth analysis of how managers make decisions implicit in the DSS approach. Similarly, many DSS are model based and typical of the management science tradition, but also tend to be fairly simple and sacrifice technical elegance in order to make them more conceptually accessible to the user. Several of the most effective DSS we are familiar with would be disdained by most management scientists.

Behavioral scientists would approve of the emphasis in DSS on the user's needs, capabilities, and procedures. They would be less likely to either understand or accept its equal emphasis on the exploitation of analytic techniques and interactive computing power. Data processing professionals really should be interested in DSS, not least because in many instances they offer a service to managers that their traditional systems have not been able to provide. All too often, though, data processing professionals overestimate the importance of large, general systems, while DSS require careful tailoring to a task and specific user(s).

Managers are—and should be—skeptical of yet another rallying cry that is similar to the five they have already heard. However, the computer field has now matured to a point where they can reliably judge what is practicable and have staff personnel (who are not necessarily skilled programmers) with access to low-cost computer resources. They are thus more willing to think about ways the computer might help them and can directly interact with a system and its designer. If they try out prototype systems, they often find that they learn and benefit from the experience. If they get involved and do not leave the computer to the high priesthood, they are able to "grow" a DSS by starting from a simple and well-defined base and gradually expanding from it. The successful application of such a DSS generally provides powerful proof of the value and practicality of the approach. The manager is at least as important as the technical professional in this process.

Many of the ideas underlying our formulation of DSS come from the perspective of managers; of all the approaches to information systems theirs is the most completely compatible with DSS. We hope their interest in and adoption of DSS will be whole-hearted. This is a central concern of this book. The computer has not really been of major and direct value to managers in their problem solving. Our starting point is that information and information-processing technology surely can be made useful to the managers, given an understanding of their needs. We then work backward from the manager to the computer. This is a book on decisionmaking rather than computers. Our discussion of DSS thus continues by examining the nature of the decision process.

MODELS OF DECISIONMAKING: PRESCRIPTION VERSUS DESCRIPTION

THREE

INTRODUCTION

Decision *support* requires a detailed understanding of decisionmaking in organizations. A descriptive framework provides the basis for prescriptive design; that is, to "improve" a decision process, one must first define and analyze it. In Chapter 4 we discuss the types of decision amenable to support. In this chapter, we present a *diagnostic*[1] approach to the study of decisionmaking, examining decisions in terms of their process and structure, in contrast to the more usual functional perspective of managers, which separates "marketing" decisions from "finance," or the analytic classifications used by management scientists, which identify "queueing theory," "decision analysis," or "linear programming" applications.

The diagnostic viewpoint helps clarify, for example, how the decision process for planning a company's strategic portfolio of business ventures is different from that of planning its portfolio of cash, bonds, stocks, and other investments. It is tempting to the systems developer to assume that the strategic planning and investment cases are essentially equivalent since both are "portfolio" problems. However, there are many differences involved, such as: (1) the type, frequency, structure, and complexity of the decisions; (2) the characteristics, capabilities, and "needs" of the decisionmaker(s); and (3) the organizational context. These differences may make a model that is effective for the investment decision totally inapplicable to the planning one.

The aim of this chapter is to provide an overview of approaches to the study of decisionmaking. Such a discussion is relevant to far broader areas of application that just DSS. However, in Chapters 4 and 6, we narrow the focus and apply the framework to the design of a DSS. It is important to stress again that decision support is close to meaningless as a concept without a broad overview of decisionmaking; unfortunately, the training of MIS and OR/MS professionals largely ignores this topic. For example, decisionmaking has only recently become an explicit subject in management education. There are two extremes in business school curricula, one based on the *functional* approach of marketing, production, finance, and so on, and the other on the *disciplines* of economics, behavioral science, and applied mathematics. Decisionmaking as such has little place in the first type of business

---

[1]The diagnostic approach requires that DSS designers ask, first of all, what is happening?, and *observe* rather than assume a priori that they understand how a decision should be made. For a more detailed discussion, see Schein (1961) and Keen, *A Clinical Approach to Implementation* (1975).

school since the focus there tends to be on the *content* of decisions. For example, the marketing aspect of the marketing problem is taught, not specifically the way to approach a decision in the marketing area. In the second type of school, aspects of decisionmaking may be included in the behavioral science curriculum but decision-making as an independent subject has not been fashionable and has not been treated comprehensively. Those interested in DSS may thus have some difficulty in getting exposure to the issues we raise in this chapter.[2]

Management science has traditionally been concerned with decisionmaking, but from an explicitly normative viewpoint. It has neglected descriptive models, focusing on how managers *should* act rather than on observing how they actually behave. This dichotomy between the normative and descriptive is important and will be discussed later in the chapter.

The literature on decisionmaking can be classified in terms of five main schools of thought. We list these below, with brief comments on their implications for DSS design and implementation. (For this approach and some of these points of view, we are indebted to G. T. Allison, whose *Essence of Decision* [1971] gives a fascinating analysis of the Cuban Missile Crisis using three basic conceptions, the "rational" actor model, the organizational procedure perspective, and the political paradigm.[3])

1. *The rational manager view:* This is the classic conception of decisionmaking in organizations, developed from the microeconomic assumption of a rational, completely informed, single decisionmaker. It is still appropriate for decisions dominated by economic factors, where an analytic definition of the variables involved in the decision is needed together with a precise, objective criterion for choice. The implementation process in this situation requires technical competence and educating those involved to adopt the rational perspective and to be explicit and consistent in their assessments. Proponents of cost/benefit analysis adopt this approach. However, many managers and behaviorally oriented management scientists reject the rational paradigm as impracticable and overidealized. Nonetheless, it remains a dominant influence in economic analysis.

2. *The "satisficing," process-oriented view:* This school of thought provided a challenge to the unnatural completeness of the rational view. H. A. Simon's "A Behavioral Model of Rational Choice" (1975) is the best-known presentation of satisficing; it focuses on how a decision-maker can most effectively use limited knowledge and skills. Simon highlights the constraints imposed by "bounded rationality"—the emphasis on heuristic rules of thumb and searching for solutions that are

---

[2]Most professional schools train students in techniques for solving a given problem. As Leavitt (1976) points out, there is far less emphasis on problem finding as opposed to problem solving. Consequently, the view of decisionmaking presented is structural and concerned with the content of decisions. It also tends to emphasize analytic methods.

[3]Allison's approach to the study of complex decision processes seems a very useful one for DSS. Rather than impose a single framework, he applies several conceptual models and asks which aspects of the Cuban Missile Crisis each explains and which it overlooks. The diagnostic strategy suggested in this chapter similarly requires *multiple* perspectives on decisionmaking.

"good enough." Applying this approach to DSS involves building a descriptive model of the decision process; the design goal is then to *improve* the existing solution (and reduce the decisionmaker's bounds on rationality), not to vainly seek for an optimum.

3. *The organizational procedures view:* This concept of decisionmaking seeks to understand decisions as the output of standard operating procedures invoked by organizational subunits. The emphasis in design is to discover what these procedures are and how some or all of them might be supported and improved. In particular, this viewpoint stresses the importance of identifying organizational roles, channels of communication, and relationships.

4. *The political view:* Here decisionmaking is seen as a personalized bargaining process between organizational units. Those who hold this view argue that power and influence determine the outcome of any given decision. Design is then less affected by the specific content of any decision than with the working process by which it is made. A premium is placed on understanding the realities of power and on the compromises and strategies necessary to mesh the interests and constraints of the actors in the decision process.

5. *The individual differences perspective:* This perspective concentrates on the individual manager and her or his problem-solving and information-processing behavior. The design and implementation strategy for building a DSS are seen as contingent on the decisionmaking style, background, and personality of the manager for whom the system is intended.

We develop these five perspectives below; each contributes to the way we think of decisionmaking, particularly as it affects Decision Support Systems. There seems to be no self-evidently right way to look at the decision process. For a given situation, the "correct" way may involve a blend of all five points of view, or the particular context may make one of them the most relevant. Because of the multidimensional nature of decisionmaking, it is critical to *diagnose* which aspect(s) is the most pivotal in any situation. For example, choosing a shipyard with which to place an order for oil tankers is likely to be dominated by economic considerations, whereas deciding the relative allocation of capital funds among divisions in some large companies is ruled in part by politics. Here we are concerned that the potential contribution of *each* of these perspectives on decisionmaking is clearly recognized so that if a DSS is warranted, it will be implemented with a strong base.

It needs to be stressed that one's concept of the decision process largely predetermines both one's response to other people's logic, behavior, and opinions, and the strategy chosen for design and implementation of any aid to "improve" the quality of decisions. For example, the rational ideal stresses the need for definition of objectives, consistency, and comprehensive analysis. The true believer in rationality thus tries to get managers to clarify their goals explicitly, to search for many alternatives, and to define utility functions. Any unwillingness to do so is obviously "pathological." The pluralist tradition in political science by contrast argues that social policy making *always* involves a multiplicity of goals and values, that objectives are fluid, and analysis situational and incremental; the rational approach may thus be inapplicable for decision support (see I. R. Hoos [1972] for a strong case against the rational model's assumptions). Some management scientists, in particular, have tended to assume that there is a single "right" way to make decisions. The central theme of this chapter is that such a prescriptive viewpoint must, at the very least, be complemented by a descriptive understanding of the decision process. Decision support involves meshing the two perspectives.

RATIONAL VIEW OF DECISIONMAKING

The rational view of decisionmaking was one of the earliest to be developed in any detail. It is highly normative, based on theorems, and focuses on the logic of optimal choice. It is idealized but has been of value in highlighting central variables in decisionmaking. It dominates neoclassical microeconomic theory. The term "economic man" summarizes this conception of how choices should be made.[4]

The modern versions of rationality relax some of its rigid definitions of a completely informed, infinitely sensitive supercomputer, indifferent to the strains, costs, and limits of cognitive effort. There are now few believers in economic man, although he remains the ideal of many economists and management scientists, who argue that the aim of analytic techniques should be to move fallible humans toward true rationality. This normative view of decisionmaking has played a major part in the development of OR/MS over the years. It still represents a useful guide to the direction in which one may wish a given DSS to move.

In the economic literature, the decisionmaker is assumed to select the most efficient alternative, that is, to maximize the amount of output for a given input. R. M. Cyert, H. A. Simon, and D. B. Trow (1956) summarize the rational choice process:

1. An individual is confronted with a number of different specified alternative courses of action.

2. To each of these alternatives is attached a set of consequences that will ensue if that alternative is chosen.

3. "The individual has a system of preferences or 'utilities' that permit him to rank the consequences according to preference and to choose that alternative that has the preferred consequences. In the case of business decisions, the criteria for ranking is generally assumed to be profit" (p. 458).[5]

Game theory and decision analysis have exploited the rational framework. Game theorists analyze the logic of choice in competitive situations (for example, bargaining, war, and "games against nature"). Decision theory similarly maximizes

---

[4]Economic man is, of course, an idealization. He appears in disguised form in such rationalistic conceptions as PPBS (Planning-Programming-Budgeting System) and cost/benefit analysis. See Quade and Bouches (1968) for a presentation of this "systems analysis" viewpoint and Hoos (1972) for a scathing assault on it.

[5]This study was one of the first that observed an organizational decision process in detail. The results supported Simon's argument that decisionmakers satisficed rather than optimized.

expected utility in situations where there is uncertainty of events and outcomes. In both instances, there is an "objective" method of arriving at a solution; given the set of consequences and one's utility function, the choice is automatic.[6]

At its extreme, the rational tradition is completely unrealistic and there have been numerous criticisms of it in recent years. There is virtually no *descriptive* support whatsoever for its conception of decisionmaking. Perhaps, though, wholesale abandonment by students of management is premature. The rational concept defines the *logic* of optimal choice; this remains theoretically true, even where it is descriptively unrealistic. Without the precision and formalism of rationalist theory, we would almost certainly have made less progress in developing descriptive insights; it has provided axioms to be challenged, hypotheses to be opposed by counterexamples, and a vocabulary that we need to use even to disagree with it. For example, the concept of consistent, absolute utility functions has been invaluable in all theories of decisionmaking, especially those that argue such functions are nonexistent.

Simon began the demolition of (rational) "economic" man. He focused on the comprehensive knowledge and analysis implied in the rational approach. He argued that it was impractical to think of generating all of the relevant alternatives. Furthermore, even if this were to be done, the "bounded rationality" of the human decisionmaker makes the information unassimilable. Simon concludes that the rational conception is completely lacking in descriptive reality and suggests a definition of satisficing man, who does the best he can but does not even attempt optimization.

From the viewpoint of this book, the rational framework is of little practical relevance. Its normative stance, however, challenges us to define the upper bounds on a system and on decisionmaking and to examine very closely the costs and payoffs from helping decisionmakers become more rational. This has been the approach of such game theorists as T. C. Schelling (1963) and decision theorists in general (for example, R. A. Howard, 1968; and R. L. Keeney and H. Raiffa, 1976).

SATISFICING AND THE PROCESS-ORIENTED VIEW OF DECISIONMAKING

The "satisficing" view of decisionmaking is an attempt to move closer to reality and to understand the world as it actually is. Such a descriptive focus provides a basis for developing prescriptions that are "behaviorally grounded" (see, for example, P. G. W. Keen's "The Evolving Concept of Optimality," 1977).[7] The main assumptions of the theory of satisficing[8] are summarized by Simon (1969, p. 64):

[6]Schelling (1963) and Howard (1968) elegantly present the case for both the logic and practical value of game theory and decision theory, respectively.

[7]Behaviorally grounded implies that the descriptive reality is a dominant constraint on prescriptive change. Clearly, OR/MS and MIS began from a prescriptive stance and have only gradually expanded their focus to include "behavioral" issues. Keen traces the history of "optimization science" and argues that OR/MS is built on a set of rational axioms that have rarely been discussed within the field because they are "obvious." The descriptive tradition essentially presents alternative axioms.

[8]While the term *satisficing* is familiar to many students of management, it has not passed into general usage; typists and copy editors search vainly for it in Webster's. Most OR textbooks devote only one paragraph to the topic. Ackoff and Sasieni (1968),

In the real world we usually do not have a choice between satisfactory and optimal solutions, for we only rarely have a method of finding the optimum. . . . We cannot, within practicable computational limits, generate all the admissible alternatives and compare their relative merits. Nor can we recognize the best alternative, even if we are fortunate enough to generate it early, until we have seen all of them. We satisfice by looking for alternatives in such a way that we can generally find an acceptable one after only moderate search.

Simon has introduced into computer-related and analytic disciplines many of the main terms and concepts of decisionmaking. As an offshoot of his work with A. Newell and J. C. Shaw on simulating human cognitive processes, he suggested that most problem-solving strategies for satisficing are based on heuristics—rules of thumb that give solutions that are good enough most of the time. For example, a standard operating procedure for many marketing managers is to set advertising expenditures equal to some fixed percentage of sales. This is clearly far from optimal; moreover, advertising should surely *influence* sales. Nonetheless, under conditions where sales and profits are adequate, this is a reasonable rule that saves immense search and analysis.

In building a DSS, this simple concept is invaluable. To understand a manager's decision process, one *must* know the heuristics he or she uses. Almost invariably, these will be effective, at little cost and effort; they constitute a general program of analysis distilled from experience. The main value of Newell, Simon, and Shaw's work in artificial intelligence is to suggest how few and how simple are the heuristics needed for effective performance in such complex problem-solving situations as chess.

Heuristics reflect "bounded rationality." That is, they are a compromise between the demands of the problem and the capabilities and commitment of the decisionmaker. One can usually improve one's heuristics, although at the often unacceptable cost of increased effort. A DSS may provide this improvement more cheaply (in terms of the manager's cognitive strain). Little's Brandaid model (see Chapter 5), for example, replaces the standard operating procedure of the marketing manager who sets advertising equal to some fixed percentage of sales by an analytic evaluation of advertising response curves and the interaction between advertising and other marketing variables. Oversimple heuristics can provide substantial opportunity for the DSS designer.

---

however, discuss it in some (critical) detail: "Satisficing is usually defended with the argument that it is better to produce a feasible plan that is not optimal than an optimal plan that is not feasible. This argument is only superficially compelling. Reflection reveals that it overlooks the possibility of obtaining the best feasible plan. Optimality can (and should) be defined so as to take feasibility into account, and the effort to do so forces us to examine the criteria of feasibility that are seldom made explicit in the satisficing process. Furthermore, the approximate attainment of an optimal plan may be more desirable than exact attainment of an inferior one. Not surprising, this type of planning seldom produces a significant break with the past. . . . It appeals to planners who are not willing to stick their necks out" (p. 443).

Eilon (1972) also suggests that decisionmakers simplify the process of clarifying objectives by treating them as loose constraints; whereas optimizing requires maximization or minimization of a precisely quantified objective function, satisficing implies getting as close as possible to, say, a profit or cost *constraint*.

Managers rely on their heuristics and are understandably unwilling to give them up. They "work" and can be trusted; a computer system, by contrast, is a "black box" whose value and reliability are hard for the manager to assess and which involves expensive new effort and learning. For this reason, a designer needs to recognize that any system that requires the user to adopt new modes of analysis may be hard to implement—although the payoff from doing so can be substantial.

Simon's third conceptual description of decisionmaking focuses on the relationship between problem-solving strategies and the nature of the task. That different tasks require different approaches may seem obvious. It is not; for economic man, each problem requires essentially the same strategy. As we shall see, researchers who view decisionmaking in terms of personality or cognitive "style" (including one of the authors of this book) would argue that some managers have an approach to problem solving that is task-invariant.

Simon introduced a distinction between programmed and nonprogrammed decisions, but he provides very little operational definition of the difference. (In Chapter 4, we attempt to sharpen the distinction.) A task that can be programmed is one for which clear rules—and potentially a computer program—can be defined, replacing the judgment of a decisionmaker.[9] For example, the complex process of production scheduling for an oil refinery is best dealt with by a linear programming model. There are very definite rules relating inputs to outputs and production to costs—the problem possesses a fundamental underlying "deep structure," too complex for the human mind to easily grasp in its detailed entirety but easy for a computer to resolve.[10] At the same time, there are many unstructured decisions; the extreme of these is summarized in J. D. Steinbruner's epigram that a man torn between love and duty is a subject for a novel, while no amount of formal analysis can resolve his dilemma for him.

Theoretically, a computer system can replace the human decisionmaker for programmed decisions, though this might not, of course, be desirable because of the economics of a given situation. With unstructured or nonprogrammed decisions, however, this is not possible, by definition. An unstructured task does not permit programming; the objectives, trade-offs, relevant information, and methodology for analysis cannot be predetermined (an example of an unstructured task in

---

[9]Newell and Simon's *Human Problem Solving* (1972) summarizes Simon and his colleagues' interpretation of their work on cognitive processes. Their theory is based on three central elements: (1) the characteristics of the human information-processing system; (2) the structure of the task environment; and (3) the problem space. A task can be programmed if the structure of the task environment permits precise rules to be defined for processing information and selecting a solution. The human problem solver is assumed to operate heuristically, since problem spaces are generally too complex for a sequential search for alternatives to be feasible.

[10]We have borrowed the term deep structure from Chomsky, who uses it to describe the fundamental syntactic structure underlying the myriad varieties of sentences and grammars apparent in any language. For more details, see Chomsky (1971). The work on AI (briefly discussed in Chapter 2) that is concerned with the representation of knowledge draws heavily on linguistic theory. In principle, any task that can be programmed has an underlying deep structure; representing the task is equivalent to identifying that structure.

management problem solving is forecasting the likelihood of major congressional tax reforms in the next 3 years and the implication for planning capital investments).

Some unstructured problems are unstructured simply because of a lack of knowledge or because of an unwillingness to explore the problem in depth. Thus tic-tac-toe, an obviously programmable problem, is not programmable to a five year old. A major aim of the rational tradition, especially in game theory, decision theory, and applied management science, has been to reveal the underlying structure of tasks that have been generally viewed as nonprogrammable. We will discuss this issue of programmable and nonprogrammable tasks in more detail in Chapter 4. The distinction is a useful one, though, like all taxonomies, a little arbitrary. Computer systems have had immense impact on programmable tasks (for example, airline reservations, payroll, and accounting). The rational tradition has often presumed that they should and would have equal impact on nonprogrammable ones. The 1960s will haunt the memories of many management scientists, who found that linear programming is not the answer for strategic planning, and MIS designers, whose All-Purpose Omniscient Answering System became a $9 million write-off on a company's profit and loss statement.

Simon, in 1965, argued that by 1975 many management decisions would be programmable. This has not happened. The computer has had minimal impact on tasks involving judgment, ambiguity, creativity, and volatility of environment. The main single reason for identifying DSS as a specific strategy for design and delivery of computer systems is our belief that the computer has already demonstrated its clear value for programmed decisionmaking and its dangerous inapplicability for nonprogrammed decisionmaking.[11] In Chapter 4 we argue that the most valuable payoff for analytic and computer-based decision aids lies in meshing the machine's efficiency in programmed functions with the individual's judgment in unstructured problems—in finding the semiprogrammable or semistructured range of tasks where the mutual symbiosis of mind and computer can be immensely valuable. Decision Support Systems are relevant over this range.

Simon has had immense influence on management thought. For many management scientists and MIS professionals, "behavioral" is equivalent to "Simon says." He has provided the computer field with most of its central ideas on decisionmaking, and no student of MIS, OR/MS, or of organizational theory can afford to ignore his work, especially *Administrative Behavior* (1976), *The Shape of Automation for Men and Management* (1965), and *Sciences of the Artificial* (1969). In the 1960s Simon was perhaps too easily considered the one true prophet and arguments against his views were overlooked. There are several powerful counters to his theories and on balance we would argue that his conception is incomplete and one-sided. While he has modified the ideals of rationality and reinforced their normative ethos, his bounded rationality is nevertheless rationality. C. Argyris (1970, 1971) has launched several telling attacks on what he feels is Simon's justification of a

---

[11]Braybrooke and Lindblom (1970), Hoos (1972), and Weizenbaum (1976), among many others, stress that techniques for programmed tasks cannot be extended to ones that are inherently nonprogrammable. They also point out the ideological and ethical implications of trying to "rationalize" multidimensional, qualitative, nonstructured decisions.

rigid status quo in organizations and denial of the validity of more emotive, intuitive, and personalized approaches to the appallingly complex process of making decisions. The pluralist tradition of political science, discussed later in this chapter, has also attacked Simon's views (see, for example, D. Braybrooke and C. E. Lindblom, 1970). J. Weizenbaum (1976) has published a detailed critique of Simon's later generalizations from experiments on limited aspects of problem solving to a universal definition of the individual as an information processor. Agreement or disagreement with these criticisms—or with Simon—is largely axiomatic. Simon's work represents the most creative and persuasive modification of the rational tradition. Given his assumptions, his arguments are hard to challenge. His critics, especially Weizenbaum, present humanistic alternatives to those assumptions. The debate is an important one and unlikely to be soon resolved.[12]

ORGANIZATIONAL PROCESS VIEW

The organizational process viewpoint focuses on the formal and informal structure of the organization, its standard operating procedures, and channels of communication. R. M. Cyert and J. G. March's *A Behavioral Theory of the Firm* (1963) is the most complete statement of this approach. Allison (1971) summarizes their work as follows (emphasis added): "In contrast to traditional theories that explain the firm's behavior in terms of market factors, Cyert and March focus—as organizational theory would suggest—on the effect of organizational structure and *conventional practise* on the development of goals, the formulation of expectations and the execution of choice" (p. 75).

Cyert and March describe the organization in terms of its coalitions, each of which has its own priorities, goals, and focus of attention. Organizational decision-making necessarily involves bargaining among these coalitions and the factoring of large-scale problems into subproblems. For example, the accounting and marketing departments are each responsible for particular aspects of overall sales activity. Each develops its own standard "programs" which are executed in response to problems as they arise. Each has "rights" to certain information and will not intrude on the other's prerogatives. Each views the corporation mainly in terms of its own department.[13]

Each subunit of the organization relies on programs or procedures that in a sense constitute its memory and store of learning. If the standard programs fail they will try to adapt some other compatible procedure; if that in turn fails they will, generally reluctantly, accept the costs and strains of creating a new routine. This viewpoint obviously implies that any system designer needs to identify these organizational subunits and their standard patterns of behavior. It is generally very difficult to institutionalize an information system that cuts across them—that, for example, intrudes on territorial rights or is inconsistent with the organization's structure and lines of communication. At the same time, where there is a stable and

---

[12]A welcome recent step that should extend the debate has been the establishment by the Association for Computing Machinery (ACM) of a journal, *The Social Impact of Computing*.

[13]Dearborn and Simon (1968) point out, for example, that the definition of corporate "profit" is different for marketing and production managers.

reasonably effective set of standard operating procedures, it is often possible to develop support packages that permit the problem-solving procedure to be executed more efficiently or modified more rapidly.

Of course, this support may reinforce the behavior of the subunits at the cost of integration. Cyert and March stress the compartmentalization and specialization of the various units in any organization; Dearborn and Simon (1968) point out that even senior executives tend to view the total market from their own functional perspective. This specialization of effort and attention is generally more efficient for a given problem but impedes integrating, changing, or evolving the subtasks of the organization. P. R. Lawrence and J. W. Lorsch (1968) describe the delicate and complex balance needed between subunit differentiation and corporate integration. As the laundry equipment case indicates (Chapter 1, pages 16 to 32), one practical value of a DSS can be its role in *integrating* subunits, in helping marketing and production, in this example, to create a joint plan rather than bargaining over their independent, often incompatible subplans.

DECISIONMAKING AS A POLITICAL PROCESS

The organizational process viewpoint is an extension of the *intendedly* rational approach—it emphasizes procedures and consistency of behavior and defines the organization in terms of its structure and operations. However, unlike the rational conception, it recognizes the relevance of such political processes as bargaining, although it does not regard them as the driving force in decisionmaking.

Many political scientists, on the other hand, view the whole decision process as essentially *pluralistic* and suggest that while the rational conception may hold for tic-tac-toe and the organizational process model for customer accounting and invoicing, neither captures decisionmaking at a strategic or policy level. Many decisions are made in relation to political constraints, aspirations, and interactions. The rational neoclassic economic theory of the firm argues that the single overriding objective of any company is to maximize its owners' utility and profit. The pluralist conception of decisionmaking as a political process emphasizes the natural multiplicity of goals, values, and interests in any organization. "The leaders who sit on top of organizations are not a monolithic group. Rather each individual in this group is, in his own right, a player in a central, competitive game. The name of the game is politics: bargaining along regularized circuits among players positioned hierarchically within the government" (Allison, 1971). This viewpoint goes beyond the organizational process in that it "sees no unitary actor but rather many actors as players—players who focus not on a single strategic issue but on many diverse intercompany (international) problems as well; players who act in terms of no consistent set of strategic objectives but rather according to various conceptions of company (national), divisional, and personal goals; players who make decisions not by a single, rational choice but by the pulling and hauling that is politics" (Allison, p. 144; we have inserted business terms and shown Allison's original words in parentheses).[14]

---

[14]See Chapter 7 for a detailed discussion of meshing a DSS into the social—and hence political—content of the system. See also Keen and Gerson (1977). Bardach (1977) provides a witty analysis of political issues in implementation.

Decisionmaking, in this conception, is not a neat, predictable, or controllable process. In general, "politics" has a pejorative overtone in organizational theory; the trend toward participative management in the 1960s, the self-images of executives as objective and acting in the company's interests, and the association of politics with inefficient government agencies have all led to a serious lack of discussion of this dimension—yet it is so obviously a major force in any organization composed of real people. The pluralists, especially Lindblom, point out that there can rarely be a single definition of goals and values, especially in social policy— what, for example, is *the* goal of education? While power, advocacy, and consensus building can be misused or hinder efficiency and effectiveness, they are legitimate and necessary. Advocacy reflects commitment. Multiple goals require discussion and bargaining. The healthy organization will always have a vigorous political life. According to Allison (1971, pp. 157–158): "Policy making is therefore a process of conflict and consensus building. The advocate of a particular policy must build a consensus to support his policy. Where there are rival advocates or rival policies, there is competition for support, and all the techniques of alliance appear— persuasion, accommodation, and bargaining."

This view of decisionmaking stresses the importance of the *implementation* process for DSS.[15] The issue is not so much the design of a system as how to introduce and position it, and how to use it. Analytic specialists disdain politics: they implicitly accept the rational view that any system should focus on the logic of the decision process and ignore such secondary and obstructive issues. They build "elegant" systems that solve the problem at hand while ignoring political factors that can make these technically excellent products organizationally infeasible. When this elegance fails, the analyst's excuse is company politics. This has been all too prevalent an attitude; it is naive and irresponsible. In Chapter 7 we present some effective strategies for diagnosing political issues and other contextual factors and for managing the entry process—of generating commitment for the system, developing a realistic contract, and building mutual trust.

The political viewpoint is especially important for DSS because it is so seldom expressed and most analysts and designers are surprised that it should be seen as relevant. It is almost totally ignored in most published accounts of information systems implementations. To suggest that managers might disagree and fight is regarded as impolite. However, as Allison and others point out, when individuals or groups are committed to a particular goal, they can be expected to fight hard for their point of view. Out of this pulling and hauling comes progress for the organization.

A corollary of this political focus on bargaining, conflict, and consensus is the concept of incremental change. This has been labeled as the "art of the possible." Given that there are many actors in any given decision situation, clear, rapid progress is rarely possible and no absolute and radical policy is likely to triumph (except in palace revolutions, takeovers, or major crises).

Lindblom's "The Science of Muddling Through" (1959) rejects both the rational ideal and Simon's and Cyert and March's neorational views. This important

---

[15]It is extraordinary how little work has been done in OR/MS or MIS on political issues in systems development even though common sense (and painful experience) demonstrates their crucial importance. Information is not a neutral commodity; it is closely linked to organizational actors' perceived influence and autonomy (see Laudon, 1974).

article is somewhat contentious but captures very clearly both the conservative, nonanalytic decision processes of many bureaucrats and managers and the reasons why these are often more effective than the formal, in-depth evaluation that a computer system or model can provide.

Lindblom goes well beyond Simon's concept of satisficing. He focuses on the same realities that make rationality impossible, for example: "Clarification of objectives founders on social conflict . . . required information is either not available or available only at prohibitive cost . . . the problem is simply too complex for man's finite intellectual capabilities" (p. 212). He argues that the decisionmaker should avoid comprehensive analysis and rely instead on the strategies of "disjointed marginal incrementalism" that are "often mistakenly dismissed as aberrations in rational problem solving." These strategies limit analysis to alternatives that differ only incrementally from existing policy. Objectives are not predefined: What is feasible may, in fact, define what the goals should be. Utopian policies are ignored as hard to assess, impossible to implement, and expensive to analyze.

The incrementalist approach is remedial—policymaking moves *away* from ills rather than *toward* predetermined objectives. Lindblom criticizes the utopian ambitions of rationality and settles for evidence of a "step forward": problems are not "solved" but repeatedly attacked through marginal adjustments. (He responds to the criticism of this as conservative by comparing it with "creeping socialism"—continuing exploration, redefinition of means and ends, and reappraisal of accomplishments make the incremental strategy far more than a second-best substitute for comprehensive and formalized analysis.)

Lindblom's theory is obviously more descriptively applicable than the rational model and explains much of the policymaking of political units in a pluralistic society. H. I. Ansoff (1968), however, argues that in crisis situations, where the status quo is unsatisfactory and incremental adjustment ineffectual, policymakers *must* (and do) go back to first principles, try to consciously define basic objectives, and look for an optimal solution. The incrementalist's strategy is limiting and in a sense pessimistic, denying the value or feasibility of planning. Any imaginative solution that is too different from the policymaker's recent experience or frame of reference will not be considered.

Muddling through is explicitly antiutopian; it is the best we can *do*. The OR/MS viewpoint is implicitly utopian; it argues that we really can do better than this, that progress need not be limited to successive approximations and timid increments.

While Lindblom's argument applies most directly to public policy planning, it is also clearly relevant for organizational decisionmaking. Many managers are incrementalists; the strategy Lindblom suggests has been very effective for them and they thus have very good reasons to resist the intrusion of rationalistic computer analysts who aim at bringing systematic methods to decisionmaking. At a conference of like-minded peers, the analytic strategy is self-evidently right; in the maelstrom of organizational activity, it may be equally self-evidently wrong.

The political view is not always relevant to the design and implementation of a DSS. However, systems have failed because the analysts viewed political issues as irrelevant, *even though they were aware of them.* Much of the mainstream work in OR/MS is methodological and based on theorems; it thus has no reason to consider politics. However, if one is interested in building systems to be *used*, the political dimension is an important constraint—and *opportunity*. We argue that most strategic errors in information systems development are caused by the technical tradition's almost total disinterest in the political perspective. By contrast, managers are generally very sensitive to politics. The work of Steinbruner, Allison, Lindblom, Bardach, and Wilensky is thus *essential* in the education of an effective systems developer (see footnote 15).

INDIVIDUAL DIFFERENCES

The final model of decisionmaking to be discussed views the decisionmaker as a unique individual, and focuses on his or her personalized strategies and abilities. It suggests that some people have very specialized "styles" of decisionmaking, effective in some contexts and less so in others. The outcome of the decision process is substantially influenced by these characteristics, and any analytic aid must be consistent with the user's style. It may also be invaluable in complementing or extending it, but incompatibility between the decisionmaker's problem-solving habits, strategies, and abilities and the implicit style of the system will generally result in it not being used.[16]

In the past few years, there has been increasing interest in this issue. There have been two broad approaches, somewhat conflicting, but both drawing attention to the need to match the system to the user's information processing. *Cognitive complexity* explains problem solving in terms of the individual's cognitive structure: People with low levels of differentiation can deal only with limited categorizations of information; they easily become overloaded. Similarly, those with low ability to integrate can be overwhelmed by too much information; they cannot absorb it into a coherent frame of reference. *Complexity theory* argues that there is an optimal balance of information input for any one individual. Too little or too simple an input load leads to boredom (for example, consider a physics professor assigned to the typing pool) and too much leads to panic.

The implications for DSS are obvious. The system should mesh with the cognitive structures of its users. C. B. Stabell (1974, 1975) and J. Carlisle (1974) have both explicitly studied the use of a DSS as a function of cognitive complexity. Stabell identified the sources of information used by investment managers and developed measures of breadth, volume, and balance. He suggests that a simple diagnostic tool such as the Role Construct Repertory Interview be used to sample and monitor managers' perceptions of information sources as a basis for developing the DSS.[17] His detailed study of a single system also highlights how little insight we have into how managers conceptualize and integrate information. The DSS he examined had been designed on the basis of assumptions about the potential users' problem solving that Stabell found were inaccurate (it needs to be stressed that the

[16]The empirical evidence to support this assertion is, at best, indirect. Churchman and Schainblatt's early (1965) experiment still remains one of the most convincing. They found that individuals will simply ignore information that is presented in a format incompatible with their own style. See also, for a similar study, Doktor and Hamilton (1973).

[17]The RCRI is derived from Kelly's personal construct theory (1955). The instrument asks managers to identify information sources relevant to their task and groups these in terms of the constructs and concepts that they use to differentiate among them.

system was still beneficial to the organization). M. L. Bariff and E. J. Lusk (1977) similarly emphasize differential responses to information and the varying levels of integrative complexity among the users of a particular information system.

Complexity theory has many advocates within OR/MS. It is a fairly precise theory with clearcut implications for systems design, particularly in its suggestion that too much information may be as dysfunctional as too little. This follows from the "U-Curve Hypothesis": "Information processing by 'people in general,' . . . reaches a maximum level of structural complexity at some optimal level of environmental complexity (point X in Figure 3-1). Increasing or decreasing environmental complexity (points Z and Y) from the optimal point (X) lowers the conceptual level" (H. M. Schroder, M. J. Driver, and S. Steufert, 1967).

Figure 3-1   The U-Curve Hypothesis (from Schroder, Driver, and Steufert, 1967, p. 37)

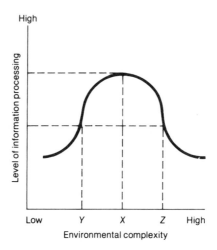

The practical applications of complexity theory seem less satisfactory than its theoretical promise. One major difficulty, common to almost all studies of cognitive processes, is the problem of finding simple and reliable measurements of complexity. Few if any of the studies are at all convincing in this respect.[18] Nonetheless, complexity theory has provided a strong conceptual base for research on information usage.

The cognitive style paradigm emphasizes the problem-solving process rather than cognitive structure and capacity. It categorizes individual habits and strategies at a fairly broad level and essentially views problem-solving behavior as a personality variable. Most cognitive style models use different labels for the same

---

[18]Psychometric analysis requires complex statistical expertise. Most researchers on cognitive processes in the management field are amateurs in this respect. Very few of them have successfully followed up their initial studies, almost invariably because validating and standardizing tests is another long and difficult research project.

general distinction between an analytic, systematic, methodological approach to problem solving and an intuitive, divergent, more global strategy. The analytic style corresponds strongly to the orthodox assumptions of the technical tradition in MIS and OR/MS: "Systematic thinkers tend to approach a problem by structuring it in terms of some method which if followed through leads to a likely solution" (J. L. McKenney and P. G. W. Keen, 1974, p. 81). Model building, from the viewpoint of the management scientist, involves exactly this—making causal relationships explicit and articulating formal criteria and sequences of analysis. This specialized mode of thought may be very different from the manager's intuitive or heuristic style: "Intuitive thinkers usually avoid committing themselves in this way; their strategy is more one of hypothesis-testing and trial-and-error. They are much more willing to jump from one method to another, to discard information and to be sensitive to cues that they may not be able to identify verbally" (McKenney and Keen, 1974, p. 81).

A consistent argument underlying the studies of cognitive style is that the intuitive strategy should be respected. Keen (1974a, p. 11) describes several experiments in which intuitive subjects outperformed systematic ones and argues that:

> Each mode of evaluation has advantages and risks. In tasks such as production management, the Systematic thinker can develop a method of procedure that utilizes all his experience and that economizes on effort. An Intuitive thinker in such a task often reinvents the wheel each time he deals with a particular problem. By contrast, the Intuitive is better able to approach ill-structured problems where the volume of data, the criteria for a solution or the nature of the problem itself do not allow the use of any predetermined method.

R. O. Mason and I. I. Mitroff (1973) extend this viewpoint in a discussion of psychological types, based on Jungian theory.[19] Individuals validate information and perceive reality in very different ways: for example, sensing versus intuition, thinking versus feeling, and judging versus perceiving. "What is information for one type will definitely not be information for another. Thus, as designers of MIS, our job is not to get (or force) all types to conform to one, but to give each type the kind of information he is psychologically attuned to and will use most effectively."

This is the obvious message for DSS development. Several researchers on cognitive style point out that management scientists tend to view their own analytic

---

[19]Their definition of the relationship between psychological type and information system is well worth quoting: "The most generic definition of information comes from philosophy: *information is knowledge for the purpose of taking effective action*. So put, the concept of information raises all of the thorny problems that all generic definitions do: What is 'knowledge,' 'effectiveness,' 'action'; and further, who defines them and for what 'purpose'? . . . It is our contention that the current philosophy underlying the design of MIS has presupposed a greatly restricted view of 'knowledge,' 'effectiveness,' 'action,' and 'purpose.' More specifically, we propose that *an information system consists of at least one PERSON of a certain PSYCHOLOGICAL TYPE who faces a PROBLEM within some ORGANIZATIONAL CONTEXT for which he needs EVIDENCE to arrive at a solution (i.e., to select some course of action) and that the evidence is made available to him through some MODE OF PRESENTATION*. This defines the key variables that comprise an MIS" (Mason and Mitroff, 1973, p. 475). See also Churchman (1971).

style as self-evidently right and to underestimate the impact cognitive style has on the acceptance and use of analytic techniques (see J. H. B. Huysmans, 1970, 1973), the desirable desire and structure of an information system (see J. W. Botkin, 1973) and the communication process between user and designer (see J. S. Hammond III, 1971, 1974; and McKenney and Keen, 1974).

The main relevance of cognitive style research for MIS has been in emphasizing the psychology of individual differences in problem solving and identifying what Huysmans terms the cognitive style constraint in implementation of computer-based decision aids. The research suffers from a lack of simple, reliable devices for measuring individuals' styles, although the Myer-Briggs Type Indicator, which defines perceptual and cognitive behavior in terms of the Jungian types mentioned above, has been found to be a valuable and very reliable instrument (see, for example, Keen, 1973; Mason and Mitroff, 1973; and R. D. Miller, 1974).[20]

The basic argument of the cognitive style approach is probably more important than specific labels any one model may use. We take our own logic for granted and overlook the many and substantial differences intelligent and effective people demonstrate in cognitive activities. In particular, the techniques of OR/MS and MIS are attractive to the systematic, analytic style; they may be less applicable for *supporting* intuitive managers, and most importantly, no amount of selling or persuasion will make them so. Botkin (1973) demonstrated that the formal structure and interface of a DSS can fairly easily be tailored to meet the needs of intuitive and systematic thinkers; however, designers continue instead to structure a system in relation to *their* view of what is relevant in the problem-solving process. They are often unaware of the users' styles and so regard them as aberrations.

The cognitive style approach suggests we look at how decisionmakers are, not how they ought to be. H. Mintzberg (1973) has extended our understanding of managers' behavior by taking the trouble to observe over a sample period exactly what they *do*. He concludes that the idea of managers as planners is misleading. The managerial world is one of: (l) brevity—they rarely spend more than 30 minutes on any one activity; (2) fragmentation—they deal with a number of problems in any one day, and any particular problem is dealt with in fragments over a period of weeks, or even months; and (3) variety—their job involves *many* types of problems and decisions.

Mintzberg observed chief executives over a 1-week time span. He does not claim his findings apply to *all* managers or to these managers all of the time. Nonetheless, the manager's day-to-day activity is very different from the analyst's world and implies different modes for planning and for the use of formal methodologies. Analysts have a few tasks that they work on calmly and completely. They view problem solving as a well-planned activity requiring full attention.

The most important aspect of Mintzberg's study is that, whatever they may actually say, executives *prefer* their world. They enjoy its challenge, excitement, and chaos. They tend to be extraverted and nonacademic, and strongly desire verbal, concrete information and face-to-face discussion rather than documents and long presentations.

---

[20]The dimensions of MBTI are: extraversion/introversion, sensing/intuition, thinking/feeling, and judging/perceiving. The labels are a little misleading; the categories specifically relate to perception and reasoning. Jung's definitions of, for example, extraversion and introversion are very different from the popular conceptions.

The relevance of Mintzberg's findings for DSS is substantial. Only a few years ago, there was a movement toward "the terminal in the executive office." The movement assumed that managers needed to be—and could be—rescued from brevity, fragmentation, and variety, and that given a powerful, flexible information retrieval system "at their fingertips" they would make substantial use of a DSS. This is an assumption too easily taken for granted. If we recognize the realities Mintzberg points to, we might design a very different system. If it is to be of real help to a manager it will have to focus either on a recurrent problem of concern or a particularly critical one-time problem. It is likely to be used for, rather than by, the manager, through staff assistants. Merely providing access to raw data that might interest managers is unlikely to pay off as the range of potential topics is simply too broad and their attention too diffused.[21]

The consistent conclusion of all these descriptive models of the individual as decisionmaker is that planners, analysts, computer scientists, and engineers all risk the success of any technical venture by assuming either that their clients are like themselves or that they ought to be. Even if this perspective provides few prescriptive guidelines, it identifies potential constraints and pitfalls in DSS design.

CONCLUSION

These five conceptions of the decision process range from the entirely normative to the entirely descriptive. Each approach highlights key issues and often directly contradicts some other one. It is obviously not easy for DSS designers to pick any one theory, and they may well view this whole issue as theological casuistry. We suggest that the best way to use or to synthesize these very divergent viewpoints is by adopting a diagnostic perspective. Designers need to be sure that they understand the realities of the decision situation and that they have a useful service to offer— they need a descriptive model as the basis for identifying a normative direction. In any particular situation, it may well be that the political or cognitive dimension is *not* relevant; designers need, however, to find this out and not to assume it in advance.

MIS and management science has almost entirely ignored descriptive models of the decision process; they are emotionally and philosophically biased toward the rational conception. This has a precision and logic lacking in the descriptive tradition, and its prescriptive implications are clear. This book is about the design and delivery of systems to help decisionmakers; it seems essential to us that any system builder be as concerned with descriptive realism as with normative idealism. The exact balance is hard to define, but we strongly recommend that every student of DSS make sure she or he understands how managers do in fact make decisions rather than focus on the logic of how they *should* do so. Analytic and technical training reinforce a normative perspective; they rarely suggest that alternate conceptions exist. Similarly, it seems useful for managers to see themselves as they are and to recognize explicitly their biases and those of the specialists who attempt to provide them with "systems" support.

---

[21]Carter (1974) argues that the *type* of information and mode of problem solving implied by an interactive computer system is not relevant to *senior* executives, whose decisionmaking is less problem specific and operation centered than that of the middle-level managers, for whom many, if not most, DSS are designed.

FOUR

INTRODUCTION

We are past the stage where we need ask if DSS can ever be of value to a manager. The examples discussed in Chapter 5 all involve situations where a DSS had a meaningful impact on important aspects of an organization's decisionmaking. In the mid-1970s there are literally hundreds of DSS in use (we willingly acknowledge that many of them are not labeled as such, but they reflect the concepts we present in this book and we modestly suggest that their designers are excellently placed to benefit from the synthesis and formalization we provide here). This fragmented but consistent growth in DSS application shifts the concern from asking if they be of help to asking *where* they can be of most help. This chapter aims at clarifying the issues surrounding this question.

Before turning to this, we need to review briefly where we stand in our argument. Chapter 2 demonstrated where DSS fit in the overall field of computer-based management information systems. We identified six rather different viewpoints on the role of computers in organizations and suggested that we need to synthesize from these a strategy for information systems development that exploits their relevant strengths and stresses the managerial and decisionmaking perspective. The viewpoints are:

1. *Computer science:* creates technology, both hardware and software. This is a necessary but not sufficient contribution to information systems.

2. *Management science:* represents the analytical viewpoint in structuring problems and develops the models so often necessary to drive information systems.

3. *Behavioral science:* provides insights into the implementation process and the human and organizational context of the system.

4. *Data processing professional:* builds the application systems the organization finally uses.

5. *Management:* understands the realities of decisionmaking and thus which systems can be effective.

6. *Decision support:* focuses attention on building systems in relation to key decisions and tasks, with the specific aim of improving the effectiveness of the manager's problem-solving process.

It must again be stressed that each of these points of view has a great deal to contribute to the rest. This is obvious, but in practice the various disciplines tend to defend their specialized perspectives, and the field is far too complex to allow a synthesized approach that integrates the insights of all the disciplines. For example, the computer science approach, as an independent activity, has played a key part in the development of more effective uses of computers. New types of hardware, better operating systems, and data management languages are built-in responses to the unfilled needs of end users of existing systems. Such feedback from the working environment shapes developments in particular fields. Thus, each can operate with minimal interaction with the others and still make useful contributions to the whole field. But we stress the critical value of getting interaction; in many respects our definitions of DSS are an effort to build a framework that can accommodate particular aspects of each approach on an opportunistic basis. Any single DSS may highlight technical, organizational, or managerial issues that seem most relevant to the decision situation.

In Chapter 3 we similarly examined conceptions of decisionmaking. Supporting decisions requires a detailed insight into both descriptive and normative perspectives on the decision process. Balancing those perspectives is difficult; support implies a descriptive focus, and improvement requires a prescriptive approach. We identified five main points of view on decisionmaking:

1. *The economic, rational concept:* this is the classical normative theory of decisionmaking, in which decisionmakers are all-knowing and able to evaluate all alternatives. They are dissatisfied with any solution but the best.

2. *The satisficing, process-oriented view:* this considers decisionmakers to be intendedly rational although cognitive limits lead to a bounded rationality; thus the goal of any decisionmaker is to get a good enough answer, not the best possible one. This point of view stresses the *process* of decisionmaking and not just its outputs; it emphasizes the relatively limited analysis and search most managers will make and their reliance on heuristics.

3. *The organizational procedures view:* this focuses on the interrelations among components of the organization. It highlights organizational structure, mechanisms for communication and coordination, and the standard operating procedures by which decisionmaking is systematized and often simplified.

4. *The political view:* this regards the participants in the decision process as actors with parts to play. They have strong individual preferences and vested interests and form coalitions of organizational subgroups. Decisions are frequently dominated by bargaining and conflict, with the result that only small deviations from the status quo are normally possible. Major innovations are (quite reasonably) resisted by those whose position, interests, or simply job satisfaction will be affected.

5. *The individual differences approach:* this view argues that an individual's personality and style strongly determine his or her choices and behavior. Personal "rationality" is subjective and behavior is very much determined by the manner in which an individual processes information.

Each of these views highlights descriptive or prescriptive issues in decision-making. In building a DSS it is essential to identify both the normative decision process that the system is intended to generate and the actual decision process that exists. The "decision-centered" approach discussed in Chapter 6 requires a careful analysis of the decision situation from all of the above viewpoints. This approach may be summarized as starting from a descriptive analysis of the existing decision processes and defining a normative model as the basis for system design. This design must at the same time be consistent with the descriptive model. *Improving* decisionmaking requires supporting managers and helping them adapt, learn, and move toward the prescriptive position. They may be both unwilling and unable to do this if the system does not start from *their* perspective.

With this broad summary of information systems and decisionmaking we now turn to an analysis of the class of problems amenable to DSS. Obviously, there are no distinctions between functional areas (marketing, production, and finance, for example) in terms of which of them are appropriate for decision support. At the same time, we distinguish very sharply between the classical use of computers in clerical replacement and data handling operations and the support of *decisionmaking* activities. Thus, for example, a DSS for the financial department's regular operations would not focus on reporting loan transactions or on shareholder records but on a decision, for example, on how to invest idle cash. Similarly, a DSS for management control might be concerned with a decision as to what next year's budget levels should be, but not with generating monthly reports and analyses of budgets and expenditures. At the strategic planning level, a DSS would not be a formal model to generate forecasts of market growth for the next 5 years; instead it would support the decision process for determining a market expansion strategy. (It is worth noting that in each of these examples the DSS is probably less technically sophisticated and for many computer specialists less interesting.) We are not suggesting that DSS are the "right" systems, but only that there is a class of problems for which such computer support can be valuable and that that class requires a different strategy from that of traditional OR/MS and MIS.

FRAMEWORK FOR DECISION SUPPORT

We need a framework in which to position where DSS are now and the directions in which they can move. For this purpose we will map decisionmaking in organizations, developing a taxonomy of decisions that will allow us to differentiate between DSS and classical MIS. It also will provide one mechanism by which an organization can check its current position with respect to information systems in general.

The framework characterizes organizational activities in terms of the kinds and levels of decisions involved. The taxonomy is broad and perhaps incomplete, but it is an essential step in developing a methodology for DSS development. It is not a theory, only a simple schema for classifying decisionmaking in relation to potential computer support. It is built on earlier, unidimensional taxonomies developed by R. N. Anthony and H. A. Simon.[1]

In *Planning and Control Systems: A Framework for Analysis* (1965), Anthony views managerial activities as falling into three categories and argues that

---

[1]Gorry and Morton (1971) provide a detailed description of this framework. See also Morton (1971).

each is sufficiently different in kind to require distinctive planning and control systems. The first of these categories is *strategic planning:* "The process of deciding on objectives of the organization, on changes in these objectives, on the resources used to attain these objectives, and on the politics that are to govern acquisition use, and disposition of resources" (p. 24). Defining objectives implies an emphasis on scanning the organization's environment. The strategic planning process typically involves senior managers and analysts and often requires innovation and creativity. The complexity of the problems that arise and the nonroutine manner in which they are handled make it difficult to appraise the quality of the planning process and to define rules for it.

The second category is *management control:* "The process by which managers assure that resources are obtained and used effectively and efficiently in the accomplishment of the organization's objectives" (p. 27). Anthony stresses three key issues in management control: (1) the activity involves considerable interpersonal interaction; (2) it takes place within the context of the policies and objectives developed in the strategic planning process; and (3) its paramount aim is to assure effective and efficient performance.

Anthony's third category is *operational control:* the process of assuring that specific tasks are effectively and efficiently carried out. Operational control is concerned with performing predefined activities (such as manufacturing a specific unit) whereas management control more often relates to the organization's policies. There is much less judgment required in the operational control area because the tasks, goals, and resources have already been carefully defined.

We recognize, as Anthony does, that the boundaries of these three types of decision are often not clear. Each area overlaps its neighbor, and the categories form a continuum. The definitions are, however, useful for analyzing information system needs and activities. The information requirements of each of the three categories are very different. The difference is not simply one of aggregation, but reflects the characteristics of the information required by managers. Table 4-1 summarizes the information needs in each category. Each of the variables in the table has different characteristics in the three stages of the continuum. The variables are:

TABLE 4-1   Information Characteristics by Area of Decision

Task Variables	Strategic Planning	Management Control	Operational Control
Accuracy	Low	⟷	High
Level of detail	Aggregate	⟷	Detailed
Time horizon	Future	⟷	Present
Frequency of use	Infrequent	⟷	Frequent
Source	External	⟷	Internal
Scope of information	Wide	⟷	Narrow
Type of information	Qualitative	⟷	Quantitative
Age of information	Older	⟷	Current

Accuracy of the information: in the case of strategic planning, accuracy is bound to be relatively low. Strategic decisions involve the future and often cover a wide range of uncertain and ill-defined variables. Operational control information, on the other hand, typically deals with very current time frames and it is generally possible and often essential to get accurate information.

Level of detail: with strategic planning the information used is normally aggregated, while operational control frequently requires detailed, specific information. For example, a decisionmaker does not need data on weekly sales by salesmen when developing a 5- to 10-year market penetration plan.

Time horizon: strategic planning deals with the future whereas operational control deals with either historical or current information.

Frequency of use: strategic planning decisions are made infrequently, while operational control decisions will be daily, weekly, and monthly. The frequency of the decision does not necessarily correlate with its impact for the organization. Any given decision in the operational control area may involve relatively little cost and risk, although the cumulative effect over a month or year can be large. On the other hand, a single strategic planning decision may have immense long-term consequences.

Sources of information: in strategic planning the information required most often comes from external sources, while operational control more frequently uses data generated within the corporation. Strategic decisions may be much more concerned with government policy, competitive activity, and economic trends than with internal company operations.

Scope of information: in strategic planning the scope of information (the type and number of variables) used in any given decision is typically very broad. Strategic planning involves examining a range of factors that often cannot be anticipated, whereas operational control frequently requires only a well-defined and narrow set of variables.

Type of information: in strategic planning, information is generally more qualitative than at the operational control end of the spectrum, where data tends to be numeric, specific, and empirical. This is, obviously, an over-generalization but the distinction is a useful one.

Currency or age of information: in strategic planning the information to be used may be quite old. In operational control it often *must* be fully current. In making a 5-year plan, for example, it is not necessary to know what sales were as of the previous day. On the other hand, in establishing tomorrow's production schedule for the factory, an operational control decision, it may be absolutely crucial to know exactly what the shop floor status was at the end of last night's work.

We will digress slightly here and stress the distinction between the *currency* or age of the data base and *response time.* This is often a confused concept. We can illustrate the difference by the example of a manager with access to some data base, which is in turn linked to operations in the corporation. The length of time between something occurring in the organization and the event being reflected in the data base defines the "currency" of the data. The response time is the length of time between the manager's querying the data base and getting an answer. It is, for example, obviously possible to have all the conditions suggested in Table 4-2.

Response time can be fast or slow, and age can be old or new. These four "cells" exist in many organizations. There are situations in operational control, management control, and strategic planning where fast response is an important need in the decision process. However, in the case of strategic planning the fast response may be to relatively old information. For example, an executive negotiating a new labor union contract may benefit substantially by being able to get a fast response to questions about the likely impact of a proposed pay raise on take-home pay or cash costs to the company, or the implications of new pension proposals. The data base, however, may contain 6-month-old data on the exact work force composition; even so, this may be far more useful than slower access to more recent data, such as this month's work force levels as revealed by payroll statistics.

Our stress on this distinction may seem unnecessary but there have been many discussions in the MIS literature where it is not made clear. For example, J. Dearden's influential article "The Myth of Real-Time Management Information" (1966) argues that managers cannot, should not, and will not ever use computer terminals in their jobs. One of the examples given is the use of a terminal to provide the president with statements on yesterday's profits by accessing up-to-date financial records. This was regarded, quite correctly, as a useless exercise. All Dearden's examples are instances of management control and strategic planning where the decisionmaker received completely current information as well as immediate response. Such a situation is indeed ridiculous. It does not, however, alter the desirability in certain situations of providing prompt response, even though the data base may be quite old. Many systems designers in the 1960s fell victim to the on-line MIS fad because they ignored this question of *how* information is used by managers in their decisionmaking. This is yet another example of the damage too narrow a perspective on information systems can produce; the fad was largely stimulated by computer scientists providing a new technology that was eagerly taken up with little debate on how such a tool should be used. The eight categories of Table 4-1 demonstrate that the information requirements of operational control decisions are at the opposite end of the spectrum from those needed in strategic planning.

The typical computer-based information system in use in a company has high accuracy and contains detailed information that is largely historical and used very

TABLE 4-2   *Currency of Data-Base Information*

Response Time	Old	New
Fast	*Terminal access to computer with disk files updated monthly*	*On-line data collection terminals with enquiry station*
Slow	*Standard manual clerical procedures*	*Standard request to normal, busy, batch processing computer center*

frequently. This information is collected mostly from sources inside the company and consists of well-defined sets of variables that are mainly quantitative and fairly current. Such a system is very specialized both with respect to the cost of maintenance, the methods by which data are collected and accessed, and the routines that retrieve and use the information. Far more importantly, it is of value only for particular types of information systems, which mainly fall in the operational control area. This "typical" system will generally have evolved from accounting systems, which are often the historical starting point of EDP. It is a mistake to assume that it can provide the base for a corporate planning system by, for example, allowing immediate access to the store of historical data. This assumption was made far too frequently in the late 1960s and again reflects a lack of focus on how decisions are made. The different needs of strategic planning, management, and operational control make the concept of a global data base for a totally integrated MIS not only impractical but also undesirable.

Anthony's framework has obvious implications for DSS. Clearly, the data base required to support a particular decision must be built in the context of that decision and not as a side effort in the course of constructing the global data base the designers hope will exist some day in the future. Only by focusing on the decision first and then defining the information required to support it, is it possible to see *which* data are worth collecting and where the collection and maintenance process should take place. With the advent of remote-access computing and distributed data bases (created and maintained locally, but accessible from all points), the system designer has far more flexibility and range of choice in this respect than ever before.[2] Applications in management control and strategic planning areas may well need to be separated from those in operational control. This is a critical but deceptively simple point. Numerous examples exist of the failure to recognize it. One of the more visible examples is demonstrated by G. Q. Gershefski's "Building a Corporate Financial Model" (1969). This describes a heavy investment in a model-based support system for strategic planning. The system failed for a variety of reasons but one contributing factor was the approach of defining the data base to be used and *then* finding the decisions it could support (see also, W. K. Hall, 1973).

Anthony's framework provides the first dimension for a taxonomy of decisions. The second comes from the work of Simon and uses his distinction between programmed and nonprogrammed decisions, discussed in Chapter 3:

> Decisions are programmed to the extent that they are repetitive and routine, to the extent that a definite procedure has been worked out for handling them so that they don't have to be treated *de novo* each time they occur. Decisions are nonprogrammed to the extent that they are novel, unstructured, and consequential. There is no cut-and-dried method of handling the problem be-

---

[2]These innovations are still too recent for clear trends to have emerged. Perhaps the potentially most far-reaching technological development in the broad field of data communications is computer networking, "a community of interconnected computers" (Tesler, 1977). The ARPANET network, which has been in use for some time, links 150 computers in over 60 locations spread across the United States. These computers are made by 13 different manufacturers. Such networks are now being made commercially available. Together with the trend toward "distributed" processing, they *liberate* organizations from many existing constraints—technological, economic, and even psychological—on gathering, sharing, and assessing data.

cause it hasn't arisen before, or because its precise nature and structure are elusive or complex, or because it is so important that it deserves a custom-tailored treatment. . . . By nonprogrammed I mean a response where the system has no specific procedure to deal with situations like the one at hand, but must fall back on whatever general capacity it has for intelligent, adaptive, problem-oriented action (Simon, 1960, pp. 5–6).

We shall use the terms *structured* and *unstructured* for programmed and non-programmed because they imply less dependence on the computer and relate more directly to the basic nature of the problem-solving activity in question. The degree of potential structure in the task predefines the procedures, types of computation and analysis, and the information to be used. In a highly unstructured task (for example, forecasting taste in men's clothing, hiring a senior executive, or R & D in the pharmaceutical industry) the decisionmaker must often rely on personal judgment, especially in identifying exactly what the problem is. By contrast, much if not all of the decision process in a structured task can be automated.

Later in this chapter and in Chapter 6, we focus on the necessary differences in design for a system to support unstructured decision tasks as compared with structured ones. Most obviously, the activities of the user are significantly more central for a DSS to support relatively unstructured tasks; the user initiates and controls the problem-solving process and sequence, and his or her judgment, personalized objectives, and interpretations guide the choice of solution. Users need models and computational aids that mesh with these activities. In structured tasks, the system will be designed to provide far more fixed routines and sequences of analysis, and to give *answers.*

The distinction between structured and unstructured decisions is a key one; we return to it in a little more detail toward the end of this chapter to establish as clearly as possible what the term unstructured means in the context of DSS.

Anthony's categories based on the level and purpose of the management activity and Simon's classification can be merged into the two-dimensional framework shown in Table 4-3, with the addition of a semistructured category, central to our concept of DSS (examples are shown for each of the resulting nine classifications).

Structured decisions are those that do not involve a manager. These are situations where the decision is well enough understood to have been given to clerks or to have been automated through the computer. Typical examples are inventory re-ordering, credit scoring, airline reservations, and even highly complex production scheduling using linear programming. The second level, of semistructured tasks, is where DSS can be the most effective. These are decisions where managerial judgment alone will not be adequate, perhaps because of the size of the problem or the computational complexity and precision needed to solve it. On the other hand, the model or data alone are also inadequate because the solution involves some judgment and subjective analysis. Under these conditions the manager *plus* the system can provide a more effective solution than either alone. This is human with machine, and the human controls the computer. The third category of unstructured decisions are those that are either not capable of being structured or that have not yet been examined in depth and so appear to the organization as unstructured. Many believers in rational man argue that there is no such thing as an unstructured decision. The pluralists counterargue that all complex social policy decisions are inherently unstructured. The debate relies on axioms about knowledge, reality, and

TABLE 4-3   A Framework for Information Systems

Type of Decision/ Task	Management Activity			Support Needed
	Operational Control	Management Control	Strategic Planning	
Structured	1 Inventory reordering	4 Linear programming for manufacturing	7 Plant location	Clerical, EDP or MS models
Semistructured	2 Bond trading	5 Setting market budgets for consumer products	8 Capital acquisition analysis	DSS
Unstructured	3 Selecting a cover for Time magazine	6 Hiring managers	9 R & D portfolio development	Human intuition

rational behavior, and is unresolvable. We suggest, on the other hand, that our taxonomy is practicable and that, indeed, there are many decisions where the label "unstructured" is a very accurate descriptor.

A lesson learned by one of the authors may help clarify the differences between structured and unstructured decisions—and the cost of not recognizing them. In the late 1950s business schools provided advanced seminars on the use of the new technique of linear programming for obtaining optimal answers to business problems. This state-of-the-art methodology seemed like magic; the student who was armed with optimal solutions would, of course, rise to the top of the organization, inevitably and rapidly. During one such seminar, the author in question was required to write a term paper illustrating the application of linear programming to a real situation. He and a friend rushed to the treasurer of a major American corporation, with whom he had some connections. The treasurer felt he had no problems for which linear programming could be at all useful but admitted that his staff members might. Further discussion with these personnel revealed that one of the treasurer's main jobs was to manage cash balances. His department was linked by teletype to the company's primary bank, which was in turn linked to 250 bank branch locations in which the company maintained checking accounts. The treasurer examined the balances in these accounts each Friday and decided how to invest this idle cash over the weekend. This was an operational control decision that generated $8 million in interest income. It involved a talented senior executive who saw it as an unstructured task.

The students examined this situation and concluded that linear programming was the obvious solution. This was clearly a *structured* task. They built a model and tested it using 6 months of historical data on actual cash balances. The LP solutions would have generated $1,750,000 of additional interest. The students presented their conclusions and generously asked for only 30 percent of the savings. The treasurer asked several questions and said he could not use the model. After the students delicately pointed out that he was old-fashioned, reactionary, narrow minded, and perhaps a little stupid, he asked what the model would do if interest rates in London suddenly rose. The LP formulation would, of course, result in all of the company's spare cash being "optimally" shipped to London for the weekend. Since the rising rates might reflect expectations of a devaluation and a consequent attempt by the London money market to prevent funds from suddenly being withdrawn, this would be a foolish and obvious mistake. The LP model would lose in a weekend more than the company made in interest over several years.

The students accepted the point and rushed off to "fix" the model. The treasurer raised a second set of questions, and a third, and then a fourth. The model grew larger and more cumbersome, no real progress was made, and the students stopped their work. The final outcome was a compromise; the treasurer got the original system and the students got no money. He had realized that the model made *better* decisions than he could for most weeks but that it also occasionally made very bad ones. He found it helpful to run the model and review its recommendations. If he found no obvious problem or felt there was no special factor to take into account, he would implement the LP's decision. Otherwise, he used his unaided judgment.

The treasurer recognized one of the main points underlying the DSS approach. The system alone or the manager alone was far less effective than the two combined. This semistructured problem could be best solved by delegating to the system routine computations and resolution of interactions too complex for the manager to perform, while leaving the judgments that the algorithm could neither make, nor recognize were needed, to the human. The students learned that there is a middle ground between the analyst's perception that problems are structured and the manager's general assumption that his or her own job is special and cannot be handled by a computer routine.

Since that time, management science, MIS, computer science, and financial theory and practice have all made great strides. The treasurer in the same company by now uses high-speed communication links to provide rapid transfer of funds, has analytic models that track activity and trends in money markets, and obtains daily reports on investments, interest rates, and balances. He still has a semistructured problem and will benefit from an interactive DSS, which will probably include an LP algorithm to support the decision on investing idle cash.

ILLUSTRATIONS OF DECISION TYPES

In Table 4-3, we showed the nine categories of decisions that result from combining Anthony's and Simon's frameworks. We discuss each briefly now to sharpen the concept of DSS as a distinctive strategy for information systems development.

Structured operational control.   An example of a decision in this cell is inventory reordering in a manufacturing organization. In the late 1940s the decision about how much and when to order parts to keep inventory levels at an adequate level required a well-paid middle manager. It was regarded in many companies as a task requiring experience and special skills. In the 1970s inventory reordering in many organizations has been delegated to a computer system that uses decision rules that require little further analysis or judgment. Such systems generally are more successful than any manager could be, in terms of consistency, cost, and reliability. It should be noted that the history of this particular class of decisions is an illustration of how the boundaries of structured, semistructured, and unstructured decisions are constantly moving as our level of knowledge increases enough to allow us to shift some problems toward the more structured area.

Semistructured operational control. There are many operational control decisions that cannot be automated but where computer support in the form of information retrieval, analytic models, or data manipulation may be invaluable. An example, other than the cash management one given, is bond trading. Virtually all major bond departments in financial institutions now have computer models accessible to their traders. There are a number of factors that the models do not take into consideration, partially because they cannot be quantified in a useful way and partially because there are so many of them, with only a few relevant in any given time period (for example, uncertainties about New York City's financial state, federal interest policy, and so on). Despite the judgments and subjective evaluations involved, there are a number of facts involving yield, maturity, and the state of the market that require careful calculation before arriving at a reasonable price. This is an instance where no automated system can make trading decisions but where the manager gains from the ease with which the machine can search a data base, make financial computations, and analyze alternatives.

Unstructured operational control. (The example below is, in fact, inapplicable. It concerns the editor of a magazine such as *Time* deciding on a front cover for this week's issue. A student who read a first draft of this book pointed out that magazine publishers have conducted detailed analyses of which issues sold well and what types of cover they had. They have correlated demographic and seasonal factors, together with key types of news items, and now have a list of cover designs suitable for particular situations. This analysis has moved the problem toward the semistructured category. However, we have left our original example unaltered to illustrate our point that structure partly reflects knowledge and perception and to suggest that a major value of the analytic approach in general is to clarify rather than solve a problem.[3])

The editor of *Time* magazine faces the recurrent operational decision as to which cover to use for the next issue of the magazine. This is unlikely to yield to analytic techniques and, indeed, it is not clear what the conditions for success are. It is a situation where taste and experience and even inspired guesswork are likely to yield a better answer than any form of support we are yet able to devise. There is disagreement in this area among those of different

[3]See Churchman (1968) and Lave and March (1975) for insightful explorations of the value of model building as a *learning* process and as a methodology for problem analysis.

philosophies as to the ultimate resolution of problems such as this. Some believe that there exists a class of problems that are inherently nonstructured. No amount of work, they claim, will solve the *Time* magazine problem. Others of a more analytical bent argue the opposite; it is just a question of working hard on the problem, breaking it into its component parts, until a solution can be found. This may be feasible but we prefer, for the moment, to use the decisionmaker's skills where those are obviously more effective than the machine's.

Structured management control.   A manufacturing facility with several factories, each able to make several different combinations of products, has complex problems of resource allocation. This decision may be facilitated by the use of a linear programming formulation or a simulation model. In either situation, managers' judgments and preferences are not critical, and it is often possible to come up with the best decision without any management involvement at all. Of course, while this is conceptually true, the problem is often too large for analytic solutions. Much of the mainstream effort of OR/MS has been to develop formulations and techniques to accommodate more and more complex structured management control problems.

Semistructured management control.   An example of this, to which we return in Chapter 5, is the development, by a marketing brand manager, of the promotion budget for a given product. J. D. C. Little's Brandaid model (see Little, 1975) is an excellent example of this use of a DSS. The brand manager's task has a 1-year time horizon. The manager must determine the timing and nature of expenditures for various aspects of marketing promotions. There is no algorithm or model that automates this, but there are structured aspects of the problem. For example, the machine can explore in detail the implications of the advertising response curves implicit in the manager's own concepts but which she or he finds hard to formalize.

Unstructured management control.   Hiring new managers is an example. This problem has defied analysis by personnel departments the world over. We are still left with the necessity of using subjective judgment in a decision as to which person to hire, or which experienced applicant should get a certain job.

Structured strategic planning.   The concept of structured planning seems unconvincing to many managers. However, there are strategic planning decisions where management preferences and judgments, although not irrelevant, are dominated by the economics of the situation. Examples of this are the location of warehouses or new factories. There are a number of generalized simulation models, sold by consulting firms, which provide a detailed analysis of the economics involved. Although managers may override the model's suggestions, they have the cost of doing so clearly before them.

Semistructured strategic planning.   A number of organizations have developed conversational support systems for the evaluation of possible acquisitions. The effect of purchasing a company at a certain price with a certain financial strategy can then be assessed in terms of its impact on earnings per share and the future growth of both companies. Clearly, this is an example of a problem that cannot be automated but where the effects of different financing strategies and assumptions can be reliably extrapolated, given the manager's judgmental inputs.

Unstructured strategic planning.   Research and development portfolio development is an excellent example of unstructured strategic planning. The choice of projects and budget allocations involve balancing uncertainty, payoffs, and the time horizon. While conceptually the formal tools of decision analysis and portfolio theory seem applicable, in practice it is almost impossible to quantify the subjective and often unanticipatable issues involved in creating new products, markets, or technology. W. E. Souder (1973), for example, found that although there are many models for R & D project selection, the average R & D manager can outperform them all.[4]

IMPLICATIONS OF THE FRAMEWORK

We have tried in this brief discussion to sharpen the definition of structured, semistructured, and unstructured decisions and to suggest the practical relevance of the distinctions for systems development. It should be stressed again that the lines that separate the cells are in reality hard to draw. Both the horizontal and vertical dimensions are continua and there are no precise divisions among any of the categories.

An additional point worth emphasizing is the difficulty of generating any comprehensive framework for discussing the use of computers in an organization. Much of the work to date has been functionally oriented, that is, it has focused on marketing, production, finance, and so on. The functional view and the data-base view are the two most prevalent in the literature today.[5] The decision-centered focus we present does not replace either, but in discussing DSS it is clearly more appropriate. We do not in any way defend our framework as more than a reasonably robust and general paradigm that clarifies some key issues in using the computer as a management tool. Our taxonomy has clear implications for the development of information systems, which is one test of its usefulness. A sensible extension of it

---

[4]Wildavsky (1964), who discusses a much broader aspect of strategic planning—budgeting within the federal government—makes a very convincing case for the innate and complete superiority of incrementalist, experience-based, and subjective strategies for analysis over rationalistic methodologies such as PPBS (Program-Planning-Budgeting System) and cost/benefit analysis.

[5]The explosive recent developments in networking and distributed processing have led to a growing focus in MIS-related research on data bases and data management. Whereas the functional view discusses systems and models in relation to classes of application (for example, accounting systems), this perspective emphasizes the role of the "data-base administrator" who "now, and in the future, is an individual who performs the function of planning, operating, and controlling the data base of an organization at both the policy and operational level" (Blasis and Johnson, 1977). This viewpoint is a useful one; it encourages the definition and building of libraries of information that decisionmakers can conveniently draw on, but it also distracts attention from the decentralized needs and activities of decisionmakers in contrast to the centralized processes of data-base administration.

may be to add a third dimension to the two we have laid out. For each of our nine cells we can add the functional dimension, giving us a set of nine cells in marketing, production, manufacturing, finance, and so on.

There are three immediate conclusions we can draw from the framework. The first of these, the shifting lines among the various cells, has been referred to. Problems that used to be seen as unstructured are now viewed as semistructured or structured. The shifting of problems toward the structured end of the spectrum has been in progress since management began. It has quite obviously accelerated since the end of World War II, largely because of OR/MS. We maintain that the advent of DSS facilitates rather than retards this movement, particularly since the emphasis on managers' own problem-solving processes helps generate the learning that leads them to identify the underlying structure of a task or decision.

The second obvious point is that the most use of computers so far has occurred for structured operational control tasks. For example, almost all computer applications in organizations today concern such activities as payroll, accounts receivable, inventory control, and financial accounting. This, of course, is obviously appropriate given the nature of the computer technology available over the past 15 years and given that it has made sense to begin with relatively simple and well-understood problems where the payoff is predictable and substantial. However, many, if not all, *management* problems fall outside the structured category, and, in fact, structured problems will naturally be delegated, since they do not involve making decisions but following well-defined procedures.[6] From this one can conclude that computers have had, at best, a second-order impact on management. We suggest that DSS can change that state of affairs. Parenthetically, we argue that a great many of the computer systems currently being installed are far more concerned with issues of efficiency of operations than with effectiveness. The aim of DSS is to increase the effectiveness of an organization through better decisions.

The third obvious implication is that DSS in the management control and strategic planning areas, and even in nonstructured operational control, are not *necessarily* dependent on the data base that exists for structured operational control. This point has been referred to earlier but it is important to stress it simply because the cost and difficulty of *usefully* linking into the data base used for structured operational control purposes is, in many cases, so high that to try to do so invites failure.

The framework also has implications for design and implementation. We discuss these in detail in Chapters 6 and 7. The list below is only a brief summary:

1.   The *people* involved in building DSS for semistructured decisions need to be different in terms of skills and attitudes from those building systems for structured decisions. For example, a systems analyst who has just completed, with considerable difficulty, the construction of a new accounts receivable system for the controller is unlikely to have much

---

[6]Many commentators have predicted that, for this reason, the main impact of computer systems on organizations will be the elimination of many middle management positions (see, for example, Leavitt and Whisler, 1958; and Simon, 1965). In practice, this process has been far slower than predicted but even so, as Hunt and Newell (1971) conclude, the growth in the number of middle managers has been far smaller than in other levels of the organization.

success in building a conversational support system for the brand manager in charge of promotion in the marketing department. Similarly, the management scientist who implements an optimization model for a company's distribution system will have difficulties working from the descriptive, decision-oriented perspective necessary for mapping analytic methods and computer technology onto the manager's problems and processes. We should not underestimate the need for a type of system designer who is currently hard to find, one who is technically competent but views her or his role as supporting the manager and understanding the manager's world. We discuss this issue in detail in Chapter 9.

2. The *technology* that supports ill-structured problems uses computer power that is altogether different from the maintenance and efficient operation of a large-scale data processing operation. Running a modern computer center, dealing with deadlines, and producing millions of pages of output is a totally different situation from the informal, flexible access required by most DSS. Recent computer developments have made it possible to obtain this access at a very low cost.

3. The *models* for the support of managers' decisions may differ substantially from the optimization algorithms used in the structured area. Small, informal models that get better answers than now exist are required, not elegant and sophisticated examples of the researcher's art. Simulation models, which represent a manager's concept of the key interactions of environmental variables, may be much more useful to her or him than optimization algorithms that are conceptual abstractions of the problem. Equally, an optimization model is desirable for solving a well-structured operational control problem for which data are available and constraints well understood.

4. The *process* by which DSS are constructed has much more the flavor of ongoing evolutionary service than the delivery of a final product that will be used repetitively. In particular, the manager must be personally active in the construction of the system since only through this process will she or he be able to use it successfully. It must be open-ended and accommodate both existing needs and learning and growth. This is a topic we turn to in Chapter 7.

STRUCTURED, UNSTRUCTURED, AND SEMISTRUCTURED PROBLEMS

The distinction between structured and unstructured problems is crucial and needs still further discussion. Simon distinguishes in the quotation we cited earlier between the two extremes of programmed and unprogrammed problems, but we are concerned with identifying the middle ground of semistructured problems. To do this properly is difficult given our current lack of understanding. For our purposes there are two key issues. The first is the distinction between perceived structure and what N. Chomsky (1971) has called "deep structure." For example, a game of tic-tac-toe has a deep structure. We can specify rules for play that will give the user, whether computer or person, a draw at worst, or, if the opponent blunders, a win. Despite the appearance of structure, however, a five-year-old child just learning to play the game regards each move as an exciting, uncertain challenge. The child cannot tell who is going to win the game and if two five-year-olds are playing, sometimes one wins and sometimes the other. They perceive the game to be unstructured. The example in the business world of inventory reordering systems has already been given. Some problems in organizations are perceived to be unstructured but their deep structure will eventually enable us to automate them completely. Others are perceived as being unstructured yet they may, in fact, lend themselves to the use of DSS in that subproblems can be structured. Yet other problems may be, in the final analysis, inherently unstructured. The recognition and correct classification of these decisions in organizations is a task we have only begun to tackle.

The question of perceived structure is dependent not only on our basic state of knowledge but on the context in which the decision is being made. An analogy with driving may clarify this. Suppose on a clear day, driving a car down a suburban street at 20 mph, we see a small child running across the road in front of the car. The problem is clear—some action must be taken or the child will be hit. There are perhaps four alternatives: (1) cut off the engine, (2) put the car in reverse, (3) swerve, or (4) hit the brakes. The choice among these alternatives has been "programmed" into us and under normal conditions we would automatically use the brakes. Change the conditions to driving on the turnpike in pouring rain at 55 mph with traffic on all sides, and a large dog suddenly dashing across the road in front of us—to hit the dog might result in the car turning over, to swerve might result in hitting the cars on either side of us, to hit the brakes too hard might result in skidding, and so on. The careful evaluation of these alternatives by, for example, looking around to see how close the nearest car is, is a theoretical possibility only if there is sufficient time, but the high speed of the car precludes all these information-gathering activities. Thus we have a situation in which all of the variables are known but where there is not enough time to do the evaluation. In such a case we argue that the context makes this an unstructured problem. Managers are often irritated by the tendency of management scientists to focus on the inherent structure of a decision, as in our example of driving, ignoring the context that makes that irrelevant.

H. L. Wilensky (1967) has shown the impact of centextual forces such as time pressure and crisis on organizational decision processes.[7] Our discussion in Chapter 3 of H. Mintzberg's studies of executives (1973) suggests that the context of managers' jobs and their own preferred modes of operation are major constraints on system design. Thus, for example, financial portfolio theory may allow the structuring of investment analysis problems, in theory at least, but the realities of the managerial world may *prevent* this.

Simon's definition of the three phases of problem solving—Intelligence, Design, and Choice—adds an important dimension to the oversimple dichotomy

---

[7]He points out, drawing on the example of the Cuban Missile Crisis of 1962, that, under pressure, groups try to simplify the problem to a point where it becomes manageable. They try to avoid searching for new alternatives, narrow the number of people involved to a select few, and make minimal use of expert opinion.

between structured and unstructured. Problems are not always structured or unstructured in their entirety but only in terms of particular phases within the problem-solving process. Simon (1960, pp. 2–3) defines the three stages:

> The first phase of the decisionmaking process—searching the environment for conditions calling for decision—I shall call intelligence activity (borrowing the military meaning of intelligence). The second phase—inventing, developing, and analyzing possible courses of action—I shall call design activity. The third phase—selecting a course of action from those available—I shall call choice activity. . . . Generally speaking, intelligence activity precedes design, and design activity precedes choice. The cycle of phases is, however, far more complex than the sequence suggests. Each phase in making a particular decision is itself a complex decisionmaking process. The design phase, for example, may call for new intelligence activities; problems at any given level generate subproblems that in turn have their intelligence, design, and choice phases, and so on. There are wheels within wheels. . . . Nevertheless, the three large phases are often clearly discernible as the organizational decision process unfolds. They are closely related to the stages in problem solving first described by John Dewey: "What is the problem? What are the alternatives? Which is best?"

By definition a fully structured problem is one in which all three phases—Intelligence, Design, and Choice—are all structured. Accordingly, we can specify algorithms or decision rules that would allow us to find the problem, design the alternative solutions, and select the best solution. The unstructured problem is one where we are unable to define the conditions that allow us to recognize the problem. In the design phase, we are unable to specify how to create methodologies to solve the problem that has been defined. In the choice phase, we do not have clear criteria for choosing a best solution from among those we created. If all three of these phases in the problem-solving process are unstructured in this way, we then label the entire problem unstructured.

Under some conditions one or two of the stages might be left in the manager's hands because we are unable to define it precisely enough. However, if the remaining phase(s) of the problem-solving process have enough structure to permit us to effectively use computer support, we label such a problem semistructured. (In all our discussions of structured and unstructured decisions we assume that the decision support is computer based. As we pointed out before, this assumption is unnecessarily narrow and in much of what we are discussing the support could come from a clerical work force or staff specialist.)

The definition of "structure" is hard to grasp and will require considerably more work over the years before it becomes precise (much of this work is already being done in AI; see, for example, M. Minsky, 1968). In addition, the strategy that focuses on *supporting* the human decisionmaker is very different from that which aims at *replacing* him or her. We maintain that a class of problems exists for which the focus on support is likely to be much more effective than that of replacement. We can illustrate these points with the simple example of games. We have already suggested that tic-tac-toe is a structured problem—it is quite simple to write a computer program that replaces a human player and plays a perfect game consistently. In checkers, a game substantially more complex than tic-tac-toe, the experience over the years has been interesting. A. L. Samuels' checker-playing program that can learn from its past experience is, in fact, capable of playing championship level checkers (see Samuels, 1959). This success, however, was not achieved by developing a computer program that uses algorithms and optimization techniques to replace the human decisionmaker. Instead, Samuels' checker-playing computer program simulates the human decisionmaker. It incorporates heuristics and rules of thumb, and learns which of these are successful and which are not and updates its own internal strategies accordingly.

The game of chess, however, shows no significant signs of yielding to either method of attack. Chess-playing programs that learn are not particularly good players and chess-playing programs that invoke algorithms are only slightly better. The computer's progress in chess playing over the past few years seems similar to climbing a tree to get to the moon. With each development we climb one step higher in the tree, but in the long run it is clearly impossible to get to the moon by climbing trees.[8] Perhaps the characteristics of chess problems indicate we would be more successful if we focused on supporting rather than replacing the chess player. If our goal is to have a given person play better chess (this is normally *not* the goal of the AI researcher who wants a computer to play chess), then a DSS to support the chess player may be one effective solution. (The former approach has resulted in not much learning for chess players and not very good chess-playing programs.) This is a purely speculative observation at this point, but our experience with some management applications suggests that it may well be valid.

The chess problem is in some sense structured since there is a board, which is finite in size, with pieces that have specific and fixed moves. The human being cannot, however, manipulate these few variables well enough to make chess a structured problem. From a practical standpoint, it is effectively unstructured and the perception of even a grand master is that the game is inherently unstructured (see, for example, R. Fine, 1967). In looking at examples of DSS in operational use, we need to keep in mind that the concept of structure in a problem evolves over time as the manager learns; we are interested in the manager's *perception* of what is structured and unstructured.

CONCLUSION

We can summarize a situation in which a DSS can be useful as also involving at least some of the following characteristics:

1.   The existence of a large data base, so large that the manager has difficulty accessing and making conceptual use of it.

---

[8]That said, after years of minimal progress with chess-playing programs there has recently been sufficient improvement for a computer to have won the Minnesota Open Championship. Also, recent advertisements for an electronic chess player, priced at a few hundred dollars, show how much advance has been made. It can play at levels of 1200, 1400, and 1650 (rated by the U.S. Chess Federation), which means that the average player will beat it 25 to 75 percent of the time and get an interesting game. Even so, no program can yet play, or recognize, a gambit (a deliberately "bad" move, such as a sacrifice, which can gain a winning position), and the general standard of achievement is well behind the optimistic forecasts found in Feigenbaum and Feldman (1963).

2.   The necessity of manipulation or computation in the process of arriving at a solution.

3.   The existence of some time pressure, either for the final answer or for the process by which the decision is reached.

4.   The necessity of judgment either to recognize or decide what constitutes the problem, or to create alternatives, or to choose a solution. The judgment may define the nature of the variables that are considered or the values that are put on the known variables.

By our definition, DSS are computer-based support for management decisionmakers who are dealing with semistructured problems. We have discussed above what we mean by this, but we have only broadly defined what we mean by support. This issue is discussed in more detail in Chapter 6 which focuses on the design process (rather than on the technical design) for delivering a system to a decisionmaker.

Support implies that the first stage in DSS development be decision analysis, with the manager defining the key decision problems. The manager can best recognize, with the designer's aid, the particular aspects that can be improved and the components that have the most overall impact on the effectiveness of decisionmaking. This first stage is descriptive and makes use of the concepts we summarized in Chapter 3.

A DSS can provide a variety of levels of support, and the exact choice can be determined only from the decision analysis. The most primitive support provides *access to facts or information retrieval.* For a manager to find relevant information in a mountain of raw data can obviously be a nontrivial task. A simple example is a manager looking at the company's price and cost history in order to assemble an argument before a federal government agency. He or she might well use oversimplified rules for analysis that could easily be supplemented by DSS routines.

The second level of support involves *the addition of filters and pattern-recognition ability to this data retrieval.* This provides managers with the ability to selectively ask for information and to give conceptual meaning to data. They may benefit from routines that provide graphical summaries or time-series analysis, for example.

The third level adds more generous computational facilities to the first two and permits the manager to ask for *simple computations, comparisons, projections,* and so on. The system is then like a sophisticated calculator, preprogrammed to include some of the manipulations the manager used by habit for such problems.

The final level of support, which we will discuss in more detail, provides *useful models to the manager.* The characteristics of "useful" here are important because the model must be designed to provide the managers with answers they can and will act on. Accordingly, it may be very simple and crude rather than mathematically sophisticated. It will often be based on heuristic rules and standard procedures for analysts. We discuss this issue in Chapter 6.

Of course, providing these four levels of support has long been the aim of many information systems designers. Recent changes in technology have now made it possible to *deliver* such systems to managers. The explicit focus on decisionmaking and decision support results in a system that is under their control. Traditional models and MIS have generally not allowed such interaction.

The first four chapters of this book present a case. In Chapter 5, we present some fairly typical DSS that are in use in organizations; these provide a basis for discussing at a detailed level the design and delivery of DSS. It is worth stressing that the systems vary widely in their formal structure and technical design. But they share a common focus on support, on *managerial* problem solving, and on meaningful interaction between decisionmaker and computer.

Chapter 5 is the midpoint of the book. The argument so far has focused on strategic issues and the context of DSS. Chapters 6 through 8 deal with tactics and the DSS itself. Perhaps the transition is too abrupt, though we hope it is eased by reviewing the examples of Chapter 5 in terms of the questions we have raised so far. Our aims are practical—to help managers and MIS professionals jointly develop more effective applications of the computer resource in organizations. The broad perspective of the first four chapters was required since: (1) there is at present a substantial gap between managers and MIS specialists; (2) the computer world is specialized and fragmented; (3) the technical, design-based tradition of MIS has rarely discussed decisionmaking, except from a normative, rationalistic viewpoint; (4) "the" computer is generally discussed as an end in itself; the idea of technology as a means to an end, seemingly obvious, is largely absent from the literature read by the MIS fraternity; and (5) decisionmaking is a very complex subject indeed and a general synthesis is both essential and difficult to provide.

We hope we have made our case. The focus of the book now switches to the practical exploitation of the DSS approach.

FIVE

INTRODUCTION

In this chapter we present brief descriptions of six DSS, almost all of which are currently in use in organizations. The systems cover a broad range of issues relevant to decision support—design aims and formal techniques, implementation, organizational factors, and so on. The case descriptions build on the arguments of Chapter 4 and provide a context for our discussion of the design and delivery of DSS in Chapters 6 through 8. We have limited our commentary to summary conclusions that highlight key features of the systems; the aim of the chapter is description not argument, and we hope that the examples are interesting in themselves and that they suggest ways in which interactive DSS may be of general value for decisionmakers.

Several general points are apparent from the detailed descriptions in this chapter:

1. DSS cannot just be plugged in; institutionalizing a system is an evolutionary process that requires careful attention to the individual and organizational context.

2. The impact of the DSS is often qualitative; it does not necessarily reduce costs or directly increase profits but "improves" the decision process. Thus it may be very difficult to evaluate the DSS, and it is essential in the design process to pin down exactly what improve means.

3. The system is what it looks like to the user; thus the software interface between the user and the underlying models and data bases *must* be humanized. The likelihood of the decisionmaker accepting the DSS often depends on how it is presented through this interface.

Each of these issues is discussed in more detail in Chapters 6 through 8.

The six systems described are:

PMS (Portfolio Management System). This DSS for investment managers is the longest example in the chapter—and it is a major influence on the ideas expressed throughout this book. PMS is a graphics-based system with a variety of fairly simple models operating on a large and complex data base. It is in use in several of the largest banks in the country.

Projector.   Projector is a system for support of corporate financial planning. Its design emphasizes the decisionmaker's ongoing learning as she or he uses the DSS to explore a complex and multifaceted problem. Projector is currently being used by six departments within a large scientific research organization to plan annual budgets for capital-intensive programs.

CIS (Component Information System).   This is a graphics-based DSS used by product planners in a truck manufacturing company. It is an ambitious system, built around a complex planning task. The design of CIS emphasizes ease of use and fast response time; these requirements were major constraints on the specification of analytic models and data bases for the system.

Brandaid.   This marketing model reflects the "decision calculus" developed by its designer, J. D. C. Little (1970). Little argues that a model for managers must be simple (but not simplistic), robust, easy to control and to communicate with, and adaptive. Brandaid is representative of a number of DSS for marketing managers developed within the past 5 years.

GADS (Geographic Data Analysis and Display System).   This is an "experimental" DSS that has nonetheless been used in several real world decision situations. GADS essentially draws maps derived from specifications in data files. The research team that implemented the DSS has paid particular attention to the issues involved in training decisionmakers who have no familiarity with computers or analytic techniques.

GMIS (Generalized Management Information System).   This is a state-of-the-art system that includes several technical and conceptual features that add new dimensions to the design of DSS. In particular, the user has access through GMIS to some unusually powerful features that permit the use of normally incompatible data bases, models, or languages. He or she may use already familiar tools (such as APL, TROLL, PL/1, IMS, or other such relatively specialized systems[1]); GMIS simulates the relevant software and hardware environment.

All six of these systems have been explicitly described by their implementors as DSS (or by Scott Morton's earlier phrase, Management Decision Systems). The label, of course, is much less important than the question of support—of using the technology of interactive systems to mesh the computer into managers' problem solving. While the technical aspects of the six systems are interesting in themselves, the key issue in each of the case descriptions is: What difference does the system make? The six DSS have many technical features in common, especially the structure and style of the software interface; we need to ask how those features contribute to the central aim of supporting managers.

---

[1]APL is an interactive and very powerful programming language that is rapidly gaining enthusiastic support (see *EDP Analyzer,* 1976). TROLL is a fairly widely used language for econometric analysis, PL/I is a general purpose higher level language, and IMS is IBM's standardized Information Management System.

PORTFOLIO MANAGEMENT SYSTEM (PMS)

Introduction

PMS is a Decision Support System for use by investment managers in a bank's Trust Department.[2] It was initially designed by T. P. Gerrity as an experiment to extend Morton's work on Management Decision Systems (see the Laundry Equipment System summarized in Chapter 1). The prototype system was extended—while the experiment was still in progress—and implemented in one of the largest commercial banks in the United States. It is still in use in that organization, 6 years after it was made operational. Since then, versions of PMS have been implemented in three other banks.

Many of our ideas in this book have come from our own indirect involvement with PMS and from the substantial research on the use of the system, generated at M.I.T. over a 5-year period. To our knowledge, PMS represents the most extensive use of an interactive system in the private sector for managerial decisionmaking in a complex, semistructured task. The system has been very successful, although as with most organizational and technical innovations, mistakes were made (especially in implementation) and the original claims, expectations, and goals were modified. The later versions of PMS have been substantially more successful than the initial one as all concerned have learned from experience. One of the lessons to be gained from studying the full life cycle of the system is a better sense of the complex interactions among behavioral, organizational, and technical variables involved over a long period of time in institutionalizing a DSS.

Our description of PMS is lengthy and tries to include the contextual issues relevant to the success or failure of DSS. We have focused on a later version of the system, implemented by the Great Eastern Bank; our reasons for this are that the designer of PMS had by then refined his design and implementation strategy and made very few mistakes indeed, and, in addition, the progress of the system in this bank has been monitored in some detail over a 5-year period.

Setting: Great Eastern Bank

The Great Eastern Bank is one of the 25 largest financial institutions in the country, in terms of total assets. It has been innovative and aggressive in developing products and services. The bank is organized into a number of profit-center line divisions. The Trust Division, for which PMS was implemented, provides investment services and manages the security portfolios of customers who range from wealthy individuals to large pension funds. The bank receives a fixed percentage of the assets managed; the percentage depends on the size of the account and the type of customer.

The Trust Division is organized into three product groups:

Personal Trust. The Personal Trust group manages individuals' assets and estates. There are 30 investment managers in this group, each of whom

---

[2]The material in this discussion is drawn from Gerrity (1971), Stabell (1974), Alter (1975), and Andreoli and Steadman (1975).

handles about 200 accounts ranging in asset value from several thousand to several million dollars. The accounts generally require close contact with the clients and substantial administrative and clerical work. Competition for new accounts is keen but it is rare for the bank to lose an existing client.

Pension funds. These funds are very large, averaging several hundred million dollars. The clients (business and labor union pension fund administrators) often have a policy of splitting their capital among four or five banks' Trust Departments and replacing the worst performer each year. Competition among banks is intense. Each of Great Eastern Bank's pension fund investment managers handles 10 to 20 accounts.

Capital Management. The Capital Management group provides services to wealthy individuals who are willing to accept high risks in the hope of getting high returns. The portfolio managers in this group are responsible for 30 to 40 accounts with an average value of a million dollars.

There is a fourth, staff support, group, *Investment Research*, whose main job is to channel information on individual securities (particular stocks and bond issues) to the portfolio managers. It also maintains a list of approved securities; the investment managers may not purchase any security not on the list. Investment Research is the training ground for future portfolio managers.

The Portfolio Manager

The goals for the accounts in each investment group are very different. Personal Trust accounts are conservatively managed. Traditionally, the "prudent man" rule is applied; the investment manager has a responsibility to preserve capital rather than get a high return. Frequently, he or she is restricted by special provisions imposed by the client, especially tax considerations or idiosyncrasies such as refusal to own tobacco stocks. Capital Management accounts are aggressively handled and require a high level of client involvement. Pension funds are not subject to taxes and the portfolio manager's central activity is making investment decisions.

The portfolio manager's job is surprisingly broad. Gerrity, in his study at the bank for which he designed PMS, concluded that the typical manager spent roughly equal amounts of time on contacting customers, reviewing portfolios, and analyzing the security market. The manager has a heavy clerical work load: written communications with clients, substantial form filling, checking on the status of trades (there is often a long delay between placing an order to buy or sell a security and the actual sale), and organizing account information for presentation to the bank's Trust Committee or to the client. In the Personal Trust group, customer relations are the key concern; C. B. Stabell (1974) found that portfolio managers rate "keeping the customer happy" as the main measure of their performance, and as far more important than the financial results of their investments. In general, if a client phones, the portfolio manager stops whatever she or he is doing to talk. The portfolio manager also has regular meetings with clients and must be ready to explain investment decisions or recommendations to them.

The traditional job of portfolio managers is to make investments. They need to keep themselves well informed on changes in the securities market. This involves daily attention to a mass of data: *The Wall Street Journal*, an average of 400 pages a month of reports from Investment Research, rumors on "The Street" (Wall Street, of course), and personal contacts with industry analysts and fellow investment professionals. The Trust Committee of the bank is both the main supervisor and constrainer of managers' investment activities. The committee, composed of Trust Division officers, senior portfolio managers, and Investment Research staff, sets the basic investment policy for the bank. For example, in 1974 it set limits on the percentage of funds that could be allocated to common stocks because of its fears of a bear market. It also periodically reviews all the accounts of every portfolio manager in relation to the bank's investment policy, the client's stated objectives, and the increase in asset value of the account (and, where relevant, its income yield).

The approved list of securities recommended by Investment Research and formally reviewed by the Trust Committee contains about 350 stocks that portfolio managers may purchase for their accounts. The client may, rarely, insist that securities not on the list be held in his or her portfolio.

Most portfolio managers regard investment as an art. They tend to rely on personal sources of information and largely ignore the formal reports they get from Investment Research. P. Andreoli and J. Steadman's interviews with Great Eastern's managers (1975) show the conservative and individualized attitude they have toward their job:

> *First Manager:* I guess a lot of it's just been a "seat of your pants" type operation; you've gotten burned on a few things and that's tried to teach you something. . . . Everything is relative in buying and selling stocks or making investments; it seems you've got to combine it with just plain common sense, and try to measure the values that are there, just using the fundamental approach. But also try to tie it into the period where you are on the stock market and what motivates people to act, aside from the fear and greed extremes. This bit of psychology has to play an important part. I subscribe to the theory that you've got to be wrong for a while before you're right in acting in the stock market.
>
> *Second Manager:* There are a lot of people here who use different types of technical methods like charts. . . . I haven't noticed anyone being any more successful than I have, using those kinds of things.
>
> *Third Manager:* I like to think I'm an individualist, though I'm not sure I am; we all move in herds just like everyone else. (Andreoli and Steadman, 1975, pp. 68–69.)

Financial Portfolio Theory

While portfolio managers regard investment as an art, there has been a wealth of theoretical research aimed at making it a science. Some of this involves the use of complex charts to locate underlying trends in the market. The most technical approach is that of W. F. Sharpe (1963) and H. M. Markowitz (1959); their financial portfolio theory argues that the level of risk and return for any given security can be quantified. For two securities with equal expected levels of return, the rational investor should obviously choose the one with the lower risk. Each additional unit of risk should be compensated by an additional unit of return. In a portfolio, total risk can be reduced by diversifying across securities whose expected trends in performance are unrelated. However, it is impossible to eliminate risk, and the portfolio should be set up in relation to an explicit goal expressed in terms of the trade-off between high risk–high return and low risk–low return. Portfolios intended as "growth funds" imply higher risk than "income funds." Tax issues are included in the theory in that stocks with high dividend yields will tend to be somewhat underpriced for nontaxable pension funds and overpriced for individual investor's portfolios. Similarly, high-risk stocks are effectively overpriced from the viewpoint of nontaxable portfolios.

Portfolio theory is complex and elegant. While it has many practical limitations (discussed below), its normative logic is convincing; the investor must think in terms of the portfolio as a whole and explicitly balance risk and return in relation to a predefined goal. Most portfolio managers have some broad familiarity with the theory; they may use its jargon terms (for example, "What's the beta for this stock?," meaning "What's the risk coefficient?"), but in general its influence on their thinking is at best indirect. The main limitation of the theory is that it is mainly concerned with the risk-return trade-off while the manager must take into account many other factors such as liquidity, capital gains taxes, client preferences and opinions, and so on. In addition, the available data are insufficient and too imprecise to allow accurate assessments of a security. Sometimes, too, a client's stated goals are not feasible, for example, high return *and* low risk, large growth *and* low capital gains tax.

The main conflict between the theory and the behavior of portfolio managers is that the traditional approach to investment has been based on analysis of securities rather than portfolios. Great Eastern's Investment Research analysts focus on particular industries or stocks and clients tend to think in terms of a given stock being an attractive investment opportunity. This securities orientation conflicts with normative theory, which argues that the decision process is triggered by a perceived discrepancy between the goals of a given portfolio (expressed in terms of risk and return) and its current composition. The investor then searches for securities that will eliminate the conflict. By contrast, in the securities-oriented process that most managers use, decisions are triggered by the attractiveness of a given security. The manager scans accounts and looks for situations where the client's goals and the current composition of the portfolio make it attractive to buy or sell the security. The securities-oriented process is most apparent in pension funds, and perhaps in large financial institutions in general, since they make frequent use of block trades (purchase or sale of a substantial number of shares at once). Block trades enable the institution to get lower brokers' commissions. In addition, since a single large trade can disrupt the market and either lead to sudden price shifts or make it hard to find a buyer or a seller, these organizations have well-established procedures for handling them. All in all, the structure, traditions, sources of information, and methods of operation of the investment world reinforce this focus on securities rather than portfolios.

Gerrity's Experiment: The Prototype for PMS

Gerrity's "The Design of Man-Machine Decision Systems: An Application to Portfolio Management" (1971) presents a "decision-centered" approach to design. He analyzed the portfolio managers' decision process in terms of five stages (derived from H. A. Simon): (1) *Intelligence*—problem recognition; (2) *Design*—generation of alternative solutions; (3) *Choice*—evaluation and selection of the "best" alternative; (4) *Implementation*—putting the chosen solution into effect; and (5) *Control*—monitoring the outcome and making necessary adjustments (which links back into Intelligence, by recognizing a new problem to be dealt with). Gerrity used this analysis to identify *operators*—components of a DSS—that can help improve the decision process. He found that the managers in Big Western Bank, the site of his study, used three formal information bases:

> *Portfolio-related* data on the holdings and structure of each portfolio. Most of this data was maintained by the accounting group and made available to the manager only on a monthly basis.

> *Security-related* data containing historical and predictive information on securities. Investment Research maintained this data.

> *Security-price* data. *The Wall Street Journal* and Quotron (a terminal-based system for obtaining up-to-the-minute stock-price data) were the main sources for these.

This information is highly fragmented and, as has already been discussed, security oriented. Since Intelligence involves the recognition of a gap between the current situation and a goal, managers tended to define problems in terms of single security holdings—their existing information system told them little about total portfolio status. Gerrity also found that the managers were far more able to make complex and subtle discriminations between securities than among portfolios; their concepts of the latter were generally naive, such as "large" versus "small" portfolios.

The Design phase was similarly oriented toward securities. Managers generally satisficed (see Chapter 3); they would scan through their portfolios looking for purchase or sale opportunities for the security they were concerned with, evaluating the portfolios in sequence, and stopping as soon as they found a satisfactory candidate. Gerrity (1972, p. 67) comments that: "This decision process is neither good nor bad; it represents a reasonable adaptation by intelligent men to limitations of the information system available to them. In fact, the group under study was achieving a very satisfactory rate of return on investment."

Gerrity used this descriptive analysis to develop a normative model of the decision process; this was strongly influenced by the *logic* of formal portfolio theory. In the Intelligence phase, managers should be provided with functions (operators) that would help them perceive the portfolio as a whole and compare it with useful standards. For example, the HISTO function in PMS produces a histogram showing the distribution of portfolio holdings along some dimension of interest, such as estimated total return. SCATTER similarly provides a two-dimensional scatter plot of the components of a portfolio (for example, price-earnings ratio versus estimated future earnings growth rate). In the Design phase, managers would need functions that would allow them to exhaustively search for alternatives. They needed to be able to scan accounts quickly and look at potential trades in terms of their impact on the portfolio as a unit.

Gerrity's normative model of the decision process emphasizes changing the existing Intelligence and Design phases. He mostly accepts that Choice was reasonably well handled, that the managers' experienced-based judgments were adequate and that no computer functions would be likely to improve them. Implementation and Control involve many interactions with the bank's accounting and trading departments; while Gerrity saw these as important he felt that a DSS should focus on the Intelligence-Design-Choice phases of the investment decision, since these most clearly affected the quality of the portfolio manager's decisionmaking.

Normative portfolio theory helped define what would be required to improve the decision process and also provided a framework for specifying the design of a DSS. Gerrity built up a list of operators; these included:

STATUS: displays the contents of a portfolio. STATUS supports the Intelligence phase by helping managers *quickly* get access to the latest data on prices and holdings; the existing reports were often out-of-date and had to be updated by hand.

TABLE: displays portfolio values and selected information on such related attributes as earnings growth rate or price-earnings ratios; this data is mostly supplied by Investment Research. TABLE supports Intelligence and eliminates the need for managers to organize, store, and remember such information and computations.

HISTO, SCATTER: graphically displays information on securities and/or portfolios. Supports Intelligence.

FILTER: searches the data base for components that meet specified criteria (for example, all portfolios where stock X amounts to more than Y percent of the total holdings). Supports Design by extending managers' ability to look for alternatives.

CREATE: generates hypothetical portfolios (for example, by making a hypothetical trade in an existing portfolio). Supports Design.

Nine such major functions were implemented in the prototype DSS. The data base for the system had two major components: (1) *portfolio structure data* (the contents of each portfolio) and (2) *security-related data* (50 variables for each of 300 common stocks). The initial design was strongly influenced by the portfolio managers, who helped specify the data and reviewed Gerrity's descriptive and normative analysis.

Eleven managers worked with the prototype PMS; the total "hands-on" usage was 29 hours spread over 31 sessions. Gerrity analyzed the managers' use of the various operators. The graphic functions supporting Intelligence (HISTO and SCATTER) accounted for over 40 percent of total usage. Analytic functions, especially CREATE, were hardly used at all. The managers were quickly able to learn how to use PMS but were easily frustrated by degradation in system response time, reliability, accessibility, and quality of data. They were able to adapt quickly and soon demanded more concise forms of command and suggested new operators.

The First Implementation of PMS

The success of the prototype resulted in the senior managers of Big Western's Trust Division proposing that PMS be fully implemented. This moved PMS from the calm world of an academic experiment to the maelstrom of organizational politics. The

Investment Research, data processing, and management science groups all had submitted proposals for new computer systems in the Trust Division. Data processing had focused on the trust accounting aspects of the investment process (these relate mainly to the Implementation and Control phases of the decision sequence, which PMS does not support).

The full version of PMS, based on the prototype, was implemented over a 3-year period. Another year was needed before the system was fully institutionalized. A number of problems hindered the development of the system; these were explicitly corrected when PMS was implemented in Great Eastern Bank. In particular, response time was often slow and the computer crashes frequent. PMS was run on the centralized computer "owned" by data processing. If a large program was being run at the same time as PMS, response time for the latter could suddenly slow from a few seconds to well over a minute.

The heaviest users of PMS were the managers who had helped design the prototype. There was little formal effort at helping or encouraging managers to learn the system. Stabell (1974) examined managers' use of PMS, in detail and over a 3-month period beginning a year after the installation of the system. He concluded at that point that the DSS did *not* lead to a more portfolio-oriented decision process. In addition, the managers' use of the full system differed very strongly from that with the prototype, as the summary statistics in Table 5-1 indicate:

TABLE 5-1   Usage of PMS, Big Western Bank Implementation

	Prototype	**Full System**
Average length of session	*60 minutes*	*5 minutes*
Average number of reports requested per session	*13*	*3*

Whereas no one operator accounted for more than 21 percent of total function use with the prototype, two functions dominated with the full system (80 percent of total system use). Our own explanation of these differences is that since the prototype was an experiment, the participants were self-consciously analytic and thought carefully about what they were doing and why. In the pressures of the day-to-day reality of brevity, fragmentation, and variety, they fell back—naturally—to their well-established habits.[3]

Stabell (1975, pp. 16–21) summarizes the reasons why the managers' decision process did not become more oriented toward portfolios:

1.   *Low capacity for change:* Managers knew their methods "worked" and they saw little potential in the information processing technology for new approaches (although they saw its value for automating clerical

---

[3]Prototypes still seem a useful vehicle for involving users in systems design. The prototype is a *concrete* example, which has meaning for users. However, it is important to recognize that it is also an experiment and that the results cannot be generalized.

operations and for calculations). In addition, their conceptualization of the portfolio investment process was a fairly fixed aspect of their thinking (Stabell examined this issue in terms of the cognitive complexity theory outlined in Chapter 3); they had a "black-white undifferentiated view of the world of information sources available to them . . . the managers do not frequently make explicit and conscious choices of how and when to use a source of information."

2. *Proposed change was not operationally defined:* PMS's design was aimed at moving managers toward a portfolio-oriented decision process but what this meant in practice was not precisely defined. Training was confined to introduction of the functions available on the system; there was no discussion of how to make investment decisions using PMS (to be fair, the managers would almost certainly have resisted such training as an intrusion on their professional role).

3. *Portfolio managers distrusted the data base:* Managers viewed the quantitative estimates on price and earnings trends provided by Investment Research as inexact, incomplete, and unreliable. The barrier between Investment Research and the managers had always been apparent; it partly reflected a conflict between staff and line, analysis and experience, specialist (the research analysts generally concentrated on particular industries) and generalist.

Stabell did not discuss political issues but it seems clear that the general hostility of the data processing group and the periodic use of the PMS project as a weapon in senior level managers' internal maneuvers led to some managers regarding it as a high-risk experiment to be avoided.

This discussion of the first effort to implement PMS has focused on its weak points. It must be stressed that PMS is still in use in Big Western Bank and that all in all it has been a success. Although it did not initially lead to a portfolio-oriented approach, many managers use it and have become both more analytic and more willing to consider quantitative techniques. In some clerical, administrative, and marketing aspects of their task, the managers find PMS an indispensable tool.

Implementation Strategy at Great Eastern Bank

In the Big Western Bank, an outside consultant had been mainly responsible for the implementation effort. For the Great Eastern Bank, he recommended that a system manager be assigned who was credible with the portfolio managers and had substantial authority within the Trust Division. Mr. Ruskin, who took this role of coordinator, had been a portfolio manager and was now in charge of planning and development within the division. He regarded PMS as an R & D investment and stressed that its benefits would be neither automatic nor immediate. He also emphasized the need to break the development of PMS into distinct phases. Phase 1, begun in late 1972, was not completed until 1974. Ruskin provided more training for the managers than had Big Western, with frequent seminars at which they could compare experiences; he pointed out that the heavy users acted as catalysts—their enthusiasm and their boasting about new tricks they had discovered were contagious especially since several of them were the perceived superstars of the Trust Division.

The initial feasibility study for PMS involved three stages of analysis: (1) defining what the system might accomplish (assuming it was implemented); (2) specifying the functions that seemed most useful; and (3) determining the monetary payoff from the system.

The cost/benefit analysis concluded that there would be savings from the increase in performance facilitated by PMS and that fewer portfolio managers would be needed as business grew. These tangible benefits had also been predicted by Big Western; however, when they did not materialize there, the sponsors of PMS found themselves in a difficult political situation (which was exploited by their rivals). Great Eastern was more concerned on the whole with the less tangible benefits; Mr. Ruskin commented:

> The intent was that the mechanics and the ability to examine alternative decisions by a portfolio manager would be facilitated by the system. He would be able to do things he might not ever have done before, plus things that he did do but which took a long time. He could do things with the system that support personnel were doing; therefore, support personnel could be reduced. . . . We examined the portfolio manager's function and tried to provide him with a tool to better perform those tasks that were programmable, not to make decisions as such, but to assist him in evaluating alternative courses of action so that he could make the right decision.

Great Eastern examined several existing on-line portfolio systems marketed by time-sharing services. These were rejected because they were expensive, had very poor response time, and did not seem to fit the evolutionary approach required. Great Eastern preferred to invest in its own "significant advance in the state of the art of running accounts" (according to Ruskin). PMS represented a risk but would be exciting, give the portfolio manager new tools, and be a valuable marketing aid, in that customers would see Great Eastern as innovative and aggressive in its use of advanced technology.

It seems clear that Great Eastern's—and, more particularly, Ruskin's— emphasis on the potential intangible benefits of PMS made implementation much easier. The earlier Big Western version (less complex than this one) had been sold as a product that would save personnel costs and lead to significant improvements in performance; when the system ran into difficulties, it was very hard to point to its intangible values. By contrast, the management of Great Eastern's Trust Division understood from the start that PMS was an investment whose payoff and progress could not be guaranteed and that the "soft," intangible benefits were in some respect more important than "hard" cost savings.

Ruskin headed an advisory committee of ten portfolio managers who helped specify both the design of the system and the phasing of the implementation process. The lessons gained from the Big Western version of PMS were valuable. At the same time, the Great Eastern implementation posed substantial new design problems. A major weakness of the earlier system had been the erratic response time and reliability caused by PMS being run on data processing's centralized computer. The Great Eastern system uses a "front-end" minicomputer (see Figure 5-1) which acts as an interface between the terminals and Great Eastern's main IBM 370/155 computer. The minicomputer (which has its own storage disk) monitors commands from the terminal and transmits them to the IBM 370/155 when they are complete. Reports are returned to the mini and stored on the disk. The output that the user sees has come from the mini. The 370/155 is thus used only for the major computations that the mini cannot handle; its resources are not wasted on local input-output operations. (The main reason that the Big Western version of PMS had such poor response time was that the 370/155 was "process-bound" so that requests or reports

FIGURE 5-1   *Portfolio Management System*

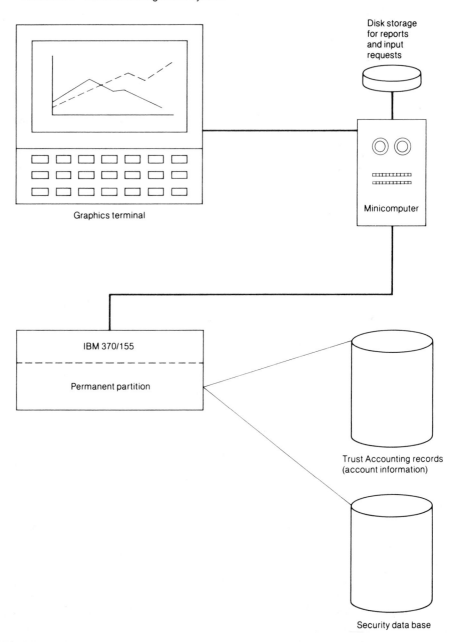

were stacked up waiting in queues.) In 1972 this combination of computers was relatively new and unproven and no software for interfacing the mini and the main computer was available "off the shelf." The effort and time needed to develop and debug the specially written software were badly underestimated, and the project fell well behind schedule. In an effort to recoup, PMS was made available to users in a fairly complete but only "95 percent debugged" form. This led to a long shakedown period but more importantly caused some users to become very frustrated with the errors in the system and initially to lose confidence in it.

Design Features

PMS is, from the user's perspective, a fairly simple system. Its complexity is beneath the surface. The system operators (TABLE, HISTO, and so on) draw on a large data base; data management and retrieval are complex in themselves and the need for fast response time meant that highly efficient programming routines had to be designed.

The data base for PMS contains two types of record:

Account data (generated by the Trust Accounting group): 190,000 "holding" records (one for each security holding in each account) for 20,000 accounts. Data elements include market value, yield, performance of the account, and so on.

Security data: each of the securities on the bank's approved list. Data elements include current market price, dividends, price-earnings ratios and estimates of betas (risk coefficients), future earnings, and so on. Much of this data is updated daily, although the research analysts submit data on securities on an *ad hoc* basis (whenever they have made new projections or obtained information on earnings, for example).

The account data is generated fron the Trust Accounting System (TAS), a batch-oriented EDP system that provides the main data base for the Trust Division as a whole. When a portfolio manager decides to buy or sell a security, he or she writes up a ticket which goes immediately to the bank's stock trader. When the transaction has been executed and booked, it enters TAS, which in turn updates PMS the same night. The normal lag between the portfolio manager's decision and the actual booking of the transaction is 5 days. Many of the portfolio managers maintain their own manual accounting system, which is more up-to-date than the PMS data base. The 5-day lag reduces the usefulness of PMS for portfolios with very recent transactions. However, before PMS, the only information on portfolio status available without immense clerical effort was a simple listing of securities; PMS transforms the TAS accounting data into portfolio decision information and encourages thinking in terms of industry diversification, risk versus return, and so on.

Figures 5-2 through 5-10 give examples of the operators available to the user of PMS (the figures are taken directly from Andreoli and Steadman, 1975). As far as the portfolio managers are concerned, the operators *are* the system. The evolution of PMS has involved the definition of new functions, one of which, the LIST operator, has led to a substantial increase in system usage. (LIST is discussed later in this chapter.)

FIGURE 5-2 DIRECTORY. This function gives a general overview of all accounts for which the manager has investment responsibility. The report is in tabular form giving, as shown, the name of the account, market values and percentage of the account's assets (broken down by the class of securities), and the other information shown.

CODE NAME	ALL AMOUNTS IN THOUSANDS					PERCENT OF TOTAL				LAST TRADE	LAST LOOK	ACCT PER- FORMANCE
	TOTAL	LIQUID	COMMON STOCKS	BONDS	PART EQUITY	LIQUID	COMMON STOCKS	BONDS	PART EQUITY			
ALPHA	1,689	1,014	47,015	22,614	355	1.2	57.8	27.7	.4	04/22	04/22	12.3
BETA	401	133	230	105	12	27.7	47.8	21.8	2.5	04/22	05/23	10.4
GAMMA	137,872	544	97,240	37,015	2,917	.4	70.5	26.8	2.1	05/22	05/28	0.7
SIGMA	139,875	2,015	31,412	5,612	0	6.1	78.9	14.1	.0	05/07	05/07	7.1
EPSILON	1,827	3	975	512	0	.2	53.4	44.4	.0	05/07	05/07	4.5

FIGURE 5-3   SCAN. This function allows the manager to view
the holdings of a particular security across all the accounts for
which he or she has investment responsibility. The manager has
the option to specify either percentages or dollars.

ACCOUNT HOLDING XYZ REFINING COMPANY										
		XYZ REFINING CO.			OIL			PETRCHM		
ACCOUNT C	TOTAL ACCOUNT MARKET VALUE	UNITS HELD	UNIT COST	PCT ACCT	#	PCT ACCT	#	PCT ACCT	ACCOUNT CASH BALANCE
ALPHA	137,071,537	120,500	30	4.4	2	6.6	2	6.6	911,245
BETA	81,688,794	110,280	28	6.8	4	8.2	6	15.0	315,260
GAMMA	217,014,862	87,240	52	2.0	3	3.2	5	12.7	1,222,637
SIGMA	39,835,820	63,100	43	7.9	1	7.9	3	37.7	29,472
EPSILON	26,727,925	30,000	22	5.0	2	21.0	3	29.4	321,354

FIGURE 5-4   GROUP. This function produces a histogram of the distribution of holdings in an account by industrial categories. The bank specified the six broad categories. The manager has the option of specifying either dollars or percentages.

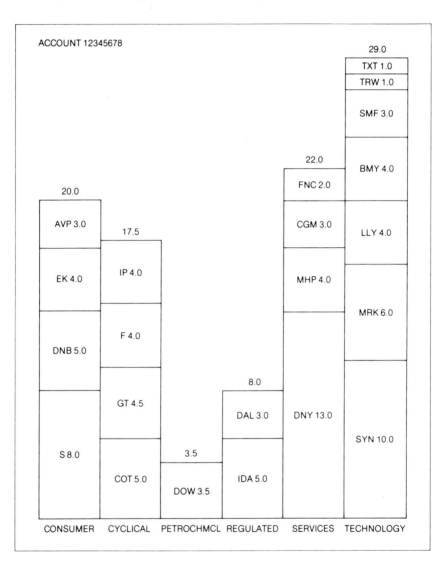

FIGURE 5-5   TABLE. This function provides the portfolio manager with the opportunity to design personal reports to review the holdings of an account. In this example, the manager has specified that the report should contain the current price-earnings ratio, the name of the security, the current market price (as of the last trading day), the current estimated earnings per share, the 5-year high and low price-earnings ratios, the security as a percent of the total common stock holdings in the account, the projected annual dividend, and the current yield on the dividend.

ACCOUNT 12345678

PRICE/EARNINGS	SECURITY NAME	CURRENT MARKET PRICE	CURRENT ESTIMATE OF EARNINGS PER SHARE	HIGHEST PRICE/ EARNINGS LAST 5 YEARS	LOWEST PRICE/ EARNINGS LAST 5 YEARS	PERCENTAGE OF COMMON STOCKS IN ACCOUNT	PROJECTED ANNUAL DIVIDEND	YIELD ON DIVIDEND
7.4	SECURITY ACB	22	3.00	15	11	16	1.50	6.74
9.7	SECURITY CBD	42	4.35	11	8	9	2.40	5.70
10.4	SECURITY BEF	21	2.00	20	10	3	.40	1.93
10.8	SECURITY FEG	44	4.00	18	12	10	.80	1.82
12.2	SECURITY XYZ	28	2.10	21	16	12	.38	3.20
17.1	SECURITY RST	41	2.40	28	19	8	1.40	3.42
22.9	SECURITY UVW	41	1.80	28	15	1	.40	1.07
26.0	SECURITY PMX	91	3.50	31	21	17	.96	1.06
27.7	SECURITY OLI	72	2.55	36	27	7	1.32	1.83
30.2	SECURITY ZGH	89	2.95	35	24	12	1.20	1.35
41.0	SECURITY BAP	74	1.80	53	36	5	1.10	1.49

FIGURE 5-6   HISTO. This function allows the portfolio manager to view the distribution of any available data item for all the holdings within an account.

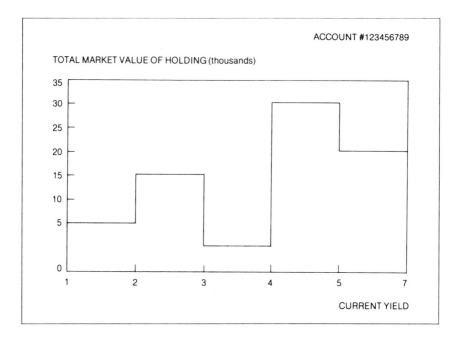

FIGURE 5-7 SCATTER. This function allows the manager to examine the relationship between two data items associated with securities held by an account. (Letters shown on the screen are the identification codes for particular securities, for example, MGI might be Magneto Industries.)

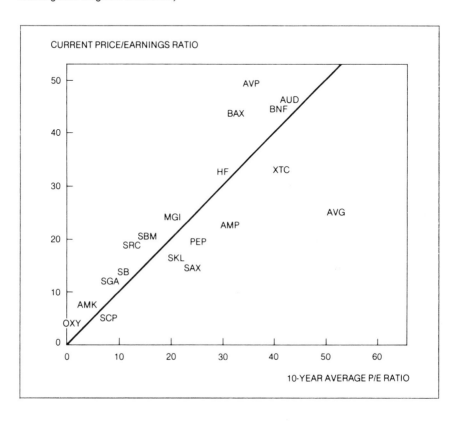

FIGURE 5-8 GRAPH. This function allows the manager to trace account performance or historical data concerning securities or market indices.

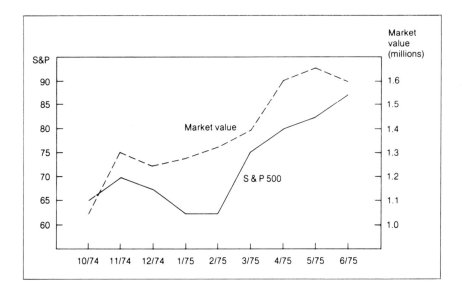

FIGURE 5-9   SUMMARY. This function contains basic data
concerning a particular account. This report is broken into five
general information groups: report heading, summary of account holdings, maturity structure of bond holdings, administrative account information, and the account title.

ACCOUNT 123456789			I. O.	F. Jones
CODE NAME XYZFGH			T. O.	K. Smith
DATE LAST TRAN 00/00/00			H. B. O	R. Doe

TOTAL MKT			
VALUE	2,775,670	100.0	
EQUITIES	2,133,527	76.9	
PFDS W/EQ	0	.0	ADMINISTRATIVE
BONDS W/EQ	0	.0	INFORMATION
PFDS	19,700	.7	
FIXED INCOME	618,076	22.3	

BOND MATURITY BREAKDOWN

MISC	0	
ONE MONTH		
LIQ ASSET	OR LESS	50,000	7.0
(EX-CASH)	4,000	.1	MONTH TO
	ONE YEAR	0	.0
PRIN CASH	365	.0	1 TO 5 YEARS	0	.0
INC CASH	21,132	.7	5 TO 10 YEARS	0	.0
	10 TO 20		
ADJ LIQ ASSETS	54,365	1.9	YEARS	0	.0
	OVER 20		
	YEARS	655,000	93.0
	TOTAL BONDS	705,000	100.0

INVESTMENT

PROVISIONS . . .

FIGURE 5-10   LIST. This function displays a standardized report concerning a specific security on the stock recommendation list.

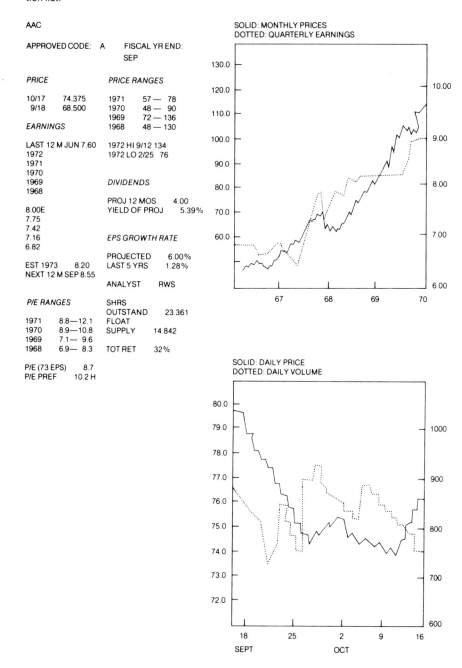

AAC

APPROVED CODE: A   FISCAL YR END:
                                  SEP

PRICE		PRICE RANGES	
10/17	74.375	1971	57 — 78
9/18	68.500	1970	48 — 90
		1969	72 — 136
EARNINGS		1968	48 — 130

LAST 12 M JUN 7.60   1972 HI 9/12 134
1972   1972 LO 2/25 76
1971
1970
1969   *DIVIDENDS*
1968
                                  PROJ 12 MOS   4.00
8.00E   YIELD OF PROJ   5.39%
7.75
7.42
7.16   *EPS GROWTH RATE*
6.82
                                  PROJECTED   6.00%
EST 1973   8.20   LAST 5 YRS   1.28%
NEXT 12 M SEP 8.55

                                  ANALYST   RWS

P/E RANGES		SHRS	
		OUTSTAND	23.361
1971	8.8—12.1	FLOAT	
1970	8.9—10.8	SUPPLY	14.842
1969	7.1— 9.6		
1968	6.9— 8.3	TOT RET	32%

P/E (73 EPS)   8.7
P/E PREF   10.2 H

SOLID: MONTHLY PRICES
DOTTED: QUARTERLY EARNINGS

SOLID: DAILY PRICE
DOTTED: DAILY VOLUME

COMMENT

10/15: NEW PRODUCT ANNOUNCE TODAY—IMPACT ON 1ST HALF '73 EARNINGS PROBABLY MINIMAL

Initial Usage of PMS

During the shakedown period, which lasted almost a year, the main users of PMS were the ten portfolio managers in the advisory group who had been responsible for guiding the development process. They obviously had the most commitment to and understanding of the system. They also had terminals next to their desks.

Unreliable system performance discouraged many managers. Some decided to wait until PMS was fully operational and others concluded that it was not worth their effort to learn a new technology. One of the main steps taken by management to institutionalize PMS was to insist that outputs from the system be provided as part of the periodic review of each account, required by law. Specific review procedures were established. PMS provided a common frame of reference for the reviews, and management gave a very clear signal that the DSS was there to stay and that they viewed it as an integral tool for portfolio management.

Ruskin held frequent seminars and discussion sessions. The managers had already been trained in the mechanics of the system; these sessions focused on meshing PMS into day-to-day decisionmaking. Frequently the enthusiasts would lead the sessions and demonstrate ways in which they used PMS; this generated new ideas and put peer pressure on reluctant nonusers.

Institutionalization of PMS

By early 1975, PMS was fully institutionalized. Usage had grown rapidly, from 2,500 reports requested per month in January 1974 to 5,700 in March 1975. Andreoli and Steadman interviewed a number of portfolio managers in mid-1975 and found that PMS was now accepted as a major tool, of particular value in customer liaison and marketing. It was being used in imaginative ways not anticipated by its designers; for example, it was of great help in cash management and in ensuring accounts were not overdrawn.

> *First Manager:* I use the SCAN function towards the end of the month to see where our overdrafts are. I'll sort the accounts on the overdrafts, then I'll have a list . . . rather than a whole set of gray books.[Gray books were the official accounting statements.]

> *Second Manager:* If I do want to buy a stock, I can see where I have cash available and know how much money I have, and the percent of liquid cash available in all the accounts.

> *Third Manager:* I have also set up an "income special table" which shows the payment dates [of dividends and other income]; I can determine when talking to a [Personal Trust] customer whether or not I can advance money. (Andreoli and Steadman, 1975, p. 57.)

Prior to PMS, a manager had no means of explaining to a client why the dividend check varied from month to month. PMS provided information that was far more precise, up-to-date, accessible, and useful than previously available.

Customer Liaison

Portfolio managers in Great Eastern generally spend between a quarter and a half of their working day dealing directly with clients, by phone or by letter. PMS has been of major impact in all aspects of customer relations. The portfolio manager can rapidly provide data about an account. The information is compact and often saves lengthy explanations and analysis. Operators such as GROUP (Figure 5-4), HISTO (Figure 5-6), and GRAPH (Figure 5-8) were designed to help *decisionmaking;* they have turned out to be invaluable as "decision conveying" mechanisms. The managers interviewed by Andreoli and Steadman claimed:

First Manager: I have created accounts. I had a customer who complained that she lost a huge sum of money over 3 years on the stocks her husband had left her and if I'd left them alone they would have performed much better than I had done. So what I did was re-create the original account at current prices and showed her what it would have been worth if I hadn't touched it and what I thought the income would have been on that basis. That was really good as there was a huge difference and I knew it would show.

Second Manager: The GROUP and HISTOGRAM are primarily to send out to customers, . . . it's easy for him to see why I want him to sell some of the stock, it makes it a lot easier to sell him on an idea.

Third Manager: For example, I find it very useful when I'm writing a letter to a customer recommending a particular program of purchases and sales by saying, "Here's where your account stood today in terms of market value, here are your holdings and values per issue"; and perhaps run a GRAPH off or a HISTOGRAM to compare the account to the averages. The customer's perception of the information you're giving them is much more concrete.

Fourth Manager: It's a confidence factor for the customer.

Fifth Manager: For instance, I went to see a gentleman here that had not expressed too much of an interest in coming in to visit with us—he was satisfied with the way things were going even though the market had been doing poorly, which is always a nice reception. I had in my folder probably eight or ten printouts I'd used as I'd looked at it from time to time and so we were able to follow a trend in the figures, aside from the GRAPH function, that showed him we *were* paying attention to his account even though we hadn't had any correspondence and very few telephone calls in between. . . . I use a TABLE as well as a SUMMARY sheet for this.

Sixth Manager: The customers' questions are typically "How much is the account worth?," "What have we gained or lost recently?," and "How much income can I expect and when?" Three sheets and you're in business and you don't have to carry tons of records on the account.

Seventh Manager: There's an example of something I couldn't have done before, a customer didn't even make an appointment, just called. When I called back, his wife said he was on his way in; of course, now I have market value lists for him, which I know is what he's going to ask for.

Eighth Manager: The best use is on new accounts; this we can get almost instantaneously. If we haven't got the figures, we can create them if they tell us what they have, even before they are at the bank. All I need is the stock symbols and I can create what the account looks like and have it there right away for the customer rather than waiting for all the stocks to go up for transfer. . . . I can come up with a lot of information on income and yield without having to spend hours [calculating them]. I can get all that on the machine right away. (Andreoli and Steadman, 1975, pp. 55–58.)

This use of PMS as a marketing tool and for communicating with clients is very differentiated; individual managers have adapted the system to their own needs and evolved new applications. The initial design of the system took into account the value of a DSS for simplifying and extending clerical operations relevant to customer liaison. However, the degree to which managers would draw on the system for this aspect of their work was not anticipated; it reflects the managers' own learning and individualized response to PMS.

Portfolio Decisionmaking

The managers interviewed by Andreoli and Steadman uniformly agreed that PMS had *not* had a real impact on their decisionmaking. It was apparent that "decisionmaking" to them meant the Choice stage, the actual selection of stocks to buy or sell. PMS mainly affects Intelligence and Design.

One supervisor in the Trust Division felt that the system had clearly influenced the portfolio managers' decision processes, by drawing their attention to issues of diversification and the "balance" of the accounts (balance between income and growth, for example) and to the overall performance of accounts relative to an industry average (for example, Dow Jones or Standard & Poor's 500). In addition, the system was increasingly used by the managers' supervisors in assessing performance: "We used to ask the manager how his account was doing. We can now say, looking at a graph, what are we doing about *this*?"

The supervisors also argued that much of the impact of the system might not be consciously felt by the managers:

First Supervisor: It gives you a different set of information than the portfolio manager was accustomed to getting. It may not be a conscious process that it's changing his way of looking at the thing, but I've seen it happen.

Second Supervisor: Everyone agrees you should be diversified, but in the typical situation of explaining to someone, you say, well 12 percent of the account is here, 2 percent's there. Over and over again I've seen us go into and out of meetings, I sat here a couple of months ago, we'd been talking to these ladies for over a year about the fact that 93 percent of the account's in cyclical stock. We laid one of these graphs on the table and 10 minutes later we had sales of over a million dollars under way. That's impact. I can't believe it doesn't have the same impact on the portfolio managers.

Third Supervisor: You look at a chart that says "consumer group" = zero and intuitively [you can see that] unless there's been a conscious decision not to buy consumer stock, there's a *gap* there, that's an impact.

Fourth Supervisor: In the old one you just had what there was, not what there should have been. (Andreoli and Steadman, 1975, p. 60.)

Andreoli and Steadman's results support Stabell's conclusion that PMS did *not* lead to a more portfolio-oriented decision process. There is little use of the more analytic operators; TABLE and SUMMARY account for 60 percent of the total requests and SCAN and SCATTER for less than 5 percent. The managers who made heavy use of the system have very individualized modes of operation, and there are few common patterns. Figure 5-11 shows the relative usage of the different operators for six heavy users. Manager B, who uses the GRAPH function more than three times as much as the others, explained that he looked at most accounts in terms of a time-weighted rate of return versus Standard & Poor's 500. He generated a simple performance line from those two graphs. Manager E uses TABLE (75 percent of his total usage) to show customers the latest status of their accounts, while Manager D uses TABLE, SUMMARY, and GRAPH for this activity.

The differentiated pattern of usage among managers is also apparent in their general feeling that they have as yet only scratched the surface. Several stated that they only occasionally found time, in a very busy workday, to experiment with PMS functions. They appreciated any help the computer staff could give them, although at least one manager was afraid he might "goof things up" while the technician was watching him.

Reliability of the system was still a problem in 1975. Heavy users commented that their lack of patience with computer malfunctions or slow response time *increased* with their own expertise. A few managers explicitly related their lack of use of PMS to its unreliability (in fact, computer crashes are relatively infrequent, although response time is often fairly slow). There seem to be no clear factors accounting for which type of person is a user or nonuser of PMS. Managers who have joined the bank recently seem more willing to try the system, regardless of their age, than those who have been at Great Eastern for a long time. Some of the older, more experienced managers delegate junior assistants or even their secretaries to run the system and generate reports. This may be due to time pressures, fear of the computer, or simply efficient delegation of effort. Very few of the heavy users of the system have a technical background or any previous experience with computers.

Andreoli and Steadman asked Great Eastern's portfolio managers if they would miss the system if it were removed. The heavy users, not surprisingly, were adamant in their view that PMS was essential to their jobs. It saved time in data gathering (especially for customers) and provided information that was unavailable elsewhere. Some of the users organized their day around the system—and, of course, were very frustrated indeed by computer crashes. For example, one manager used the SCAN facility at 9:30 every morning "to get my cash working for me."

The LIST Function

Gerrity's prototype system for his experiment at Big Western Bank had included a CREATE operator. This allowed the user to design a hypothetical portfolio and then operate on it as if it were a real one. In the experimental situation, CREATE accounted for only 1 percent of total usage. HISTO and SCATTER, by contrast, accounted for over 40 percent. In retrospect it seems clear that to managers, problem solving in an experimental laboratory situation was not representative of their behavior in the day-to-day pressure of their job.

HISTO and SCATTER account for only 15 percent of Great Eastern's usage but LIST, the equivalent of CREATE, has been of immense value. In the 6-month period following the introduction of the fully debugged LIST function (mid-1975), total usage of PMS doubled. LIST allows a manager to set up a new account and show what this account would look like if certain transactions had or had not been made, or to test the effect of implementing a possible decision. It adds a "what if" capability to the manager's problem solving. LIST was not included in the initial set of operators for the system, partly because of the technical problems it posed but mainly because the experience with the prototype system did not indicate its potential value. A major advantage of the design of PMS is that such operators can be added to the system easily.

FIGURE 5-11   Relative Usage of PMS Operators for Six Heavy Users

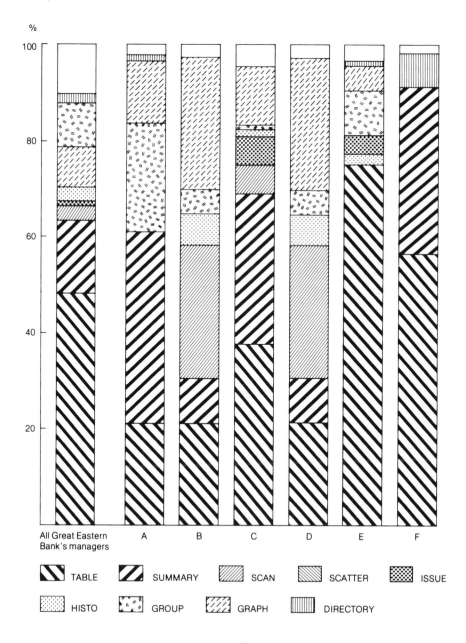

Summary: Is PMS a "Success"?

The portfolio manager's job is multifaceted. The portfolio-composition task, which PMS was primarily intended to support, is only one part of his or her overall activity. In fact, the manager's *daily* activities center around client liaison and clerical operations. PMS constitutes a *repertoire* of capabilities that can be integrated into these activities. Little's concept of a decision calculus (1970) is directly relevant here. The managers do not have to use PMS; if they decide to do so, they adopt and adapt it in the ways most useful to them. This process reflects their perception of what is important in their job. Their use of PMS is somewhat different than was anticipated, but the system clearly supports their existing decision process.

The weaknesses, unanticipated problems and successes, and lengthy institutionalization of PMS mentioned in the above descriptions indicate how difficult it is to evaluate a complex tool that aims at supporting and improving a managerial task. PMS is clearly a major success in Great Eastern. It has led to important changes in procedures (account reviews, supervision of managers), to increased effectiveness in the important area of customer relations (the managers believe they are primarily evaluated by their superiors in terms of "keeping the customer happy"), and to new approaches to cash management. Although the Trust Accounting System had important effects on the portfolio manager's job, it was not seen as useful and it was not integrated into his or her activities. But PMS has subtly changed the way managers think and act.

There are still problems with PMS. Its evolution and institutionalization have been fairly slow. The primary aim of facilitating portfolio-centered decisionmaking is still not fully met and system reliability is not always satisfactory. Three years ago, the system was operational but observers were generally pessimistic about its chance for success. A major lesson to be gained from the Great Eastern experience is that: "With evolutionary systems, there is a danger of evaluating results too soon. To change an ingrained method of working requires a considerable period of time and evaluations after 1, 2, 5, and 10 years may give quite different results" (Andreoli and Steadman, 1975, p. 116). Decision support in itself implies evolution, integration, and learning. The PMS experience raises many issues of design, implementation, and evaluation which are discussed in Chapters 6 through 8. Above all, it stresses the need for a broad perspective. The "system" is not an artifact, a set of computer routines, but a dynamic interaction among task, individual, organization, and technical components.

PROJECTOR

Introduction[4]

Projector is a DSS for financial planning. Developed by C. L. Meador and D. N. Ness, it has been used in several experimental settings as well as in the planning units of a large scientific research organization. In one of the "experiments," a presi-

---

[4]The material here is condensed from Meador and Ness (1974) and from personal communications with them.

dent of a small manufacturing company used Projector to evaluate the acquisition of a subsidiary and the introduction of a new product line (discussed below).

The initial design aims for Projector were (1) to integrate a range of advanced tools for financial planning into a "user-oriented," interactive computer system and (2) to provide an effective learning device for graduate students and managers interested in studying financial management. The second of these two aims led to a strong emphasis on evolutionary design and on providing informative messages, suggestions, and warnings—a genuine dialogue between user and system. Figure 5-12 is an example of this interchange.

Projector's English-like dialogue conceals—or makes less intimidating—some complex tools, including multiple regression, exponential smoothing with trend and seasonal analysis, goal programming, and optimization algorithms. The system allows the user to specify any single criterion or multiple criteria for evaluating alternatives (for example, net present value, return on sales, profitability index, minimum cost, profit margin, payback period, and so on). This obviously gives decisionmakers complete freedom to explore their problems in their own terms. Projector asks, in a conversational form, only for data relevant to the current application; the software includes "knowledge" about what factors need to be considered in, for example, assessing internal rate of return. This knowledge is used to provide prompts and warnings (see Figure 5-12).

Projector contains four types of model: merger/acquisition, project analysis, forecasting, and cash-flow analysis. The models link into a user data base. Additional FORTRAN routines may be provided by users or their staffs.

Projector is highly generalized. Any one application is likely to draw on only a few of its facilities. The designers of the system aimed at a compromise between support "which is so general that it is of little direct relevance to the problem and support which is so specific that it can only be useful in solving (or operating on) one particular problem" (Meador and Ness, 1974, p. 52). Meador and Ness emphasize the "setup" costs involved in learning to use a new system. The manager must first get a passive understanding by using the system to operate on his or her problems. This too often requires a large investment of time and energy:

> With the technology described here, there is an attempt to avoid this problem by constraining the manager in some dimensions, which may not be extremely material to him, and in doing so provide him with some prior structure. This allows him to obtain some desirable returns with relatively little investment in either effort or time and thus substantially limits the risks involved in deciding to use such a support system (Meador and Ness, 1974, p. 52).

This emphasis on support and learning dominates the formal design of Projector. From the user's viewpoint, the system *is* the software interface: the flexible, English language dialogue that provides help and that does not interfere with the user's preferred sequence of analysis. Projector does not look like a complex analytic tool; the goal programming algorithm, exponential smoothing, and regression routines are hidden; the "vocabulary" of the system is the user's own. Obviously, this approach to design is effective only if the user can trust the system. Meador and Ness'

FIGURE 5-12   Example of Dialogue between Projector and User

> NPV OF CASH FLOWS FROM PERIOD 0 TO PERIOD 9 AT 10%

NET PRESENT VALUE @ 10.00% = $ −107.70

> INTERNAL RATE OF RETURN

INTERNAL RATE OF RETURN: 49.66% (EFFECTIVE ANNUAL RATE)
                          10.61% (PERIODIC RATE)

> INCREASE CASH FLOWS BY 17%

CASH:	−1170.	117.	117.	117.	117.	175.
175.	175.	234.	351.	292.	281.	234.

>CHANGE THE CASH FLOW OF PERIOD 1 TO 2210.

CASH: 2210.0

> INTERNAL RATE OF RETURN

INTERNAL RATE OF RETURN: 1489.47% (EFFECTIVE ANNUAL RATE)
                           99.67% (PERIODIC RATE)

> CHANGE THE CASH FLOW OF PERIOD 2 TO − 3450.

CASH: −3450.0

> INTERNAL RATE OF RETURN

WARNING: STREAM OF CASHFLOWS IS NOT "PURE".
         IRR WILL YIELD INAPPROPRIATE EVALUATION CRITERION.
         FOR MORE INFORMATION REQUEST INFO ABOUT IRR
         RESTRICTIONS.

————DCF————·

> WHAT ARE THE USAGES OF THE INTERNAL RATE OF RETURN COMMAND

    INTERNAL RATE OF RETURN SUBCOMMAND

————USAGES————
(1)   PROJECT ACCEPTANCE: ACCORDING TO THE IRR CRITERION, AN INVESTMENT
       SHOULD BE ACCEPTED IF ITS IRR IS ABOVE THE COST OF CAPITAL OF THE FIRM.
(2)   BOND YIELDS: THE IRR IS THE SAME AS THE YIELD TO MATURITY ON A BOND, I.E.
       THE RATE OF DISCOUNT THAT EQUATES THE PV OF ALL FUTURE INTEREST AND
       PRINCIPAL PAYMENTS WITH THE BOND'S MARKET PRICE.

> WHAT ARE THE RESTRICTIONS

        INTERNAL RATE OF RETURN SUBCOMMAND

————RESTRICTIONS————
BECAUSE THE MODEL ASSUMES THAT THE INFLOWS (RECEIPTS) CAN BE REINVESTED AT
THE COMPUTED INTERNAL RATE OF RETURN IRR, THE IRR CRITERION HAS NO
SIGNIFICANCE FOR A "NONSIMPLE MIXED" STREAM OF CASHFLOWS (I.E. ONE WHOSE
NET CASH OUTFLOWS ARE INTERSPERSED WITH NET CASH INFLOWS THROUGHOUT THE
LIFE OF THE PROJECT, AND WHOSE CUMULATIVE PRESENT VALUE PROFILE COMPUTED
AT THE PROJECT'S IRR IS NOT NEGATIVE OR ZERO THROUGHOUT THE PROJECT'S LIFE).
SINCE "MIXED" PROJECTS ARE PARTLY INVESTMENTS AND PARTLY OVERDRAFTS, THEIR
RETURNS TEND TO VARY WITH THE FIRM'S COST OF CAPITAL. USE NET PRESENT VALUE
AS A PROFITABILITY CRITERION FOR "MIXED" CASHFLOWS.

> MULTIPLY ALL CASH FLOWS BY 1.15

CASH:	−1346.	2542.	−3968.	135.	135.	201.
201.	201.	269.	404.	336.	323.	269.

> ADD 2800. TO THE CASH FLOW OF PERIOD 2

CASH: −1168

studies and those of the GADS team (see pages 147 to 160) suggest that decision-makers will indeed accept even complex mathematical programming methods on faith if the interface is well designed [see also, C. A. Holloway and P. E. Mantey's (1976) discussion of using GADS to set up school district boundaries].

The Acrofab Study

Acrofab is a small New England manufacturing company, whose president had a master's degree in management and felt fairly comfortable with analytic techniques. Acrofab was considering the incorporation of a new subsidiary, Vehicle Security Systems, which would market a device named Interceptor. This product was technically superior to any other currently available and tests suggested that it could compete well with the existing systems that held 95 percent of the market for security devices. The president was very concerned that the company not commit too much of its own capital to the venture because of the risks involved in challenging well-entrenched nationwide organizations in a specialized industry. He brought in a technical consultant to help him set up a formal planning model to assess Vehicle Security Systems. While he had no clear idea of what type of model was needed, he had some well-defined issues he wished to explore and had collected a substantial amount of data. "As a result he had more data than ideas of how to use them" (Meador and Ness, 1974, p. 61).

The questions of most concern to the president were:

1. The inventory and working capital requirements for given production and sales levels.

2. The impact of rapid changes in production or sales on cash flows.

3. The sensitivity of total project profitability to changes in assumptions about the product's life cycle.

4. The financial impact of specific marketing strategies.

5. The interrelationships among working capital, total production, variable costs, and project acceptability.

Several types of models were considered by the consultant and the president. While a large-scale probabilistic simulation would facilitate the most useful and detailed analysis, the president felt that he could provide point estimates of parameters such as sales and marketing expenditures but not cumulative probability functions, correlation coefficients, and expected values. He understood and appreciated the logic of stochastic models but could not personally identify with this statistical approach to analysis. He preferred a simple—and cheap—model that would give him immediate assistance.

The consultant suggested that Projector be used since it was a relatively simple and interactive system that could be quickly implemented. It would allow a broad exploration of the problem and identify sensitive issues to be followed up in more detail later. The president found it easy to learn how to use Projector, mainly because of its English language mode of interface. He made a preliminary analysis of the Vehicle Security Systems division, in terms of the discounted cash flows for the investments involved. He then felt ready to add in more complex assumptions and variables. After several sessions working at the computer terminal, he moved on to sensitivity analysis and multiple regression routines for evaluating market and cost data.

The president felt especially concerned that he understand exactly what the model's assumptions and conclusions were. He did not feel there was enough time available for him to learn sophisticated financial techniques. His whole approach to the analysis was to add complexity to his original cash-flow model gradually and only as he himself saw fit. Nonetheless, he soon was making very sophisticated demands on the system and complaining that he needed additional flexibility and complexity that Projector did not provide.

Since Projector does not produce "answers," it is difficult to assess its impact on the president's decision process. He stated that his time-effectiveness was improved "by a factor of at least 20" over his usual planning methods and that he could perform sensitivity analysis through Projector in less than 1 percent of the time it would otherwise take. He also said that: "He would never under any circumstances have made such a thorough and confidence-inspiring analysis of the ramifications of his new division proposal without the computational support, flexibility, and ease of operation provided by the interactive planning model" (Meador and Ness, 1974, p. 65).

The president had several criticisms of Projector. There were four computer crashes that led to the loss of painstakingly entered input data. The slow, noisy terminal irritated him, and after a while he found Projector's English-like interface verbose.

As a result of using Projector, the president made substantial changes in the marketing strategy for Interceptor and completely rewrote major parts of the Vehicle Security Systems division plan. He found that Projector alerted him to issues he would otherwise have ignored. For example, early sessions with the model indicated that profits were extremely sensitive to small variations in inventory levels and that he had greatly underestimated working capital needs.

Conclusion

Projector is a prototype and has had limited use so that it is difficult to draw general conclusions from Meador and Ness' report. The system is now being used by six decentralized units in a (profit-making) scientific research laboratory to determine operating plans and budgets. It is run at least twice a month in each unit.

The emphasis in the design of Projector is on "humanizing" the interface. The system is polite, instructive, and easy to learn. It also includes some *knowledge*—the system has built into its routines data on financial concepts (see, for example, the warning in Figure 5-12 on "pure" cash flows). However, most of Projector's analytic functions are available elsewhere; most time-sharing services provide financial models and routines. Projector is distinctive in that it packages such routines through an interface that helps structure the problem-solving process and provides real *communication*. A set of financial models is not at all the same as a DSS; Projector helps make the models accessible and meaningful and encourages managerial learning and exploration. The interface and methodology defined by Meador and Ness make the system a far more dynamic tool than a set of independent models would be.

CAPACITY INFORMATION SYSTEM (CIS)

Introduction

CIS (Capacity Information System)[5] is an interactive graphics DSS used by Ztrux, a major manufacturer of trucks, to assess the impact of changes in product plans on the organization's overall manufacturing operations. Ztrux's 12 product planners are "fast-trackers," middle-level managers with an above-average performance record, who are assigned to this planning job for a 2-year period, mainly as training for a senior line executive position. They are each responsible for a major truck component (for example, transmissions, engines, axles, accessories). These components involve substantial capital investments and complex production scheduling. Ztrux has over 50 manufacturing locations and 20 major product lines. The product planners have frequent direct contact with top management.

The major decision supported by CIS is the creation and modification of the 1-year plan for the key investment items in a truck, such as the type and size of the engine. CIS does not make product plan decisions or generate the investment costs associated with a plan. Its main value is to help identify production bottlenecks and assist the user in building realistic plans that can be evaluated and later presented to top management. Modification of existing plans is fairly frequent and is caused by short-term fluctuations in sales or by environmental pressures. For example, in mid-1975 there was substantial discussion of downgrading the engine size for small trucks to improve fuel economy. An engine product planner would need to assess how much downgrading could be achieved without incurring substantial plant and equipment costs or causing shortages, excess supplies, or production bottlenecks. (While sales forecasts are made on an annual basis, manufacturing operates on a daily demand schedule.) CIS provides very few *answers* to such questions but helps the planner close in on feasible plans quickly and simply.

The Product Planning Process

The product planners have primary responsibility for profits (based on unit costs of truck components) and for ensuring availability of supplies for the manufacturing division. They interact with the sales and R & D departments and with production engineers and plant managers. The initial plan is based on corporate sales forecasts, which are used to generate a component product demand schedule. Each major component (engines, axles) is broken down into specific component products; for example, engines will be classified by number of cylinders, performance type, and so on. Each truck type is listed in the plan in terms of the percentage of sales that use a specific component. For the class A/3 light truck, for instance, 7 percent of the units will have high-performance, eight-cylinder engines, and five-speed transmissions. Twenty-two percent will use economy-performance engines, with three-speed transmissions. There are over 500 distinct component products.

Once total component product demand has been determined, the detailed manufacturing requirements must be calculated. A linear programming model is

---

[5]This discussion is based on an unpublished case study, disguised to maintain confidentiality.

used to allocate production to each plant. In many cases, additional capacity will be needed to make the product plan feasible. The annual investment involved is well over $100 million.

It is not difficult to generate aggregrate component product demand from the annual sales forecasts, but the detailed allocation to the plants is extremely hard to specify. The initial plan may also need to be changed several times during the year. Actual sales may deviate from the forecasts. The product mix may change even though unit sales are as predicted; for example, perhaps 10 percent of the A/3 truck sales are for the high-performance engine, instead of the expected 7 percent. Such deviations may not seriously affect the aggregate plan but they drastically alter the allocation schedule.

About 10 percent of next year's components are not in current production. This figure rises to 60 percent for 5 years ahead. These high percentages of component product for which no accurate data exists severely degrade the accuracy of the initial plan and the usefulness of the allocation analysis.

Modifications of product plans are generally initiated by the planners, although they must work very closely with other departments. A typical situation would be a truck line manager suggesting that engine size be upgraded to counter lower than expected sales. The product planner might feel that no alteration to the overall plan is needed. If it is required, he would generate feasible alternatives and assess them with manufacturing and engineering personnel. If the changes involve additional investments, they must be justified to top management in a formal presentation. Manufacturing will be responsible for implementing the modifications to the plan.

Sometimes a modification is based on estimates of costs, time, and capital requirements that turn out later to be very inaccurate, and the modification is in fact infeasible. The major stimulus for CIS was the product planning department's embarrassment at the acceptance—after substantial study and their personal justification of the proposal in front of senior line executives—of plans that were impossible to implement. For example, inaccurate estimates of production rates for a new front-wheel drive mechanism led to bottlenecks that affected virtually all product lines for a 2-month period. In this and most such cases, the product planners consulted the engineering and manufacturing units and figures were supplied in good faith. The complexity and detail involved in generating modifications of product plans too often made it impossible to test the impact of changes in estimates. CIS was partly intended to speed up the process of analysis and thus to allow the planner to examine "what if?" issues.

CIS

CIS supports the plan modification process. The system uses a T-shaped video display screen, which is split into three sections (see Figure 5-13):

1.   The *work section:* this is the main area of the screen, above the T. Data and analysis output are displayed in this space.

2.   The *system commands:* these are shown to the left of the stem of the T. These are the CIS commands the user may choose from at any given point.

FIGURE 5-13   CIS Screen Design

3.   The *menu selection:* this shows the routines and outputs that the user may obtain at this stage in the analysis.

A light-pen is used to select system commands or menu options.

The advantage of the screen format is its simplicity. The user does not have to remember what commands are allowed; only the relevant ones are displayed. Typing is minimized by the use of the light-pen. The log-on and log-off procedures for CIS are designed to be quick and easy (see Figure 5-14). Response time is fast. Every effort was made to obtain hardware peripherals (for example, terminals, disks) and software that ensured almost immediate response. Even the choice of an algorithm for the plant allocation analysis was constrained by this need. The designers felt that the product planners would never accept a system that kept them sitting and waiting for even a few minutes. The planners were generally seen as hard-driving and aggressive and under substantial pressure. They were not used to computer systems and spent most of their time in face-to-face discussions with other people or on the phone.

FIGURE 5-14   Log-on and Log-off Procedures for CIS. In log-on, the user types in surname after ENTER PLANNER'S NAME. The session is ended with the log-off entry, GOODBYE.

ENTER PLANNER'S NAME:

PASSWORD _____

.

.

.

GOODBYE

Sample Session

CIS is best described through the example of a session. The following sequence is reasonably typical, although the user will generally go through several iterations, generating a forecast, analyzing capacity, modifying the forecast, reanalyzing capacity, and so on.

Step 1. After the user has logged on, the screen appears as shown in Figure 5-15. The work section is blank since no analysis is in progress. The user selects the FORECASTS option from the menu and asks for forecasts for light trucks only. The screen then appears as in Figure 5-16.

FIGURE 5-15   CIS Screen Design After the User Has Logged On

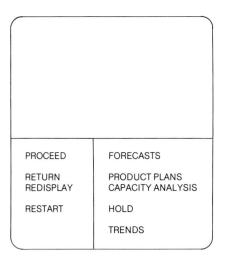

PROCEED	FORECASTS
RETURN	PRODUCT PLANS
REDISPLAY	CAPACITY ANALYSIS
RESTART	HOLD
	TRENDS

FIGURE 5-16   CIS Screen Design Showing FORECASTS Option from Menu Selection

	US SALES	CLASS A LIGHT TRUCKS FOR 1977	
LINE	SALES	PRODUCTION	COMMENTS
A-1/10	450	487	Forecast updated 6/5/75
A-1/12	86	92	
A-2/B15	626	608	
.			
.			
.			
G-7/2	50	0	Discontinue line 6/77
TOTAL/A	2065	2430	
TOTAL/IND	10306	9805	Forecast for ind from LREGR model

PROCEED	FORECAST REVIEW	DELETE FORECAST
RETURN	COPY FORECAST	CHANGE CLASS
REDISPLAY	UPDATE TRUCK LINE	
RESTART	INSERT TRUCKLINE	
HOLD	DELETE TRUCKLINE	

Step 2. The user revises the forecast for this line of trucks and next specifies PROCEED. The available menu options are shown. He requests the current product component demand schedule and asks for this to be updated to include the changes just made to the original forecasts.

Step 3.   He now requests a capacity analysis, using the revised demand schedule. The system allocates demand to plants through a linear program algorithm (response time for this step is about 1½ minutes—the calculations are considerable). Several levels of detail can be chosen, such as plant, component, component group, and truck line, and reports on allocation, bottlenecks, product mix, and so on can be obtained. Figure 5-17 shows bottlenecks in the Transylvania plant and the impact on production of adding an extra assembly line (INC 1 on the screen). The output of this stage of the analysis almost always needs to be reviewed with other departments, especially manufacturing.

FIGURE 5-17   CIS Screen Design Showing Capacity Analysis with Several Levels of Detail Requested

AXLE	BOTTLENECKS PROBLEM LIST FOR TRANSYLVANIA PAS-61/8 ALLOCATION				
PROBLEM BOTTLENECK		PLAN DEMAND	OTHER DEMAND	TOT CAPAC	INC 1
1	DIFF CASE SC/1000	1780	25	1805 1700	1850T
2	CARRIER & CAP AS	2067	0	2067 1920	2080
3	HYPOID DRIVE GEAR	1890	73	1963 1650	0
.					
.					
.					
10	PS PINION FLG&DE	1890	0	1980 1500	2300

PROCEED	SELECT A PROBLEM NUMBER TO GET
RETURN	TRUCKLINES AND PRODUCTS AFFECTED
REDISPLAY	BY BOTTLENECKS
RESTART	SWITCH PLANTS
HOLD	SWITCH PRODUCTS

Step 4.   Each plan or modification has a unique, user-supplied label that allows it to be saved and later compared with others. The "owner" of the plan is indicated. The user in this example now checks the new plan against those of several other product planners. (However, differences cannot be resolved by CIS.) He then asks for a summary of bottlenecks and for a list of the product lines affected by them (see Figure 5-18).

FIGURE 5-18   CIS Screen Showing Requested Summary of Bottlenecks and Lines Affected by Them

PROB 3 CONSTRAINT IS CYL & CASE L4				COMPARE ALLOCN NUPLAN AND C77-6/5 PLAN
ENGINE	PLANT	DAILY 1	DEMAND 2	CONST IS USED BY FOLLOWING
140-1P	TORONTO	200	200	H, H-S, USP
140-2P	LEGMONT	308	297	CANBOP, H
122-EP	HAGENBRO	406	521	CANBOP, MIN

Step 5.   The user saves the new plan for future reference, under the name C77-8/9 PLAN. He then logs off the system. He can get printed copies of all the displays generated; they are saved on tape files for a month.

System Design

The example illustrates many of the major features of CIS. The mode of interaction between user and system is simple and rapid. The system is virtually "bomb-proof"—the user cannot generate nonsense results through misuse of commands—and is also highly reliable. The design team emphasized human engineering issues from the start. They specified the *output* from the system well before the routines that generated it were ever discussed. This had several additional advantages; it provided a clear criterion for assessing hardware and peripheral equipment and gave top management a fairly precise description of what they were being asked to approve. Users had a clear idea of what the system would look like, well before the development effort got underway. CIS was thus designed mainly in terms of the software interface between the user and the system.

This emphasis on the interface and on response time and ease of use strongly constrained the design of the other two aspects of the DSS, the data-base management component and the analytic routines. The choice of an algorithm for allocating component product demand to the manufacturing plants posed several dilemmas. Obviously, the routine should produce accurate and realistic results. At the same time, it should not consume too much of the computer's resources. Several of the mathematical programming routines considered for CIS required large amounts of core storage, computation, and input; the resulting costs and response times were unacceptable, regardless of the quality of the solution generated.

Initially, the head of the system design team (who was a staff specialist in the product planning department) tried to incorporate a scheme that would let the user make personal allocations of demand to the plants. This approach was quickly discarded; the number of products and plants was so large that a formal algorithm was essential. However, it was not clear what variables should be included in the allocation routine. Since the overall goal of CIS was to generate the capital investment associated with a particular sales forecast and product plan, it seemed reasonable to use investment cost as the objective function in the optimization routine. The transportation costs involved in shipping subassembly and finished products between plants might also be included in the analysis and the profitability of each product plan might be assessed. Each of these approaches required substantial input data, some of which (for example, capital expenditures) could only be estimated. The final design of CIS did not include any of this investment data.

Four different mathematical programming codes were considered. Integer and mixed integer programming methods required heavy use of scarce computer resources; in addition, there were no reliable software packages available. A network representation of the allocation problem was rejected only because the design team could not produce a formulation that would be easy to implement and maintain and for which the computer costs would be reasonably low. In the end, a standard linear programming routine was chosen. The LP minimized overtime and excess capacity utilization. The allocation was constrained to meet all component product demand implied by the sales forecast and product plan. A priority scheme, rating each production process, was used to make sure that the least cost was incurred by the allocation.

The LP was a compromise choice and has several major limitations:

1.   Since transportation costs are ignored, demand may be badly misallocated. For example, the LP solution may specify that the

western Pennsylvania plant produce component products for use in the Ohio assembly plant when in fact the Ohio *engine* plant is much closer.

2. The data files for each plant list manufacturing output rates per day and not unit cost for each production process. This could result in demand being allocated to a high-cost instead of low-cost plant. (The priority scheme used to minimize total costs, mentioned above, does not take into account plant differences.)

3. Because of the difficulty in obtaining and maintaining capital investment data, the analysis does not provide the planner with the one figure really needed to evaluate a particular plan—the cost of the additional plant equipment required to implement it. The planner needs to follow up the analysis by more detailed discussions with the manufacturing department since CIS provides only a preliminary solution.

In spite of these limitations, the LP provides a believable allocation of demand, which in turn realistically identifies the major bottlenecks, which can then be examined in more detail.

The data files used by CIS were almost all generated by the manufacturing units. (The truck sales forecasts created by the corporate staff were already available on computer tape.) Manufacturing played a key role in the design of CIS by classifying component product types and identifying relevant production processes. The system designer asked manufacturing to provide information on production process changes that involved more than $3 million of investment or took over 60 days to complete. This information was collected for every plant.

The process of defining the data files for CIS revealed some surprises. The product groupings or product differentiations used by the planners were not the same as those used by manufacturing. For example, the distinction between manual and automatic transmissions for engine components is not relevant to the product planner but is critical to manufacturing.

The plant data files include detailed figures on capacity. Each production process can be expanded by some logical increment, such as a new assembly line. In addition, overtime may be used to increase output even though the overtime rules and constraints can be fairly complex. Some components require (or may be more efficiently produced by) specific pieces of equipment. All the plant data were developed by manufacturing, which was also responsible for maintaining it. The reluctance— or at least, the stated inability—of manufacturing to provide consistent and realistic cost data for capacity increases frustrated several of the designer's main aims for the system. Without investment data, the scope of CIS is limited to the decisions on bottlenecks and feasibility.

Implementation

CIS took almost exactly 2 years to implement. The mandate to develop a proposal was given in July 1973. In January 1974, the design team made a formal presentation of the intended outputs of CIS to top management. Over the next year, the system designer and two programmers worked full time on CIS; substantial time was spent on developing criteria for selecting hardware, software, and peripherals. They also wrote 40,000 lines of FORTRAN code. The system was made operational in January 1975 but another 6 months were needed to make modifications and adjustments. These 6 months were highly frustrating to the designers; all the "creative" work had been completed, but many wrinkles remained to be ironed out.

The product planners were slow to accept CIS. The heaviest users are still those in charge of accessory components; the engine, axle, and transmission planners have not become particularly active users. In part this is because they prefer face-to-face transactions with managers in their own and other units to building a plan by themselves at the terminal and then exposing it to other interested parties. Face-to-face development of plans involves advocacy and argument and it is important for their careers that they be highly visible to senior managers. Other reasons for the limited use of CIS may reflect the limitations of the system itself, in particular the lack of investment cost data.

The system has, on the whole, been a success. There are fewer infeasible plans accepted, and, in addition, the planners have been able to pinpoint bottlenecks much earlier in their analyses. There are virtually no complaints about the quality of the system; to a large extent, the planners take for granted its reliability and ease of use. Ztrux remains fully committed to CIS; no major design modifications have been proposed, and the general expectation is that the system will be used more and more as the product planners come to accept it as a tool of their trade.

BRANDAID

Introduction

Developing the annual marketing plan for most consumer products generally involves a preliminary sales forecast and estimate of overall profitability. These figures are used to specify the budget for the marketing "mix," for example, price, advertising, promotion, sales force activities, and so on. Brandaid is an interactive DSS that supports this decision process. Designed by J. D. C. Little, Brandaid reflects the criteria for building models for managers that he summarized as a decision calculus (Little, 1970; ADBUDG, the model discussed, is a precursor of Brandaid). According to Little, a model should be:

1. Simple and easy to understand (though not simplistic).

2. Robust: a user should find it hard to make the model give bad answers [A. Malhotra (1975) uses the term "bomb-proof" in this context].

3. Easy to control: a user should be able to make the model behave the way she or he wants it to.

4. Adaptive: it should be easy to update in terms of both parameters and structure as new information becomes available.

5. Complete on important issues: in conjunction with simplicity, this implies an optimal level of detail and complexity, which balances precision with scope. According to Little, "An important aid to completeness is the incorporation of subjective judgments."

6. Easy to communicate with: a user needs to be able to change inputs simply and obtain outputs quickly.

among these is multiplicative: $1.06 \times 1.32 \times .98 = 1.371$. Sales revenue is estimated to be 1.371 times the reference value of \$520,000.

FIGURE 5-20   Response Curve for Promotion

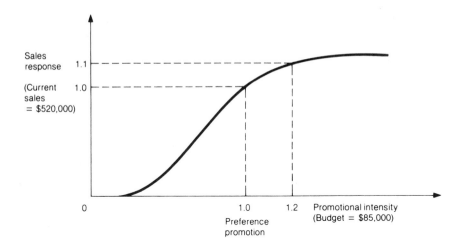

This approach to calibrating the model relies on managers' judgments. The exercise of developing a consensus on the exact shape of the response curve is often valuable in itself for a group of marketing managers. The model combines the individual consensual judgments, on price, advertising, and so on; in effect it extrapolates the implications of the managers' beliefs in a way that they themselves cannot, because of the human mind's limited ability to integrate complex masses of data. Brandaid shows how the computer and the manager can combine their relative strengths in a semistructured task.

Implementation

Brandaid has been used in many organizations for about 7 years. Although it is clearly a successful system, institutionalizing it has often been a slow process, partly because some managers are unwilling to adjust their mode of analysis to models.

Little reports that most successful implementations of the DSS occurred when the following types of people were involved in the project (see Little, 1975, pp. 656–657):

1. A senior staff member who was the internal sponsor.

2. An appropriate marketing manager who saw opportunities in the project for both his product and his own career (Little implies that cognitive style is relevant here: "A good person is someone who likes the style of thinking represented by a model").

3. "A models man on location" who was able to devote his full effort to the project.

The steps involved in adapting Brandaid to a new context comprise a 1- or 2-day seminar for management on the state of the art in marketing models. The aim is to establish realistic expectations about the role of models in decisionmaking. Next a team is formed; the leader should be a *marketing* manager and not a technician. A models specialist and someone from marketing research who knows what data are available and can locate people with special skills in particular areas are also needed. Ideally, the team selects a problem of current concern to the company and of manageable size. The model *evolves;* it starts from a simple structure that is gradually elaborated (this may require 1 or 2 years, although, according to Little, "Initial problems have been treated usefully in 4 to 6 months"). Possible starting points are the geographic allocation of advertising, the development of national marketing budgets, or the planning of promotions. The general model is customized to fit the particular situation.

The team members assemble historical data and specify reference conditions. They may also use statistical analysis to help define response curves. The model is tested and calibrated, mainly drawing on the knowledge of the marketing managers and staff. The model can then be used to analyze specific strategies, and the results are presented to senior management. The accepted plans will be entered into the model data base, and over the next few months actual sales will be compared with those predicted by Brandaid. As unexpected events occur in the marketplace, the DSS will be used to reevaluate the current plans. Discrepancies between Brandaid's forecasts and actual sales may be due to poor calibration or an inappropriate model structure, but most often they are caused by some phenomenon not included in Brandaid. In several instances (see the discussion below of the Groovy case), the manager was alerted to important shifts in the market environment by such a discrepancy (Brandaid is a system for learning, not a "solutions" model). Little emphasizes the importance of "stabilizing" the system—institutionalizing its use, identifying direct payoffs gained from it, and helping managers adjust to it. Turnover of key personnel involved in the project is a major destabilizing force: "This turnover can mean virtually starting over."

Calibrating the model involves finding a set of values for the input parameters through judgment, historical analysis, "tracking" (running the model with past data and getting managers to review the results and, if necessary, redefine parameters), field measurement, and "adaptive control." Managers must feel they can trust the parameters selected; no set of issues raises more concern in the minds of potential users. Little strongly recommends using judgment, obtained in an organized way and from more than one person. Generally, a group of knowledgeable in-

FIGURE 5-21   *A Judgmentally Determined Curve of Sales Response to Advertising (from an Application)*

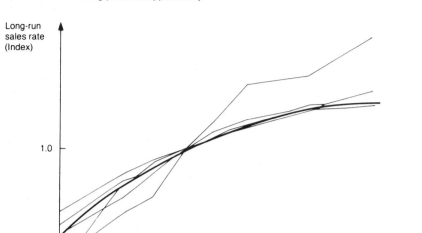

When the model had been calibrated, several different project levels and allocation schemes were assessed, using Brandaid. These stimulated new plans and variations on existing ones. The results were presented to senior executives by the Groovy product manager; his recommendation, calling for an additional promotion and increased advertising, was only partially accepted by them since they were unwilling to rely on the advertising response estimates.

After this initial use of Brandaid, the implementation team carried out several tracking studies, comparing the DSS's predictions to actual sales. Little emphasizes the simplicity of the structure of the model underlying the Groovy DSS. Even so, after it had been recalibrated to take into account incomplete and, in several cases, missing data, it proved to track well with historical information.

This lengthy calibrating and tracking process helped build confidence in the DSS. Groovy managers used it for "firefighting"—testing proposed price and advertising charges—and for dropping and subsequent reinstatement of promotions. One example of how the DSS led to a decision that would otherwise not have been made occurred about 2 years after the initiation of the system, in June 1971. Year- to-date sales were substantially ahead of the previous year. However, the brand manager

FIGURE 5-22   Groovy Sales for 1966–1968

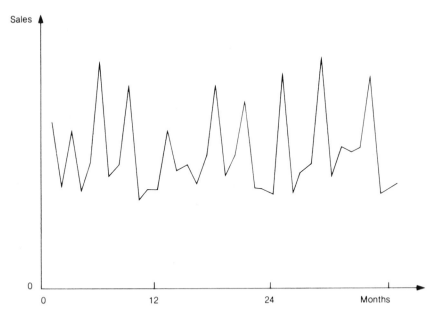

announced that the product was in trouble. His team had been doing regular tracking with Brandaid and had become aware of important differences between this
year, when a promotion had been run in January and price increased in March, and
the previous one. The effects of the price increase had been masked by a large corporate television advertising campaign, supported by coordinated promotions that
had included Groovy. The team made several detailed studies that showed that,
now that much of the advertising money had been spent and the impact of the pro-
motional activity was fading, the sales for the rest of the year would be very poor.
The manager proposed to senior management an additional promotion, and the
recommendation was accepted.

Brandaid is a learning system. The trading and calibration described in the
Groovy case alerted the brand team to important issues, without giving them
"answers." "The process is not one of sudden breakthroughs, but of modest advances, which bring about gradual integration of new techniques into the existing
system" (Little, 1975, p. 670). This integration often leads to unexpected results. For
example, Little and his colleagues assumed the main use of the DSS would be in
developing the annual plan:

> Presumably, after completing the plan, brand management would turn its at-
> tention to carrying it out. The model would then be put on the shelf until the
> next year, when it would be dusted off, updated, and used again. Instead, we
> have found that tactical changes in which the model can be of assistance occur
> frequently, although somewhat unpredictably. Thus we learned that the
> model should be available on a moment's notice. (For example, in one in-
> stance a brand manager heard a rumor that his advertising budget would be
> cut in half. By 5 o'clock he had a complete analysis of what he felt the effects

of this cut would be on this year's and next year's sales and profits for his brand.) . . . The most unexpected result, however, is the new feedback loop stimulated by tracking. Periodically, the marketing actions actually taken, including notable competitive moves, are put into the model. Any discrepancy between predicted and actual quickly confronts the model's team. The pressure to understand the reason is great. Not to understand is to say that the model is wrong, which in effect means the team does not understand what is going on in the market (Little, 1975, pp. 670–671).

This learning process, stimulated by Brandaid, has resulted in significant improvements in the planning process; in particular, the feedback of predicted versus actual performance (see Figure 5-23) into Market Diagnosis, which generates problems and opportunities for Operations, and an updating of Model (the conceptual model, as much as the formal structure of Brandaid). The final plan, which used to be seen as a "bible," is now reviewed regularly and Brandaid is used as a key part of the marketing control system.

FIGURE 5-23   The Role of a Model in the Market Control System

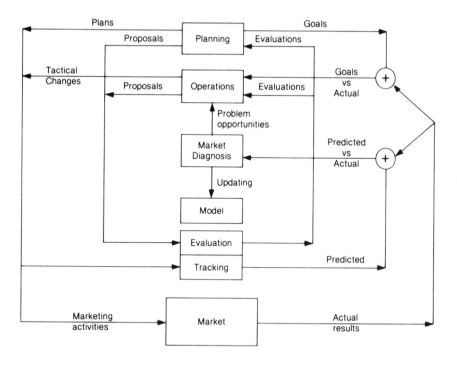

Conclusion

Brandaid is a marketing "model." In describing it as a DSS, we may seem to be relabeling a successful management science application to suit our argument. However, Brandaid is very different from most such models, not just because it is interactive or simple to use. Its design—and, more generally, Little's definition of the decision calculus—strongly reflects a central focus on decision support and only a secondary concern for technical structure. The task Brandaid assists is semistructured, and Brandaid encourages rather than dispenses with managerial judgment. It is used in a variety of ways as an integral tool within the marketing planning process. The implementation strategy is evolutionary and the managers have integrated it into their own problem-solving processes. It provides insight rather than solutions.

Of course, institutionalizing Brandaid is not always easy. In some situations, organizational factors have limited the usefulness of the DSS. In Connoisseur Foods (discussed in S. A. Alter, 1975), for example, the brand managers' superiors allocate marketing funds to a group of products. They do not have any DSS similar to Brandaid. They are concerned with "cannibalization," where a brand increases sales at the expense of another of the company's products. Brandaid does not take this into account. Because of these factors, the advocacy value of the DSS is reduced; its outputs are not seen as important by the product group managers and there is thus less incentive for the product managers to use it. (This is in contrast to Great Eastern Bank, where the senior Trust Division managers require PMS to be used in their annual review of each account.) Nonetheless, Brandaid has been successful and influential, mainly because of its focus on decision support: "Models are inherently inward-looking; that is, by themselves they suggest only those actions that are encompassed within the model structure. The diagnosis step [Figure 5-23] opens up people's thinking and invites new marketing ideas and model improvements, both of which effects tend to produce better decisionmaking" (Little, 1975, p. 672).

GEODATA ANALYSIS AND DISPLAY SYSTEM (GADS)

Introduction

GADS is an experimental system developed by the IBM Research Division to study the use of DSS "by nonprogrammers to solve unstructured problems effectively."[9] It has been implemented in several real world situations, so that the label "experimental" is misleading. Applications include planning for urban growth, designing police beats, and redefining school district boundaries. In all these instances, professional personnel in nonbusiness organizations worked with the DSS; only in the urban planning case did they not report that the system had been of substantial help to them in reaching a decision.

GADS is an interactive graphics system that essentially draws maps. Whereas Brandaid and Projector are model-based systems, GADS provides decisionmakers with tools for analyzing data categorized in terms of geographic coordinates. For example, this DSS was used to redesign police beats (see E. D. Carlson and J. A. Sutton, 1974). The end product was a map dividing the city into 35 zones. The initial data selected for the analysis was a random sample of "calls for service" from the previous year's police records. These showed the type of call (for example, crime in progress), the police unit assigned, the disposition of the call, and so on. Each record contained a geographic identifier; the city had previously been divided up

---

[9]Material in this section is taken from Bennett (1975), Carlson and Sutton (1974), Grace (1975), and Holloway and Mantey (1976).

(for purposes of this analysis) into 248 "beat-building blocks" based on natural and neighborhood boundaries, traffic patterns, previous call levels, or whatever criteria seemed relevant to the police personnel carrying out the study. (These basic units were later redefined, as the officers responded to information and insights gained from the initial stages of the project.) The problem was to combine the blocks into beats. The criteria for this were multiple and judgmental. For example, some officers aimed at balancing the work load, others at ensuring that the beats reflected neighborhood characteristics. Later in the analysis, several users of GADS changed from balancing calls for service to balancing the total time required for the calls. In all these instances, the basic data involve a large table of values for each building block that decisionmakers must scan, compare, and combine. The DSS automates the organization and retrieval of this data, leaving the system user to concentrate on shaping a solution.

Several of the DSS described in this chapter reflect an assumption that graphic displays are more useful in the problem-solving process than static tables of numbers, which lack patterns and are hard to assimilate. For PMS and the laundry equipment DSS, for example, the most expensive components of the system hardware were the graphics terminals. GADS obviously is specifically intended for applications that involve data most meaningfully presented and interpreted visually. Much of the improvement in the planning process in the laundry equipment case seems due to the value of graphs in communicating information quickly, highlighting key trends and problems, and in helping the user focus attention on the overall situation rather than on details isolated from their context.

The designers of GADS emphasized the need for high-quality graphic display devices. The initial version of the system used a terminal that provided adequate resolution (1,024 by 1,024 characters could be shown on the screen), but the amount of flicker was unacceptable. More recently, a terminal with color capabilities, minimal flicker, and a larger display size has been developed for GADS. The user can specify colors, to highlight boundaries or special zones or simply to organize the map to make it most striking or easy to look at. This new capacity adds a powerful tool for problem solving; users can relate more quickly to information that is in effect three-dimensional and where key variables or relationships can be brought to their attention and others kept in the background. The GADS research team has not carried out any formal studies as yet of the differences color graphics make in the problem-solving process. Our own assessment is that the perceptual assimilation of information and even one's response to data—in an almost emotional sense—are dramatically changed.

The technical details of the GADS design are summarized in Carlson and Sutton's case study of the police project (1974). The system requires complex data management software and data preparation. Figure 5-24 is a summary of the system. Source data files, generally maintained by the organization for other applications (for example, the historical police records on calls for service), are used to generate an extracted data base for analysis through GADS. Each record must contain a geographic code, such as a street address. A Geographic Base File contains computerized maps which are used to transform the code into x, y coordinates. As mentioned, the beat-building blocks defined by the police study group organize the city into 248 zones; this information is stored in special-purpose maps. Extraction specifications are provided by the user to select, organize, aggregate, and label data values from the source files. The extracted data base is a set of tables. The extraction

FIGURE 5-24   GADS Architecture (from Carlson and Sutton)

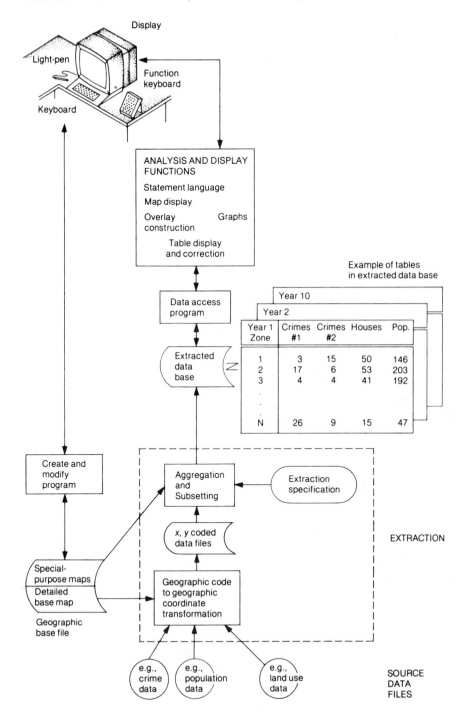

process may be handled on-line, but more generally staff specialists will create the data base as a separate step so that the user is largely unaware of the data management operations.

The GADS user is most concerned with its display functions. These include commands to create maps, to display them with symbols showing selected values, to overlay several previously defined maps, and to use a light-pen in effect as a pencil (eliminating boundaries between zones or creating new ones). Data may also be shown in graphs or tables.

The GADS design group has carried out several detailed case studies, which have focused on how nontechnical professionals have used GADS and which compare various modes of training and of interaction with the DSS ("hands-on" versus "chauffeur-driven"; see Holloway and Mantrey, 1976, and Grace, 1975, for more details).

The Police Beat Design Project

The use of GADS to redesign police beats, briefly discussed above, was the first major application of GADS. An earlier project which used the DSS for planning urban growth had been less successful. The model used to analyze the relevant data for the urban project was too complex for the users to understand and they could not validate it. They rejected both the model and the analysis. Later implementations of GADS emphasized the need for the user to be able to trust the DSS; according to Holloway and Mantey (1976), "The model could be validated by trying it on several examples and comparing the results with the users' intuition and also through a partial understanding of the process."

The beat plan in use at the start of the study had been devised almost 10 years earlier and revised 18 months before. It was unsatisfactory from the viewpoint of police officers, police management, and citizens. The work load was unevenly distributed, leading to poor morale, and 70 percent of calls for service were being answered by officers not assigned to the beat where the call originated. There were complaints that officers were unfamiliar with the neighborhoods in which they worked. Supervision was difficult.

A team of four police staff and lieutenants had been assigned to redesign the beat plan. A third party brought them in contact with the IBM Research Division personnel developing GADS. This group provided substantial support throughout the project, helping define and create the data base, providing training in the use of the DSS, and assisting users at the terminal. Fourteen police personnel worked on the project. There were five main users of GADS: two lieutenants from Field Operations, one from Research, a staff assistant from Research, and a sergeant assigned to communications. Five other field personnel were brought in when special knowledge of local conditions was needed. Over 350 hours of effort were required to create the data base, and IBM personnel spent 6 months developing programs for data management and 40 hours entering the special-purpose map defining the beat-building blocks. This is obviously a fairly high setup cost; while much of the effort was needed only because the system was experimental, it is clear that the manual steps involved in defining, collecting, and checking out a large set of source data are often the most complex aspect of a special study such as this.

The criteria for defining a beat plan are multiple and mainly judgmental. There is no clear "best" solution; an optimization algorithm could perhaps be defined to minimize, for example, response time to calls for service or to level out the police officers' work load. However, there are many other requirements. The deputy chief in charge of Field Operations aimed at assigning officers to a beat for 2 years with minimal rotation, to establish their identity in the community, define clear responsibility for crime prevention, and improve field supervision. Natural and neighborhood boundaries needed to be respected and communication between the field and the central operations unit needed to be enhanced.

The police personnel spent over 200 hours constructing proposed plans. They worked in teams of four, each of which developed very personalized ways of approaching the analysis. Eight solutions were finally proposed. The average time to generate a plan using GADS was 15 hours and the minimum, 3. Much of the time was spent discussing which zones to combine into beats; patrol officers and communications personnel were brought into these sessions. (The police personnel worked on the DSS in the IBM Research Division offices.)

Carlson and Sutton describe differences between the police department's problem-solving process with and without the system. While their analysis is informal, it seems clear that the DSS stimulated new and useful ways of resolving a problem that had up to then resisted a solution. Previously, only two personnel (both of whom were also users of GADS) worked on the beat study. The graphical display capabilities of the DSS made it easy for patrol officers, watch commanders, and communications staff to join in the discussions and provide extra expertise. Eleven officers actively worked with GADS.

At the start of the analysis, the police personnel found it hard to make their goals operational. There was general agreement that work loads should be leveled, for example, but little agreement on what this really meant. Some goals, such as respecting neighborhood boundaries, were never fully operational, but, on the whole, as users became experienced with the DSS, they were able to articulate—and better communicate with each other—what their goals and criteria were. Most of the officers changed their goals during the study; for example, leveling work loads was initially defined in terms of leveling calls for service but later revised to leveling time spent serving the calls. The users' decision rules became more complex and generally then required more data and more computations. This seems likely to be due to the reduction in effort required to explore the large data base in more depth and to refine generalized goals and heuristics. Whereas there had been only one solution proposed before GADS was used, eight solutions were generated with the DSS, each substantially different from the existing beat plan and fairly different from each other. It is worth emphasizing that GADS did not reduce the amount of time or cost involved in the manual approach. The officers were given 8 hours of training and spent far more time using the DSS than had previously been required in generating beat plans.

Carlson and Sutton (1974) comment on the value of the DSS in communicating ideas [their comments are similar to Scott Morton's (1971) assessment of the impact of the laundry equipment system in helping production and marketing managers work together]. One of the reasons the officers found it hard to make their goals operational was that they placed different values on constraints and relationships among variables. But they were able to articulate these values through the displays provided by GADS. They could look at different combinations of solutions and decision rules and compare them with their own proposed plans. The teams worked toward a consensual solution in this manner, explaining why a particular decision rule was necessary or unacceptable, examining where one member's rule or implicit value was in conflict with another's, and so on.

The police personnel all had other responsibilities in addition to constructing a beat plan. They were impatient with the 8 hours of training and felt that 4 would be adequate. They were rarely able to spend more than 4 hours at a time working with GADS, and tired quickly. They wished that a terminal were available so that they could play with the system during meal breaks or after working hours. They seemed to have little difficulty operating the system; there were always IBM personnel available to help them during their sessions at the terminal. As they became more familiar with the DSS, they also became more demanding. They expected the response time for trivial operations to be less than 2 seconds and 2 to 5 seconds for more complex ones. The IBM staff "improved" the system during the progress of the study. If these improvements changed any operations with which the users were already familiar, they would generally retreat and avoid using the new routines.

Each user (or group of users) drew on only a fraction of the system's resources at any one time. For example, 750 variables were available (25 data items for each of the 30 days in the sample) but users manipulated only 2 or 3 at once. Only two variables (total time and total calls) were included in most analyses. Each user converged on a "working set" of data, a small set of relatively constant variables and a larger number of infrequently used ones. They had little sense of data representation and thought in terms of aggregates; they found it difficult to think of a variable as an array of values. The main problem they encountered was the clumsy statement language used to create new symbols for a map and create new variables (the expression "*: TOT__POP (44)/TOT__H) > 3.5," for example, results in an asterisk being displayed in each zone where the average population per household, given in one of the tables, exceeds 3.5).[10] They were also surprised to find that they would be operating the system themselves; they had assumed that a technical specialist would be provided.[11]

Design of School Boundaries

Holloway and Mantey (1976) used GADS to help a school supervisor and his senior staff define a districting plan they could present to the school board.[12] They integrated a districting model, which used a special-purpose linear programming

---

[10]This language was based on FORTRAN. Obviously it is difficult for any DSS designers to provide a general purpose, humanized, and English-like interface of this sort. One advantage of the use of an intermediary or "integrating agent" (see Chapter 7) is that he or she can work directly with the system, defining new data items or routines and *translating* the user's specifications.

[11]Grace (1975) comments that most professionals and managers do not have an image of themselves as direct users of systems. They need to be carefully introduced to the terminal and in some cases simply will not sit down and operate it. Carter in his paper on "The Executive and the Terminal" (1974) suggests that senior managers are unlikely to change their attitude easily.

[12]The DSS extended earlier work by Holloway on algorithms for *solving* this problem (see Holloway et al., 1975). The DSS *supports* the decision process and the algorithms are now embedded in the system rather than being the system itself.

algorithm, into the GADS structure. The model had been implemented before; the researchers felt that it would be far more effective embedded in an interactive DSS, which would provide flexibility and ease in formulating problems and rapid feedback of information. The model is a fairly complex multiperiod assignment routine which establishes a set of constraints on moving children from one district to another as they progress through their school years. Geographic characteristics, especially freeways or major intersections, may be included in the constraint set. Upper and lower bounds are defined for each school, in terms of the number of students to be enrolled. The user may specify a variety of objectives and special considerations. The objective function tries to create compact school districts rather than optimize a single criterion; the constraint set includes the major criteria the user feels relevant. This districting model is a sophisticated but relatively standard operations research application.[13] The GADS user does not see the model; the "system" is the DSS software interface and display functions.

The incentive for this study was the need to redesign school district boundaries as a result of declining enrollments. Two elementary schools had been closed and plans were under way to eliminate several others. The school superintendent's office was responsible for making recommendations to the school board. The issue was politically sensitive.

Six school officials worked with the DSS: the superintendent, the associate superintendent, two assistant superintendents, the leader of a school reorganization study, and a data processing staff member, who was the only one with direct experience in using computers. The group met over a 1-month period; another month was required to finalize the proposal to the school board. Whereas in the police case, the users operated the terminal, an "indirect mode" was employed here. Holloway and Mantey and other consultants operated the system and helped the school officials formulate the problem.

The group began by examining *ad hoc* alternatives and tried to develop a process for handling a situation in which there were no clear guidelines for analysis. The initial time horizon of the school officials was 1 year—they had a problem that needed immediate resolution and they focused on the tactical issues of getting an acceptable plan for the coming school year. The analysis proceeded interactively. The districting model generated an initial assignment of students to schools that took into account the predefined constraints. The school officials then responded to the resulting displays and introduced additional constraints. Figures 5-25, 5-26, and 5-27 show typical displays from the analysis. Figure 5-25 shows the number of students currently assigned to each district, the upper and lower bounds for each school, and how far the number of students enrolled exceeds or falls below the bounds. This display indicates the feasibility of the plan; in this example, schools 5 and 12 are below the lower bound and schools 1, 2, 3, and 13 are above the upper one. Figure 5-26 shows the number of students in each basic zone, the school to which they are assigned, their previous assignments, and the number of times a zone has been reassigned. Figure 5-27 shows a map of the boundaries for the current alternative; the symbols represent the district or school.

The school officials found the system very helpful. They had no difficulty in accepting the validity of the model and data (partly because they initially tried out alternatives and tested them against their local knowledge and intuition). They were

---

[13]It provides a limited multiobjective capability in LP techniques and works by searching for feasible solutions that are iteratively adjusted to provide an optimal one.

strongly influenced by the structure imposed on them by the model. (This contrasts with a follow-up study of graduate students who used the same data and problem statement; they generally expressed a wish to include more qualitative issues.[14]) The school officials were able to accept the mathematical programming algorithm by visualizing it as checking all possible assignments and selecting the one that met the constraints and was the most compact. They found the system particularly useful in eliminating potential solutions and in generating insights. Because the DSS was operated in an indirect mode they perceived the information flow to be very uneven; they would have to wait 2 to 5 minutes while the "driver" of the system explored a suggested alternative. Then they would be overloaded by a sudden flood of output.

FIGURE 5-25   Feasibility of Current Alternative for Redistricting Plan

ASSIGNMENT FEASIBILITY DISPLAY

SCHOOL NO	LOWER BOUND	NO. OF CHILDREN	UPPER BOUND	EXCEEDS LOWER BOUND BY	BELOW UPPER BOUND BY
1	200	294	281	94	-13
2	200	360	357	160	-3
3	200	341	306	141	-35
4	200	320	332	120	12
5	200	178	255	-22	77
6	200	301	357	101	56
7	200	280	306	80	26
8	200	237	255	37	18
9	200	233	255	33	22
10	200	252	281	52	29
11	200	275	332	75	57
12	200	131	255	-69	124
13	200	282	281	82	-1
14	200	194	230	-6	36
15	200	240	255	40	15
16	200	231	255	31	24
17	200	237	281	37	44
18	200	374	459	174	85
19	200	375	383	175	8

TIME	1	DISPLAYS FOR TIME		CALC	SCHOOLS		
INITIALIZE		FEASIBILITY			CURRENT		
SAVE AT TIME	1	ASSIGNMENT	ST.D		1	FEASIBLE	NEW BMAP
RELEASE FUNC		FRACTIONED	ST.D		1	COMPACT	GET BMAP
RELEASE	0	REASSIGNED	ST.D		1	RETURN	

[14]Of course, for them this was simply an experiment so that, as was the case with Gerrity's prototype for PMS, they ranged more imaginatively than they might under the pressures of a real decision situation.

B. F. Grace (1975) had earlier studied the use of GADS in a similar situation, where a school superintendent, a committee of five parents, urban policy analysts, and IBM personnel worked together on a school district problem, which involved reassigning students to four elementary schools. The major constraints included a requirement that minority students should be at least 34.4 percent of the total enrollment, that busing should be minimized, and that attendance boundaries should be maintained over the next few years. Over a 4-month period, the staff specialists defined the problem, generated the data and maps for input into GADS, and verified the information base. According to Grace, "The judicious choice and careful preparation of the relevant data was a significant phase of the project, making overall success possible." Grace provided the senior staff analyst with 12 hours of training over a period of a month so that he could operate GADS. The analyst validated the data and met with the district principals to formulate four proposed solutions. Only at this stage were the superintendent and parents brought in. They met with Grace and the staff analyst in two 3-hour sessions, which resulted in the formulation of four new plans, one of which was adopted by the Board of Education.

FIGURE 5-26   Summary of Student Assignments to Schools

			ASSIGNMENT DISPLAY		
			PREVIOUS		NO. OF TIMES
NO. OF	FROM	ORIGINAL	ASSIGN-	ASSIGNED	REAS-
STUDENTS	DISTRICT	DISTRICT	MENT	TO SCHOOL	SIGNED
34	1	1	12	12	0
19	2	2	12	12	0
19	3	3	12	12	0
1	4	4	11	11	0
18	5	5	12	12	0
34	6	6	11	11	0
21	7	7	11	11	0
22	8	8	11	11	0
27	9	9	11	11	0
13	10	10	11	11	0
36	11	11	12	12	0
22	12	12	9	9	0
17	13	13	9	9	0
10	14	14	9	9	0
18	15	15	9	9	0
19	16	16	9	9	0
17	17	17	9	9	0
15	18	18	9	9	0
36	19	19	11	11	0
15	20	20	11	11	0
34	21	21	11	11	0
40	22	22	11	11	0
17	23	23	10	10	0
47	24	24	10	10	0
4	25	25	10	10	0

TIME	1	DISPLAYS FOR TIME		CALC	SCHOOLS		
INITIALIZE		FEASIBILITY				CURRENT	
SAVE AT TIME	1	ASSIGNMENT	ST.D		26	FEASIBLE	NEW BMAP
RELEASE FUNC		FRACTIONED	ST.D		1	COMPACT	GET BMAP
RELEASE	0	REASSIGNED	ST.D		1	RETURN	

FIGURE 5-27   Map of Proposed Districts, with Schools Shown by Symbols

MAP FOR T = 1   CURRENT SUPERZONES

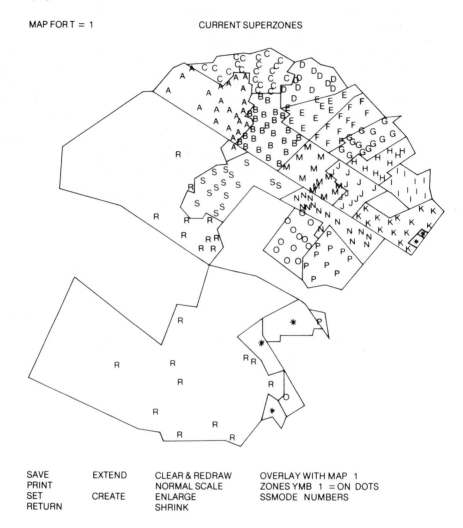

SAVE	EXTEND	CLEAR & REDRAW	OVERLAY WITH MAP 1
PRINT		NORMAL SCALE	ZONES YMB 1 = ON DOTS
SET	CREATE	ENLARGE	SSMODE NUMBERS
RETURN		SHRINK	

Grace discusses the training process in detail.[15] She points out that users generally have a low tolerance for training and that nontechnical individuals, such as the superintendent and parents, do not expect to operate the terminal; doing so conflicts with their self-image. The analyst was needed as an intermediary between the DSS and the users.

---

[15]Grace (1976) also describes an interactive training methodology that involves generating a manual containing sample sessions, couched in terms of the user's problem and vocabulary. This manual is generated by special software, for a particular application.

In the first of the two problem-solving sessions, the analyst presented the four proposed solutions, with no displays generated by GADS. The superintendent rejected all the alternatives. This was a highly charged political problem, in which parents and educators had differing goals and interests. Some reasons for rejecting the initial proposals were problems with creeks and dead-end streets, the effects of new townhouses and homes, and the superintendent's wish to fill up a particular school. The analyst suggested that the group work at the terminal and explore other combinations. Initially, the superintendent asked the analyst questions and the group waited, at some distance from the terminal, for the answer. Fairly quickly, however, they began to make more active suggestions. One parent proposed a modification to the current alternative that would reduce the need for busing. She verified that the figures on the map generated by the analyst in response to her idea were accurate in relation to her own locality. The superintendent said, "We have good data," and his confidence in the system and in its potential value clearly increased from that point.

The group met again 4 days later. The superintendent needed results that night. He had created two new alternatives which Grace and the analyst had entered into the DSS over the preceding weekend. The analyst had added explanatory symbols and labels so that it would be easy to respond to other ideas and modifications. In this second session the analyst or Grace acted as "chauffeurs," pressing the buttons and wielding the light-pen. There was substantial interaction among all the participants and frequent use of "hard copy" printouts of displays from GADS. The group analyzed, modified, and created multiple solutions. The parent who had proposed the earlier modification continued to push her argument and used GADS to help her make adjustments to it to bring it back into favor when the others rejected it because certain schools would not have enough minority students enrolled. Grace had designed a possible solution, which was viewed as unacceptable because one neighborhood was split and certain parents had been "almost promised" that their children could attend a particular school. It was easy to bring in these issues and use GADS to help resolve them.

Four new solutions were generated in this session, together with 50 sheets of supporting analysis derived from the GADS data base and displayed in graphs and tables. The superintendent closely examined, throughout the session, minority percentages and enrollment figures, shown by symbols on the maps produced by the DSS. The final analysis of each alternative included a breakdown by grade in each school so that he could also check how close the student-teacher ratio was to particular multiples. The study had begun with explicit constraints (such as the lower limit of 34.4 percent minority enrollment). The interactive problem solving brought out a far larger number of implicit constraints, such as transportation patterns and walking times, the feeling of parents in certain localities, and the effects of residential growth and school capacity adjustments (this last issue would have been included as an explicit constraint if the superintendent had been brought in earlier).

Grace calls attention to the importance of such implicit constraints in semistructured problems. "Only when the superintendent and parents were actively involved in generating and modifying alternatives was the GADS system truly effective. [It] . . . is in sharp contrast to typical operations research approaches which generally produce an 'optimal solution' based upon explicitly stated constraints with no convenient method of introducing implicit constraints" (Grace, 1975, p. 23).

The superintendent was very satisfied with this experience. He felt that he would be frustrated in similar situations in the future if he did not have access to a DSS of this sort. He stated that he had learned that a number of variables, which could not be processed manually, needed to be included in the analysis. In a previous instance involving redistricting he had been able to generate only one solution and estimated that GADS had reduced the time required by a factor of at least 2 over manual approaches.

The "Chauffeur"

An important aspect of all the GADS case studies is that the IBM research team took an active role in training users and helping them make use of GADS. J. Bennett (1975) emphasizes the value of an integrating agent (his remarks specifically apply to the police beat design case study but seem equally applicable to the school districting examples):

> A great deal of the success experienced by the users was due to what could be called "expectation creation." One of the GADS project members spent much time going over the details of the problem with the prospective police users as the data was being prepared for system use. His interest and guidance helped them understand what would be expected of them and how the system could help them solve their problem. . . . During the use of GADS, the staff member effectively served as an "integrating agent." Because the police had identified with him as a friend, found him knowledgeable about GADS functions, and had recognized him as a person who understood their problem, he could help them overcome the obstacles presented by an experimental system. . . . the agent was a catalytic factor in successful use of the system.

Bennett suggests that the integrating agent has four main roles:

1. As an *exegetist* who explains the system and interprets the concepts and objectives underlying its design. He or she can help the user get started on the DSS, beginning with simple functions and approaches.

2. As a *confidant* who provides support, helps overcome misconceptions, and encourages the user to view the system as a tool under personal control rather than a threat.

3. As a *crusader* who can demonstrate the power and value of the DSS. A new system often involves substantial costs in terms of time, effort, and learning. Once the novelty of the system wears off, the user is aware of these immediate costs, while the benefits are less clear and more distant. The integrating agent can point to these benefits and maintain the momentum of the project.

4. As a *teacher* who can be far more effective than manuals or seminars, particularly with nontechnical professionals, in tailoring the training to the individual. She or he also can help structure problems to exploit the system's capabilities.

The agent obviously needs many skills: to be familiar with the DSS; experienced in problem formulation, analysis, and interpretation of data; and responsive to the users' needs and moods. P. G. W. Keen (1976) built on Bennett's ideas in defining a strategy for developing DSS for senior managers. He argues that the intermediary may be far more effective than a software interface, that the "system" is the DSS and a skilled integrator. One problem with this and with Bennett's recommendation is that individuals with all the needed abilities are hard to find and generally aim at far more senior jobs. Nonetheless, the GADS experiments suggest that an intermediary can substantially improve the likelihood of a DSS being successful. The experiments also highlight the complex issues involved in introducing a personalized problem-solving aid—it cannot be plugged into the organization and left to sink or swim. The user must first gain *confidence,* partly by learning how to operate the DSS, partly through developing trust in its reliability and accuracy. As the user begins to see where the system can provide new approaches to problem solving, additional insights are gained, and the DSS is incorporated into everyday decision-making.

Holloway and Mantey (1976, pp. 21–23) compare four modes of using a DSS (see Figure 5-28). In mode 4, separate individuals or groups operate the terminal, decide what functions or sequence of analysis is required, and respond to the system output. In mode 2, a technician or staff specialist interacts with the system but the decisionmaker defines what is to be done and interprets the results. Mode 3 is the chauffeur-driven mode used in the situation described by Grace, where the school superintendent and parents were the consumers of the information generated by the analyst's use of the DSS. Mode 1 was used by the police officials, who operated the terminal, decided what functions to choose, and responded to the output. (In Great Eastern Bank, the assumption of the designers of PMS was that mode 1 would generally be used. Some managers in fact preferred mode 2, leaving the physical operation of the system to a secretary or staff assistant.) Holloway and Mantey suggest that "psychological validation"—building trust in the DSS—will be most difficult with mode 4 and easiest with mode 1, where the user can directly test ideas and develop a highly interactive sequence of analysis. Information flows will be perceived as most uneven in mode 4.[16]

Conclusion

GADS is an experiment. It is therefore difficult to generalize from the case studies of one-shot decisions, where the DSS was specially brought in, with much support from the research team, to help a small group of professionals. However, the experiences reported by the IBM researchers point to some important aspects of DSS design and development. Most obviously, they indicate the value of powerful graphics-based systems for a class of problems involving geographic assignments, balancing activities or levels in localized areas, and processing substantial volumes of data. They also show that a DSS will be accepted by decisionmakers who on the whole have virtually never used computers in their planning and decisionmaking.

---

[16]Holloway and Mantey point out that mode 4 is the one most users of computer systems encounter. Batch processing involves clear separation between system operation, process control, and information consumption. Alter (1975, pp. 153–155) comments that users of DSS value time-sharing mainly for the *access* it permits; in effect it allows them to select any of the four modes.

FIGURE 5-28 Models of Using a DSS (from Holloway and Mantey, 1976, p. 23). A, B, and C are individuals carrying out the indicated tasks. In mode 1, all three tasks are handled by the same person. In mode 2, individual A is responsible for system operation and B is responsible for process control and information consumption. In mode 4, a different person carries out each activity.

		Organization for Analysis and Evaluation			
		1	2	3	4
	System operation	A	A	A	A
Function	Process control	A	B	A	B
	Information consumption	A	B	B	C

School superintendents and police officers are not likely to welcome the intrusion of an unfamiliar technology into their professionalized activities; however, they seem to have had little difficulty in adjusting to GADS.

GENERALIZED MANAGEMENT INFORMATION SYSTEM (GMIS)[17]

Introduction

There has been—deliberately—little discussion of technology in this book. The emphasis has been on decision support and the system has been viewed as a means to an end. In Chapters 1 to 3, we suggested that the focus of computer scientists on technology as an end in itself has generally been less effective, in terms of impact on managerial problem solving, than the DSS approach. It is important to recognize, though, that many such applications are made possible *only* by technical developments. The last DSS discussed in detail in this chapter represents a significant and very complex advance in software design. It provides an excellent illustration of both the concept of decision *support* and the need for and exploration of technical developments.

GMIS (Generalized Management Information System) was developed at M.I.T. by a group led by J. J. Donovan and S. E. Madnick. It was designed

> To allow for the rapid assimilation of "seemingly incompatible" computer programs and data series. That is, a necessary analytical program may exist on one computer while another computer may have a needed data base management capability, yet the two systems are incompatible because they run under different operating systems. . . . By being able to combine such facilities, the analyst can respond to a policymaker's request more generally and at less cost by building on existing work (Donovan and Madnick, 1976, p. 16).

[17]This discussion is mainly based on Donovan et al. (1976).

Donovan and Madnick distinguish between *"ad hoc"* and "institutional" DSS. Most of the situations discussed in this book relate to institutional systems, where the decisions to be supported are recurrent and the DSS evolves over several years as users learn and extend their needs and capabilities (PMS, for example). An *ad hoc* DSS supports decisionmaking for a wide variety of problems that are not usually anticipated or recurring. Examples of such problems are new product introductions and capital acquisitions such as the Acrofab study discussed in the description of Projector. Public sector decisionmaking frequently involves such problems, where policy choices, responses to legislative changes, or assessments of the impact of economic or social factors must be determined quickly. GMIS is designed to support these *ad hoc* decisions; its main application has been in the NEEMIS project (New England Energy Management Information System). NEEMIS uses a DSS, based on the GMIS software and accessed by governors' and congressional staff, state energy administrators' offices, and M.I.T. researchers concerned with legislative and economic issues in energy planning. The incentive for the NEEMIS project was, of course, the energy crisis in the winter of 1973–1974.

> Consider the range of problems that must be addressed by a regional public policy decisionmaker in New England. At the height of the energy crisis . . . the main concern was managing the distribution of oil to minimize the impact of shortages throughout the region. Less than 6 months later the problem had changed completely. New England was no longer in a shortage situation, as there was a backlog of full tankers in Boston harbor. Instead, the region was beset by a new series of problems, primarily economic. . . . As the region realized its vulnerability to price fluctuations in energy, the problems of the policymaker shifted from ones of handling shortages to ones of analyzing methods to conserve fuel; analysis of impacts of tariffs, decontrol, and natural gas or oil prices on different industrial sectors and states within the region; analysis of impacts of off-shore drilling on New England's fishing industries. These are but a few of the problem areas which New England policymakers face and on which they need effective decision support (Donovan and Madnick, 1976, p. 8).

In such a situation, data needs and functions cannot be predefined. An institutional DSS can be built around a detailed analysis of the task to be supported and a menu of user options provided (and evolved). As Table 5-2 shows, an *ad hoc* DSS requires very different tools. It needs to be stressed that the concept of decision *support* still holds and that the underlying problem is semistructured. NEEMIS is not a system for making strategic choices (unstructured) or for allocating supplies (structured). The examples of how NEEMIS has been used, given below, emphasize the balance between human judgment and control of the decision process and the analytic power provided by interactive computer technology.

Design of GMIS

The GMIS software is based on the concept of a "virtual machine," which allows several apparently different computers (virtual machines) to be simulated on a real one. For example, one analyst may wish to use a model written in a language such as APL/EPLAN (designed for econometric modeling and forecasting). A suitable data base exists but it is stored on another computer and uses SEQUEL, a struc-

TABLE 5-2   Comparison of Institutional and Ad hoc DSS

Characteristics of Decision Situations	Institutional DSS	Ad hoc DSS
Number of decision occurrences for a decision type	Many	Few
Number of decision types	Few	Many
Number of people making same type decisions	Many	Few
Range of decisions supported	Narrow	Wide
Range of users supported	Narrow	Wide
Range of issues addressed	Narrow	Wide
Specific data needed in advance	Usually	Rarely
Specific analysis needed in advance	Usually	Rarely
Problems recurred	Usually	Rarely
Importance of operational efficiency	High	Low
Duration of specific type of problem being addressed	Long	Short
Need for rapid development	Low	High

tured, English-like query language. Another analyst also wishes to access this data base, from a third computer, and prefers to work in PL/I, the language with which she feels most comfortable. Obviously, the only real choice generally available to the personnel involved in such a project is to convert the models or data base to a common language on a single computer (although the advent of computer networks and distributed processing makes the latter requirement less binding). The effort and delay involved are likely to be unacceptable for an *ad hoc* decision situation in which responsiveness and time pressure are critical. GMIS allows each user to work with the tools he or she prefers. In this example, the analyst who wishes to use the APL/EPLAN model simply requests access to the SEQUEL data base; the virtual machine manager (a GMIS program) retrieves the data base from the relevant virtual machine and, if necessary, reformats the data. The PL/I user may *at the same time* access the same data base. The analytic tools in this instance are fundamentally incompatible. APL/EPLAN and SEQUEL are "stand-alone" systems not designed to interface with other programs or languages. SEQUEL also has its own special-purpose operating system which would not allow the PL/I program to be run.

The GMIS virtual machine approach allows access to a range of powerful analytic tools. Available modeling languages include TROLL (for analysis of econometric time-series data), TSP (Time Series Processor), DYNAMO (the simulation language used in the famous Limits of Growth World Model by the Club of Rome), and APL/EPLAN. Other languages include FORTRAN, APL, and PL/I and statistical packages and data-base management systems. These constitute an immensely powerful set of analytic techniques. The whole is far more than the sum of the parts; only through the virtual machine concept can they be combined. The tools are fairly specialized and hard to learn. GMIS reduces the need to relearn. An analyst who works mainly with TROLL need not be at all familiar with SEQUEL. The virtual machine approach to providing the user with an interface combining the available models and data resources is a major development in the process of "humanizing" the computer and making it easily accessible and responsive to users—it clearly extends the type of support a DSS can provide.

The NEEMIS Project

The NEEMIS project is a joint venture between the New England Regional Commission (NERCOM), the New England state energy offices, IBM, and several groups at M.I.T. It was begun in early 1974. Its main mission is to provide the region with the capability to respond quickly and effectively to energy problems. It has four main resources:

1. GMIS, the "advanced computational facility."

2. Data on demand, supply and relevant constraints (2,300 data series with an average size of 4,000 records).

3. Large-scale computer models for analyzing economic impact, which forecast and assess demand and conservation issues (12 main models).

4. A range of specialists in the areas of energy, economic and policy planning, and data processing.

The New England state energy offices all have had computer terminals installed since 1975 to access resources. At any one time, there will generally be 12 NEEMIS users simultaneously working with the DSS.

The NEEMIS project has had top-level support from both federal and state authorities, with several glowing statements of praise from governors. The DSS has been used as an integral part of studies made by the project. These included contingency plans for shortages of natural gas, evaluation of trends in automobile registrations, analysis of the merits of refineries and the impact of alternative pricing schemes for electricity, and forecasts for future energy demands. Donovan and Madnick give several illustrations of the value of an *ad hoc* DSS. For example, when the governor of Connecticut requested a 5 percent decrease in energy use in state buildings in the winter of 1975–1976, a DSS, using the models and data series already contained in the full NEEMIS system, was created with the aid of state planning agencies. Connecticut was able to reduce consumption by 7.5 percent (a saving of over $1 million). The *ad hoc* system was then used as the basis for an institutional DSS, which was adopted by several other states.

An extreme example of the flexibility and responsiveness made possible by the GMIS software occurred late in 1975 at the New England Governors Conference. The governor of Rhode Island requested an analysis of the impact of a proposed federal decontrol program on his state, in the light of likely price increases by

OPEC. He wished to use the results in a meeting that afternoon with President Ford. The various tools contained in the NEEMIS facility were used to construct an *ad hoc* DSS to provide the necessary analysis. This example demonstrates both the advantages of the GMIS approach and of the DSS concept. There is no supermodel here, no large-scale computer system that provides "answers"; instead, the whole intent of the NEEMIS project has been to make available analytic resources (people as much as models) when needed. To the user, the NEEMIS *ad hoc* DSS is a black box in most respects; he or she is most concerned with his or her own decision problem and process. At the same time, without the complex of tools and the integrating vehicle GMIS provides, it would be virtually impossible to build a DSS responsive and flexible enough to handle the *ad hoc* nature of those decision situations.

Institutional DSS: An Example

Donovan and Madnick (1976, pp. 23–29) describe in some detail the development of the institutional DSS for conservation monitoring and analysis, mentioned earlier in relation to the governor of Connecticut's request for a 5 percent saving in energy use in state-owned buildings. All six New England state governments felt that their own buildings would be the best starting point for a major conservation effort because of the potential cost savings, the availability of federal funds for this purpose, the need to slow the growth in state budgets, and, of course, the visibility and example that this initiative would provide. It was decided to make a cursory analysis of and to monitor monthly consumption in all state buildings and to make a more detailed analysis of large buildings to identify where and how savings could be made. The project was begun early in the winter of 1975–1976.

Substantial amounts of data and output reports were needed for the monitoring and cursory analysis. For example, (1) building characteristics: locations, floor space, type of usage, data on vendors, and deliveries of heating fuels; (2) supplemental data: administrative hierarchy (agency, special characteristics), buildings owned; (3) weather data (to normalize for weather conditions by location and date); and (4) executive reports: monthly consumption figures, list of fuel oil suppliers to the state, and comparisons with prior years. Assembling all these would require months, probably years, using standard computer programming techniques. In addition, the data and reports would need frequent revision. Actually, many changes occurred *after* the *ad hoc* DSS was operational. The prototype was used partly to help structure the problem and thus to define the data, reports, and data collection methods that were really needed.

The DSS used APL/EPLAN and SEQUEL. It was completed in time for use that winter. The "cursory" analysis identified which buildings were most relevant for more detailed study. The most useful reports were graphical [see, for example, Figure 5-29, which compares *(a)* the monthly consumption of two buildings and *(b)* consumption normalized to take into account floor space]. As with all semistructured problems, the outputs of the DSS are informative but do not provide solutions. In Figure 5-29, for example, building A has higher consumption and higher consumption per square foot. It is a likely candidate for conservation; storm windows could be added or the heating system changed. Choosing a method of conservation could be done through several fairly expensive methods—direct experimentation in the building itself or the development of detailed computer models. In fact, three general building analysis models were already available.

These were added to the GMIS facility and integrated into the DSS through the virtual machine software. This was accomplished before the end of 1975. The new models could access the existing data base, although this was designed in SEQUEL.

FIGURE 5-29   *Heating Oil Consumption for Buildings A and B, 1975–1976. (a) Actual Consumption. (b) Consumption Normalized for Size.*

(a)

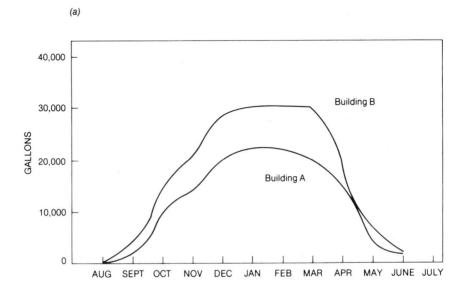

(b)

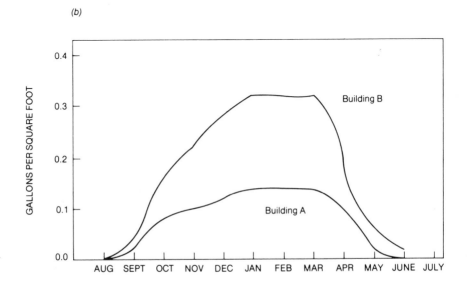

They were used for detailed assessment of individual buildings. One model developed by NASA required the collection of additional data for a large medical laboratory building. This took 7 work days to gather but was easily added to the system.

It is difficult to see how this type of responsive, flexible DSS could have been developed without GMIS. Each of the individual tools is in itself highly flexible. The APL language, in particular, reduces the time required to define, design, and test a program by a factor of at least 5 over standard languages such as FORTRAN. SEQUEL similarly allows flexible access to data. The two systems, however, normally cannot be linked. The DSS encouraged staff working under great time pressure to locate and integrate new tools, such as the general building analysis models. None of them had to learn new skills or convert existing programs and files.

Conclusion

GMIS is a relatively new addition to the technology we may draw on for decision support. The intent of this description is to demonstrate how such developments extend the range of strategies and applications available for DSS. We argue throughout this book that the techniques of computer science should be viewed as means, not ends. GMIS is partly an end in itself—a potentially important contribution to the field of virtual systems. The NEEMIS project used it as a means; it allowed professional planners, researchers, and state political leaders to draw on analytic and computational aids that had direct value to them in *helping* them with, although not resolving, complex *ad hoc* decision problems. It would be a risky overstatement to say that it was the decision support approach that made this possible. Nonetheless, any survey of computer models for public policy planning and analysis reveals extremely little application in real world situations. GMIS suggests that such application requires both powerful computer tools *and* an emphasis on decision support.

THE DESIGN PROCESS: DECISION ANALYSIS AND EVOLUTION

SIX

So far, we have discussed the general context of DSS and have given some representative examples. We now turn to the tactical and operational concerns involved in building such systems.

Our experience with the design of DSS is too recent for much more than broad principles to have yet emerged. Nonetheless, the *strategy* for DSS design is clearly very different from much of current practice in MIS. In particular, design and implementation are inseparable and evolutionary. DSS deal with semistructured problems that, by definition, are hard to define. As a result, the initial design will prove more or less incomplete. This is particularly true as the decisionmakers learn more about the problem and the problem-solving process through analysis, implementation, and usage of the DSS—they grow and their perception of the problem changes. Thus there is no clear break between design and implementation. Similarly, there may be no precise end to implementation; evolution of ideas, the users' ongoing learning, and a shifting environment lead to new adjustments and developments.

The next three chapters discuss the integrated process of design, implementation, and evaluation of DSS. While it would be far better to examine them as a whole—one of the major weaknesses in the technical tradition has been to separate design from delivery—a single chapter would be, unfortunately, clumsy and much too long. So, in this chapter we will focus on design—but the *process* of design rather than the technical characteristics of a system. This is really the process of *support*; the strategy we present emphasizes analysis of the decision situation and definition of the criteria for the technical structure and routines contained in the DSS.

Obviously, the first step in design is to select the right problem to work on. Historically, computer specialists have tended to either pick the technology first and then look for a suitable application or to accept the client's definition of the problem. The decision-centered approach to DSS clearly requires us to avoid the temptation to argue that conversational terminals and interactive problem solving are in themselves desirable. (This is a strong temptation. The DSS movement is based, like most rallying cries in MIS, on faith and zeal; we find ourselves too often responding to a manager's description of a problem or need by asking, "What kind of DSS should we suggest?").

The "problem" does not come neatly packaged. It is really a symptom, a sense of some deficiency or opportunity.[1] Also, the problem will be defined by different units of the organization mainly in terms of their own perspective. This obviously makes decision analysis both complex and political since the interested parties often take up a strong advocacy position.

The Portfolio Management System (see Chapter 5) provides a useful example of differing responses to a symptom. When the question of "doing something" in the investment division was first raised, the following groups submitted written proposals to senior management:

> *Investment Research:* "The 'problem' requires more high-quality investment analysts who should be hired as soon as possible."

> *Data Processing:* "There is an urgent need for an improved Trust Accounting System, for handling and record keeping." The Data Processing department argued strenuously and loudly in favor of this solution and made it a highly political issue.

> *Management Science:* "Obviously, we need to and can build a set of models to optimize the investment portfolio."

While the last proposal had little support elsewhere in the organization, the first two were seen as attractive ways to improve the effectiveness of the investment department. They each imply a very different definition of the "problem." Data Processing views it from a technological perspective and emphasizes issues of efficiency. Investment Research, in almost complete contrast, focuses on "artistic" and conceptual considerations. (Management Science in some ways ignores the specific situation and defines it as a special case of the general issue of optimization.)

The distinctive contribution of T. P. Gerrity to this debate, which led to his developing PMS, was to focus on the portfolio investment decision itself. This required a number of iterations through several levels of the organization. Such analysis also involves a very clinical assessment of the context of the decision.

The very different proposals of the Investment Research and Data Processing groups clearly suggest that decisions have several facets and many interdependencies. The Trust Department of the bank in which PMS was developed was a profit center, and the head of the group was concerned both with his position and the ability of the department to handle the obvious challenges and strains of the next decade. His strategic planning group's analysis suggested that while the bank's competitive position was satisfactory, there would be some very difficult times ahead. This led the department to think in terms of becoming an asset management service, one aspect of which would be trust business. It chose to focus on ways to improve revenues and profits over the coming decade in the face of strong competition from other banks, mutual funds, and investment services. The bulk of the revenue (and profits) came from the fund management business. This consisted of trust, pension, and investment advisory funds, as described in Chapter 5. Fees (revenues) were charged as a percentage of the market value of the assets. Increased revenue thus required increasing the asset base.

---

[1]Gore (1964, p. 37) points out that the first stage in decisionmaking is one of determining a level of reaction (routine, innovative, or crisis, for example) *before* identifying what the problem in fact is. Pounds (1969) similarly distinguishes problem finding from problem solving.

There seemed to be two ways of increasing assets: expanding the base by attracting new funds or managing the existing base better by increasing its market value without adding significantly to risk. The first strategy was implemented immediately: a marketing group was formed to promote the department's services. However, the second strategy, better management of assets, was hard. Further analysis revealed that the key activities were the specific buy and sell decisions of the individual portfolio managers and the definition of overall investment strategy. This latter decision proved to be unstructured in its most critical dimensions, and the department head took steps to hire a seasoned professional with an established track record.

During this period of discussion, the department agreed to support an experiment by Gerrity (his Ph.D. thesis) to develop a methodology and a design for a prototype DSS. The attraction of this for the bank was the insight into the key issues in the investment decision process the experiment would generate and the possibility that a DSS (or a "Management Decision System," the terminology then in use) could be of value. Gerrity's research brought in a fresh viewpoint and Trust Department personnel were very willing to talk aloud and reflect on their job, information needs, and so on.

Of course, since PMS was the solution finally selected, it is easy in retrospect to pick out the features of the investment decision that made the DSS an attractive alternative. However, before tracing through the decision analysis and design process for PMS, it is worth describing the symptom/problem from the perspectives on decisionmaking presented in Chapter 3 (it would be belaboring the obvious to do so for the viewpoints of Chapter 2; the responses of Data Processing and Management Science, mentioned above, are illustration enough). In fact, the options the bank considered correspond fairly closely to these perspectives.

The Economic Man

Economic, rational man is clear on what to do. Normative portfolio theory (see, for example, W. F. Sharpe, 1963; and H. M. Markowitz, 1959) provides a clear base for design by viewing the portfolio management task as highly structurable. According to C. B. Stabell (1974, p. 201):

> The manager makes portfolio composition decisions, consistent with account objectives, based on a couple of summary statistics for individual securities: the beta or volatility of the security returns, and the expected return of the security relative to the market. The main information processing task is located in the (research) analyst function, responsible both for estimates of the relevant individual security data, and for estimates of overall market performance.

The bank had made several expensive efforts to use portfolio theory. In practice, the theory is currently of minimal practical value, largely because its simplifying assumptions do not fit with the realities of clients' objectives and attitudes (for example, tax considerations, fluctuating cash streams for new investments, uncertain payout, and so on). In addition, portfolio managers are reluctant to trust analysts' estimates and rely far more on their own feelings.

The fact that this normative mathematical theory is *currently* not useful is, of course, not a real argument against it. The theory does draw attention to what Gerrity and Stabell saw as the key weakness in the existing decision process. The portfolio managers made investment decisions mainly in terms of *securities*, not portfolios. They would decide that security X was a good buy and then scan each of their accounts to decide whether or not to add the security to it. This approach eases cognitive strain. It simplifies the process of analysis but it is clearly suboptimal. The logic of portfolio theory is unassailable: the decisionmaker must consider the portfolio as a whole and balance risk and return. The economic viewpoint is a strong argument in support of continued research to extend portfolio theory and make it more practicable. Anything else is a suboptimal compromise.

The Satisficing Perspective

The satisficing perspective agrees that normative portfolio theory provides a far better solution, conceptually, than current practice. However, it argues for a less abstract and more short-term approach. The starting point for improving the decision process should be to *understand* it, to identify and evaluate the heuristics and decision rules that portfolio managers actually use. One way to do this is by building a simulation model and examining its behavior (which is, of course, a direct analogue of the manager's); this is G. P. E. Clarkson's (1962) methodology.[2] Another is to compare the heuristics of the most capable performers with those of the average ones and try to synthesize a general set of rules.

The satisficing perspective does not in itself contain guidelines for improving existing heuristics. It argues mainly that these decision rules reflect, on the whole, the best the real world manager can do. They constitute the major constraint for any prescriptive technique or decision aid. They can be strengthened or fine-tuned and obviously inadequate rules can be improved—but they cannot be ignored. A satisficer would probably recommend a consulting team be brought in and perhaps a staff specialist be added to the department to provide training and joint discussion with the managers of methods and strategies.

The Organizational Procedures Approach

Waiting in the wings, in fact, are many traditional consultants whose natural focus is on organizational procedures. They would point out that the portfolio manager's task is not self-contained. For example, there are at least three well-defined groups within the Trust Department with operating procedures of their own: (1) The Administrative group handles clerical work; (2) Investment Research generates the approved list of stocks that managers may include in their portfolios and also does research on markets, industries, and stocks; and (3) three separate subunits of portfolio managers: Pension, Personal Trust, and Investment Advisory. Each of the investment groups has its own method of analysis which defines its needs for information and decision support.

The organizational procedures viewpoint is probably the most common one among management consultants. Here it is clearly applicable. The important linkage between Investment Research and the portfolio managers is obviously working badly; the managers tend to ignore the analysts' recommendations, and the

---

[2]Dutton and Starbuck (1971, pp. 18–22) suggest that Clarkson's persuasive methodology simply does not work. Whether this is so or not, his experiment provides an insightful approach to the study of complex decision processes.

information flowing between the two groups is frequently incomplete and not up-dated regularly. Similarly, clerical operations are inefficient and even inaccurate; most portfolio managers maintain records of their own as a double-check.

The "traditional" consultant would probably recommend rationalization of these communication links and the generation of better information flows. He or she might well also suggest a restructuring of the Investment Department with clear-cut allocation of responsibilities. The information systems proposed would be very differentiated, acknowledging the differences among the Pension, Personal Trust, and Investment Advisory groups.

The Political Viewpoint

The political perspective would find the bank to be a rich source of opportunities. There are clearly several powerful units competing for resources and influence. The relationship between the research department and portfolio managers is volatile and uneasy. The research group represents the academic perspective. Many investment managers view its work as essentially irrelevant and rely instead on personal con-tacts and "inside" information. Investment Research was strongly in favor of any computer-based decision aid since it would give it direct influence on buy-sell deci-sions. Similarly, the Data Processing group was anxious to maintain its position as the centralized coordinator for data and information systems. This is the reason for its strong advocacy of a new trust accounting system. (It was also strongly opposed to PMS, which was developed and implemented by an outside consulting firm.)

In addition to these different professional interests, individual managers had much to gain or lose in this debate. For a variety of reasons, there had been several management changes in this area of the bank; some individuals had gained visibility and influence and others had clearly lost power. Several of these changes were linked to "empire building" in the information systems department.

All these political undercurrents were easy to identify, although not often openly discussed. The technical tradition (and, in this instance, several of the com-puter personnel involved in presentations and analysis) tends to regard them as un-fortunate interferences with the process of rational decisionmaking. However, all the "actors" in this political play very reasonably adopted a partisan perspective and tried to convince others to follow the course of action they themselves were pro-fessionally or personally committed to. While it is outside the scope of this book to discuss in detail these political maneuvers, they had substantial impact on the im-plementation process for PMS.

The political viewpoint would stress that political forces will always be both relevant and discernible in a major project that will change organizational relation-ships. The system developer must make sure that a proposal is organizationally feasible and has strong support from its management sponsors. She or he must also be sensitive not only to the positive payoff from the system but to the "downside" risk, the personal costs, career interests, likely oppositions, relative perceived gains and losses, and so on.

The political viewpoint does not have many specific prescriptions for improv-ing decisionmaking. It would probably argue that in this instance the proposal for the DSS should be supported. It had the active backing of the top management of the department and the support of a key group of portfolio managers. The primary recommendations in any such situation are: (1) make sure that what you propose can be implemented; (2) before you design anything, be certain that you understand the political dynamics of the organization and the stake key people have in the status quo; and (3) lobby and follow through—do not imagine that the logic of your presentation is all you need. In many ways, these recommendations correspond to the strategy for implementation that we present in Chapter 7. They also stress the need for substantial diagnosis of the organizational reality *prior to design.*

The Individual Differences Perspective

The task of portfolio management is extremely complex. There are no clear rules for analysis or for balancing risk, return, growth, and individual customer goals. There is substantial cognitive strain and a need for very specialized strategies for problem solving. A natural starting point for "improving" decisionmaking would thus be to analyze in detail the strategies portfolio managers use to simplify their task. This approach emphasizes *support:* any formal system should aid or extend the decision-maker's methods of problem solving. In the situation in the bank, the proponents of this "introspective" view (this term seems to capture the similarities underlying the different theories of cognitive structure and style) would suggest that managers be interviewed and observed at their work, in order to get preliminary answers to at least the following questions: (1) What information do portfolio managers actually use? Why? Can we help them make better use of this information or provide more? (2) How should information and analytic aids be presented to the managers so that they both accept and gain from them? (3) How do the managers *learn?* (4) What are their striking strengths or weaknesses? Can these be exploited or remedied? (5) Are there clear differences among the managers? (6) Can we build a helpful relationship with the managers?

The introspective view seems fairly applicable here; the portfolio managers are a small, distinctive professional group and success in the *investment* task obviously depends on their own problem-solving skills. The bank should therefore focus on building personalized information and decision systems for the portfolio managers. The Data Processing group's proposal is not relevant from this perspective since it deals with the wider context of organizational procedures (the focus on the individual is an obvious limitation of the introspective approach). The Investment Research group's position would be of more interest because of the "artistic" aspects of the decision process. However, the introspective view would emphasize that the portfolio managers and research analysts have different concepts of "information" and "analysis" and that these may be hard to integrate.

It is worth noting that the introspective view is more likely to be supported by the manager than by staff and technical personnel. Gerrity's "decision centered" research adopted much of the introspective approach; the managers of the investment department found his concepts innovative and insightful. PMS was not initially included in the proposals discussed by the bank. It was brought in during a later stage and was finally chosen as the solution. Management's interest and support were obviously critical here.

All the viewpoints we have briefly discussed are relevant both to the bank example and DSS in general. Gerrity's design methodology included almost all of them; it was perhaps weakest in terms of recognizing political dynamics. (The implementation strategies presented in Chapter 7 strengthen the decision-centered design approach considerably.)

THE FIRST STAGE IN DESIGN: IDENTIFYING
THE KEY DECISION

As the discussion so far implies, design is not a linear sequence of well-defined steps. The differences in perspective, organizational coalitions, definition of the "right" solution, and so on make it particularly hard to know exactly where to start. However, we suggest that one early step is to apply the framework discussed in Chapter 4 to particular functional area(s) involved in a manager's or group's operations and to lay out the key decisions in each of the nine cells (see Table 4-3). This helps identify which decisions are of most importance for effective performance and, of course, which may benefit from decision support. If one then assesses the quality of informational and analytical aids for each key decision, one can begin to get a sense of potential priorities for more detailed analysis.

Of course this is not a trivial task but it is simplified by making sure that the predesign cycle, outlined in Figure 6-1, involves at least two iterations before the detailed, more formal definition of the system design is begun. This cycle begins when a potential area for support has been identified and the designers begin their descriptive study of the relevant decision processes.

The right-hand column of Figure 6-1, Entry, relates to essential initial steps in the *implementation* process: building momentum for change and developing a "contract" for action that involves realistic, mutual expectations and commitment among the parties involved. In some instances, this initial diagnosis may make some of the decision analysis inapplicable; for example, it may be that the "best" solution is a large-scale systems development effort that requires a level of support from senior management in several departments that is clearly lacking. There are then two obvious choices:

1. Recycle through Entry and try to build that support.

2. Recycle through Decision Analysis and reassess the problem situation and the "best" solution given this new constraint.

A major aim in this predesign cycle is to make sure that the right problem is worked on. (It is worth noting in passing that the individual perspectives on information systems and decisionmaking discussed in Chapters 2 and 3 too easily ignore this issue; they jump to design immediately or ignore one column of the cycle—the rational tradition focuses on the left and the political and behavioral perspectives on the right-hand column.) There are, of course, many interactions within the cycle; objectives influence what the key decision will be and the areas to be supported partly define available resources and vice versa.

In the PMS example, Gerrity's decision analysis revealed two critical issues not explicitly recognized within the organization:

1. The portfolio managers' information processing was *security-oriented;* they thought in terms of particular stocks and bonds and not in relation to the individual portfolio.

2. Their task consists of three distinct components: *(a)* investment, *(b)* administration, and *(c)* client relations (the portfolio managers interviewed by Stabell (1974a) felt that management measured their performance mainly in terms of this aspect of their job).

FIGURE 6-1   *The Predesign Cycle*

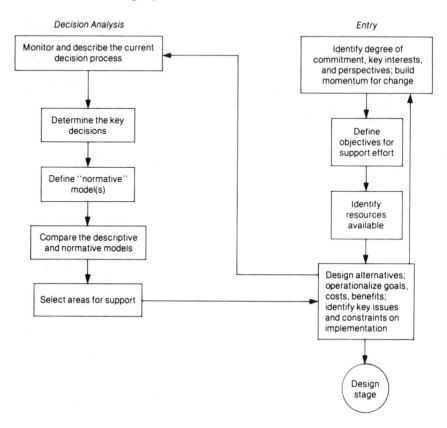

The "key" *decisions,* not surprisingly, were concerned with making investments for the customer portfolios.

The development of *normative models* is the next key stage in the predesign cycle. The descriptive analysis of the decision defines a reference point for discussing improvement. In many situations, it also indicates the status quo, which will naturally be preferred by the decisionmakers over new systems and procedures—unless the change is seen as beneficial to them. The normative models are proposals for change: they define the potential range of designs for an information system. For example, in the bank situation, financial portfolio theory explicitly prescribes a solution that is very different indeed from the existing process. If the theory can be effectively implemented, then the potential payoff is huge. So, too, are the potential risks. The degree of change (the distance between the descriptive and normative model) is generally a measure of both payoff and difficulty of implementation. The cognitive style perspective, as presented by J. L. McKenney and P. G. W. Keen (1974), recommends matching the information system to the decisionmaker's current processes. This involves very little distance, if any, from the descriptive model: it implies easy implementation but probably relatively low payoff in that the existing procedures are reinforced rather than altered. (There may, however, be long-term payoff if the system facilitates learning and willingness to explore analytic techniques and other computer-based aids; however, in the portfolio management situation, there would seem to be little value in reinforcing existing heuristics and strategies.) Figure 6-2 shows designs based on the cognitive style and portfolio theory perspectives, in terms of their implicit degree of change. The figure specifies normative models, in the plural. For a nonstructured decision, there is no one best solution but rather a range of potential designs. It seems useful to view a DSS project as an R & D situation involving a trade-off between risk and return. Risk is represented by the degree of change and return by the payoff from attaining this "improved" decision process. The choice among the designs should be made by *management* rather than by the technician, and there should be explicit recognition of the R & D aspects of the trade-offs.

This use of normative models in conjunction with descriptive analysis is the key aspect of the design strategy we recommend for DSS (it is based on Gerrity's work). A major implication of the approach is that management can consciously balance risk and potential payoff. It can decide how much change it believes is feasible, how much (resulting) effort will be needed, and how much commitment it is ready to make. Chapter 7, on implementation, discusses organizational change in more detail; it is worth stressing here that change is generally *incremental*—that individuals and organizations can rarely implement utopian advances in a simple step. In terms of Figure 6-2, which schematizes the descriptive-normative comparison, financial portfolio theory involves far too big a step. But, as Gerrity points

FIGURE 6-2   *Designs Based on Cognitive and Portfolio Theory Perspectives*

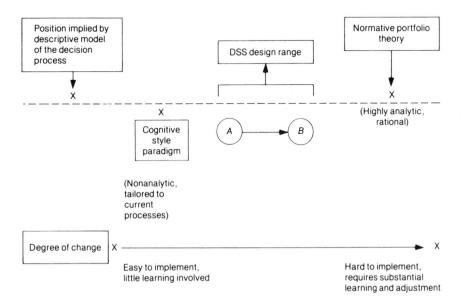

out, it still represents a desirable direction; what is needed is a design that begins from a position close enough to the descriptive model for implementation to be practicable and to permit further evolution. Whereas the design for a structured problem is generally "final," a DSS often requires a more open-ended structure. This will be discussed in much more detail later in this chapter.

In Figure 6-2, the DSS design is shown as a *range* of choices. Gerrity concluded that portfolio theory represented the right direction, but was infeasible. He thus specified a system that included many routines to support the current process (point *A* in Figure 6-2) and others to encourage change (toward point *B*). For example, PMS includes routines (see Chapter 5) such as SCAN, DIRECTORY, and GROUP that speed up or simplify the portfolio managers' routine procedures. SCATTER and HISTO are more analytic and represent a shift from the current decision process.

The predesign stage should generate several designs. The final design may well be a synthesis of these; for example, PMS combined insights from portfolio theory with those of the introspective and satisficing approaches. The use of the normative models has several side benefits:

1.   It helps clarify the choices and risks involved and ensures commitment and realistic expectations.

2.   It allows the multiple theoretical, political, and organizational viewpoints to be explicitly compared in that each of them implies a design choice.

3.   It encourages the use of research and theory, even when these cannot be directly implemented.

This predesign cycle is completed with the selection or synthesis of a specific design alternative (Figure 6-2 reflects synthesis: the definition of a *range* of choice). Of course, it may be necessary to repeat the cycle several times. In some instances, the descriptive analysis will suggest that only a small subset of the decisions involved justify the use of a DSS, and the normative analysis will imply no payoff from such support. Some of the key decisions will be highly structured and thus best dealt with through batch computer systems or analytic models (for example, if the descriptive analysis identifies administrative and clerical operations as key in the portfolio management case, then the trust accounting system would seem a far better choice than any DSS).

The final choice of a design alternative is mainly judgmental. The issues to be discussed still center around risk and payoff:

1.   Which alternative(s) offers the most improvement to the existing decision process? What are the likely economic payoffs? What is the cost of the organizational or behavioral gains?

2.   How difficult will it be to implement this degree of change? Are we ready to commit the dollars, time, prestige, and support necessary?

3.   What are the downside risks—if the system falls behind schedule or meets resistance, what are the costs (financial, behavioral, political, and so on)? Does the system permit a phased, evolutionary development?

In a complex task, important to the organization, it is extremely unlikely that any one design will stand out as the best. This "entry" stage will clearly require consensus, compromise, and frequent reassessment. It establishes *criteria for design* and focuses on context rather than on techniques.

AN EXAMPLE OF THE PREDESIGN CYCLE

A manufacturing firm, most of whose business was based on special contracts in the $300,000 to $800,000 range, was concerned that its bidding and pricing decisions were made erratically. It felt that a DSS might be of assistance. Pricing decisions were made by an executive vice-president with frequent recommendations from the Accounting Department.

The descriptive analysis indicated two key decisions:

1.   The Accounting Department's estimate of direct and full costs, taking into account special conditions for the contract.

2.   The executive vice-president's modification of the resulting standard price (cost plus markup) on the basis of his estimates of such factors as competitors' prices, production levels, and so on.

The full descriptive model is shown in Figure 6-3 (with an asterisk indicating the key decisions).

An immediate issue raised by Figure 6-3 is the relevant organizational level for analysis. Initially, it appeared that the Accounting Department staff were the focal unit in the decision, but the entry stage clearly indicated that the executive vice-president was the central figure. He personally made the final choice of bid. More importantly, he could and would override the recommendations of the Accounting Department. However, he was not the initiator of the DSS study, which had been sponsored by the controller. This made it essential to recycle through the process, especially the entry steps, and make sure that the executive vice-president was ready to get involved, allocate resources, and, of course, to use any suitable decision aid resulting from the study. The key decision, from this new perspective, was the price modification process (box 2 in Figure 6-3). The executive vice-president—and other senior managers—felt that the standard cost markup process was generally reliable and that the Accounting Department's existing decision rules were acceptable.

The next stage in the cycle was to develop normative models. These were:

Optimization: Several analysts argued that this problem was essentially one of constrained optimization. They proposed a linear programming model, with complex sensitivity analysis reports. The executive vice-president could use these to test the impact of changes (or inaccurate estimates) of competitors' actions, the firm's production schedules, and so on.

Competitive simulation: This was a simple probabilistic model to develop a pricing strategy, given various assumptions of competitors' responses. The proponents of this model felt that this was essentially a bargaining game (in the sense of game theory) and that the aim should be to maximize the probability of winning the bid, given profitability and production targets.

FIGURE 6-3   Descriptive Model of Bidding Decision Process

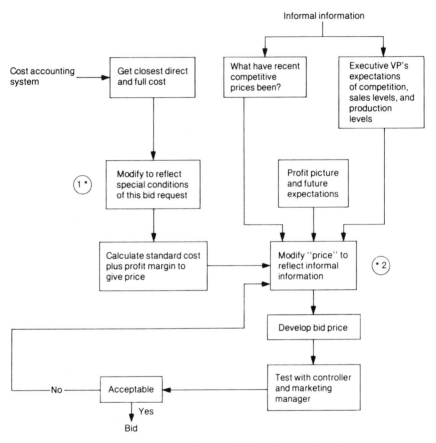

Strategic intelligence system: This would be a large-scale information system to gather data on competitors' announced sales, estimated inventory levels, this company's bids and the outcome, and so on.

The executive vice-president rejected the first proposal out of hand. He felt he could not trust such a system; he was unwilling to treat this problem as one of resource allocation. He felt that the other two proposals were both acceptable in concept. The third one would involve major new procedures for data gathering and system maintenance. He commented that a major outcome of the study so far was its identification of the need for a *strategy:* he felt he was too tactical in his approach, viewing each bid in isolation.

The degree and type of change involved in the three proposals and the perceived payoffs were:

Optimization: This involved a major change in concepts and analysis; additional coordination among Accounting, Production, and Sales departments; increased role for the technical staff in the planning units; and a potentially substantial payoff if the company continued to operate at or near capacity.

Competitive simulation: This involved relatively little change, except perhaps in the development of probabilistic parameters; relatively little payoff was seen by the executive vice-president, in that he felt he operated on this same basis now; however, he believed he could benefit from a formalization of his approach.

Strategic intelligence system: This involved little change in concepts and attitudes; substantial change in organizational operations; difficulty of gathering the required data; and a potentially large payoff from developing a strategic sense and a broader picture.

Figure 6-4 summarizes the proposals.

The system that was finally defined was a DSS, the Bidding Intelligence System, a modification of the third option. The prototype BIS was a simple retrieval system that used an interactive terminal. The executive vice-president used it mainly to review historical data. He found it helpful to examine such questions as: Where do we tend to lose large bids? How often are we badly overpriced or underpriced? Can we guess our competitors' general strategies from this data?

BIS evolved over a 3-year period. The system software was designed to allow easy addition of new routines. The executive vice-president soon found he needed analytic functions and models. He also commissioned a study by a junior analyst of the impact on prior years' profits and sales of particular changes in his own strategy. This led him to develop general conclusions—several of which ran counter to his prior assumptions—such as: (1) with any large contract ($750,000 or more), beware of a low price since there is often an opportunity cost in tying up substantial capacity; (2) company A's bids can be reliably forecast, while company B's depend very heavily on external factors; and (3) the greatest long-term profitability seems to result from a strategy of bidding very low on medium-size contracts, high on large ones, and eliminating where possible the small ones.

BIS cost around $200,000 over 3 years. The executive vice-president estimated it probably contributed at least $400,000 of additional profits. The main point to be made here is that the system design differed from the three original proposals. The descriptive and normative models and the predesign cycle clarified both

FIGURE 6-4   A Summary of Normative Models and the Degree of Change Involved in Each

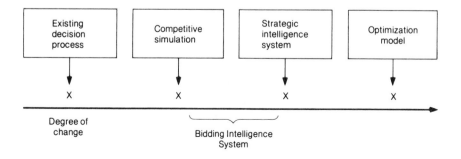

the criteria for design and the positioning of the DSS. BIS was also *planned* as an evolutionary system, which began from retrieval routines and expanded to more complex analysis.

THE DESIGN STAGE

There can be no cookbook for designing a DSS. We discuss some of the key components in this section and conclude the chapter with a simple diagram (Figure 6-5, page 186) designed to provide some sense of perspective.

At this point, when the predesign cycle is complete, the design specification is at best a statement of intention. It is thus essential to focus on what the DSS is intended to *do*, not what it should look like. Frequently, some aspects of the planned design turn out to be far more difficult or easier to accomplish than was predicted. The designer then needs clear criteria for deciding whether to drop, modify, or add particular functions and routines. The key questions to be asked at the start of the design stage are:

1.   What do we want the DSS to accomplish?

2.   How will we recognize when the system is complete—that is, when it has met its design objectives?

3.   What are the priorities and/or sequence of stages planned to meet the design aims?

In the predesign stage, objectives are fairly broad and commitments and expectations are general. These now need to be pinned down very precisely since they constitute the main criteria for and constraints on the formal design. In the BIS example, the broad aim was to develop a strategic intelligence system. Making such an objective operational can be very difficult indeed. There is often a tendency for the design team to focus on the system as an artefact and lose sight of what it is to accomplish. It is not enough to define BIS in terms of inputs and outputs and specify particular data and reports. *Design must be based on usage:* what will we *do* with BIS? The executive vice-president, a skilled executive who was determined that this would be *his* system, defined his aims as:

> I want BIS to give me easy access to all the contract and bid data that I feel is relevant and that we can collect. I want it to start small; I'll be happy initially if I can get answers to reasonably free-form questions like: Who got most contracts of this type? What was the average spread in prices for . . .? What's the biggest contract ABC got this year? I don't yet know what analysis I'll need; I'd like the system designed so that a programmer can bring up new routines very quickly. I want BIS to be used by other line managers, especially in marketing, so keep it simple. I see this as an open-ended project. I'll be happy if we get the system so that it answers 90 percent of the questions I'd like to ask. I don't want us to get bogged down with big reports and data bases. The sooner I can start playing with the system, the better.

(It is worth noting that the executive vice-president clearly sees BIS as evolutionary; the initial system will provide the base for learning and for further design features.)

The BIS design team translated these statements into technical specifications. While each DSS is unique, the BIS example shows the features common to DSS design in general (see, for example, the descriptions of PMS and GADS in Chapter 5). For example, the question, *What does the system do?*, can be answered best by defining "imperatives" or commands.[3] S. A. Alter (1975) points out that most DSS—from the user's perspective—can be viewed as a set of verbs or imperatives that "do" something: for example, "show me," "find," "extrapolate," and so on. A. Malhotra (1975) similarly suggests that most requests in a data-based DSS fall into adverbial categories: for example, "why," "who," "what," "how much," and so on. Rather than define reports or routines, the BIS (and PMS) design team identified the "do something" commands implicit in the executive vice-president's statement.

From the user's perspective, BIS is simply a set of verbs, many of which (FIND, DISPLAY, PLOT) are common to almost all conversational information systems. Others are specialized and complex (and less verblike). SPREAD, for example, performs statistical analysis on bid prices and GUESS is an experimental routine for comparing actual competitive or winning bids with the executive vice-president's original estimate and for forecasting future bids. Almost all the DSS we know of use some version of this command-driven approach.

BIS consists of a software interface that communicates with the user and that links to these imperatives. As far as the user is concerned, the interface is the system. PMS, for example, appears fairly simple to the user; it consists of a set of "do somethings" (SCAN, TABLE, and so on). Behind the user interface is, however, an immensely complex set of routines for retrieving data, interpreting commands, and so forth. The design of a DSS really involves three almost separate areas: (1) the "user" design, defined in terms of the imperatives, (2) the interface or "driver" which links them, and (3) the data-base management design. We discuss the last two of these areas later in this chapter.

How will we recognize when the system is complete? This question transfers attention from the imperatives to the interface. BIS is in one sense never complete. New routines have been added on a regular basis. It was, however, self-sustaining and operational once the first set of routines, all for data retrieval, were *usable*. The executive vice-president criticized several aspects of the system in the early months of usage; he disliked its cryptic error messages and found it hard to shift from one set of data to another. Major modifications of the software were needed. The BIS design team was frustrated by this; their early focus on the imperatives led them to underestimate some human engineering issues. Because the routines worked and the initial design of the interface had been approved, they felt they had met the design objectives. This is a common situation. The preliminary design turned out to be inadequate in particular areas, and the executive vice-president was able to define

---

[3]Keen, "The Intelligence Cycle: A Differentiated Perspective on Information Systems" (1977), and Berry, "The Democratization of Computing" (1977), similarly argue that systems should be designed in relation to *verbs*. Berry, for example, describes how an economist's problem-solving activities in predicting commodity prices can, through empathic interaction with a system designer, be translated into a verb such as *smooth*, which in turn can be turned into an APL routine. Keen suggests a conceptual investigation of the general verbs required in the full problem-solving sequence.

what he really wanted only when he had a real system to experiment with. The design specifications had been met but not the design *objectives.* The system was incomplete.

It seems essential to emphasize usage of the DSS and what it *does* rather than what its technical characteristics are. BIS was "complete" in terms of design when the executive vice-president felt comfortable with the interface and had the dozen routines needed for him to be able to answer "90 percent" of his questions. Of course, he soon impatiently asked for additional routines, but accepted that these represented "the next step," the start of an evolutionary movement.

What are the priorities and phases for the system? The executive vice-president defined BIS in terms of evolutionary design. For most DSS, a few routines will be seen as essential and a whole range of others as of value for particular users or situations. Priorities can be assigned either on the basis of user needs or technical feasibility. Obviously, the user should define the priorities wherever possible. A major reason for separating the interface from the imperatives is to facilitate phasing in of additional routines and modification or extension of the system over time. In the BIS case, this was fairly easy. The executive vice-president wanted the initial phase of the evolutionary design to emphasize data retrieval. He planned on adding in analytic and model-based routines but had no clear idea of what these would be. The design team thus made sure that the interface was sufficiently flexible to allow this evolution.

THE SOFTWARE INTERFACE

The system, as seen by users, *is* the interface. They are—and should be—uninterested in the clever coding, hierarchical structuring, relational data bases, table-driven command software, and so on that carry out their requests. *They are very sensitive to the quality of the interface.* (See J. D. C. Little, 1970, and T. D. Sterling, 1975, for excellent definitions of essential requirements for the interface.[4]) The following list is highly incomplete but indicates some of the issues designers *must* deal with:

1. *Communicability:* The system must be genuinely conversational, with a well-defined, simple process for submitting requests, switching to new data or routines, and so on. It should be "polite" (Sterling) and informative. Error messages should be helpful; "unidentified UUO at USER Loc 6078E" is useful to the programmer of the system, but infuriating to the user. It also seems desirable to use English-like commands where possible, to minimize typing and to provide lucid, brief responses.

2. *Robustness:* The DSS should be "bombproof." It should contain internal checks to prevent users making mistakes or nonsensical output being printed. For example, one of BIS's forecasting routines occasionally produced estimates that the winning bid for a contract would

---

[4]Sterling includes, in what amounts to a user's "bill of rights," such issues as helpfulness and politeness. In effect, the software interface is a staff assistant and the user can reasonably expect it to provide similar services.

be a negative price; the executive vice-president found this very disturbing and assumed that the routine was programmed incorrectly. Of course, the real problem was that the particular input data, although valid, did not meet the requirements or assumptions for this type of statistical analysis. C. L. Meador and D. N. Ness' Projector (1974) avoids such difficulties by providing frequent warnings of likely sources of error. In the BIS case, a response such as "No forecast possible; analysis suggests negative bid. Please check data," would prevent a potentially expensive loss of user conficence in the system.

A second aspect of robustness is, of course, system reliability. Computer crashes naturally anger users, especially if there is no restart procedure that allows them to pick up again without having to retype all the data or requests they have just submitted. Program errors obviously irritate, as do invalid data; these problems can be difficult to eliminate. The initial implementation of PMS included all these problems. The system was behind schedule and the design team submitted to pressures to allow use of PMS before it was really ready. This turned out to be a bad mistake. Users' confidence in the system was damaged and their frustration was high. A key determinant of DSS success is the users' trust in the system. They are asked to make a commitment of effort and to learn a new technology; they require in return that the system will not crash, give garbage answers, or make mistakes. Robustness is a central need in the DSS interface design.

3. *Ease of control:* This is an extension of communicability. The DSS programming personnel should remind themselves daily that "this is the user's system, not mine." A side-benefit of the descriptive decision analysis is that it can give designers a sense of what the users will require to feel comfortable when operating the system: which type of routine they will generally need, their likely sequence of analysis, and so forth. It may be useful to create a prototype system, a mockup of the interface, to check that the users feel they can operate the DSS in *their* way and not feel forced into a sequence or vocabulary unnatural for them.[5]

Designing the interface is often the most difficult aspect of a DSS, both conceptually and technically. It is hard to anticipate user needs and the software overhead can be immense. The GADS system, for example, is on the whole easy to use. Its weak link is the method for defining new variables. For example, to generate total income figures for a geographic unit, the required input command might be: TOTINC (I) = MINC (I) * (WPOP(I) − SCHOOL (I)). This is easy for anyone with minimal experience with a programming language such as BASIC, COBOL, or FORTRAN to deal with. It was, however, highly frustrating for many users of GADS, and important features of the DSS could not be exploited by them. The

---

[5]Once again, it is important to remember Gerrity's prototype for PMS; the experiences with this experimental system did not provide a reliable indication of users' later behavior with the full DSS.

GADS input conventions will need to be changed; this requires substantial programming to accomplish something that can already be done efficiently but that does not meet the needs for communicability and ease of control.

DATA MANAGEMENT

The third aspect of system design, data management, is not unique to DSS. Computer science and data processing professionals have focused increasingly on the technology for handling complex data structures over the past few years (see, for example, J. Kanter, 1977, Chapter 4). A difficulty for many DSS is that they require fairly large data bases and complex retrieval facilities with infrequent access to most of the data. It is hard to get *efficient* software to handle this combination. By far the major effort in the PMS design, for example, involved data management.

Apart from the software needed for data management and retrieval, the organizational processes can also be difficult. It is easy to specify a data base, but harder to collect and validate the data, and frequently close to impossible to maintain it. This is especially true for nonroutine data. For example, it was assumed in the design of PMS that analysts' forecasts of earnings and prices would be accurately updated. This simply did not happen. In general, an individual (or unit) who either does not have to update data as part of a routine task or who does not gain something from doing so, will be very unlikely to maintain the data base (Alter found this to be a major problem for most information systems). The BIS data *was* well maintained since the problem was anticipated and a staff analyst was specifically assigned to collect, validate, and maintain the needed information.

We have no specific recommendations to offer concerning data management for DSS, except to mention C. A. McCoubrey and M. Sulg's rule: "Assume the data you want doesn't exist, no matter what people tell you" (1975). The organizational aspects of data bases are often harder to resolve than the technical issues where DSS can draw on the ongoing work in computer science on data-base design and software.[6]

COMPLETING THE LOOP:
THE POSTDESIGN PROCESS

The phrase *evolutionary design* has been used frequently in this chapter. Evolution does not mean one should just make a first cut at design, get it working, and see what ought to be done next. Evolution, experiment, and learning are closely linked. A major assumption of the DSS faith is that competent managers will learn from using the system and begin to extend their analysis; they will then require additional levels of support. For example, the executive vice-president began by using BIS to answer questions. He then started to specify quantitative approaches to analysis that went far beyond anything he had done prior to the implementation of the DSS. The evolutionary approach to DSS design assumes that this learning will occur and that the system should facilitate it.

---

[6]This work, still mainly conceptual, aims at providing efficient ways of accessing complex information from a large data base. For example, Chen (1977) recommends a hierarchical, Codd (1970) a relational, and Donovan (1976) a virtual machine approach.

Figure 6-2 suggests what this means in practice; the initial design of a DSS is positioned to support much of the existing decision process (point *A*) and to encourage movement toward point *B*. This means that the first stage in the long-term process of evolution should be, as it was in the BIS example, to design and deliver a system that is seen as usable and useful *now*; but the interface software should be flexible enough to allow rapid extension and addition of routines. The second phase, which would probably begin after 3 months to 1 year of experience with the original system, will involve design of a few powerful new routines that extend the decisionmaker's efforts and abilities. In one organization that implemented PMS, the initial system was reasonably successful although not strikingly so. However, when a new function, LIST, was added, usage of PMS accelerated almost immediately and continued to double every 6 months for 2 years. Clearly, evolution is possible only if the users play a full role in the design process. The initial system, even if designed in cooperation with potential users, is an uncertain venture; managers are not used to inventing computer systems. However, once they are experienced users, they and not the technician are generally best able to design new features.

The process of evolution of the DSS is also one of change in the managers' decision process. A new design phase for an existing DSS requires the same basic sequence as before; it starts from a descriptive analysis of the decision process. This will have changed—hopefully in the direction implied by the normative model used as the basis for the DSS. The decision process will have become more effective. (It is naive to expect either dramatic or continuous improvements; nonetheless, if the DSS has had any impact, some shift should be apparent.) This new analysis forms the basis for evaluating the system and allows managers to compare achievements against expectations and to plan the next design iteration. They must then decide if there is a potential for further development and, if so, whether or not they are ready to commit the necessary resources. This means repeating the predesign cycle. Evolution is a conscious *strategy*, with explicit phases and design objectives, and not open-ended and unplanned.

CONCLUSION

This chapter has focused on designing rather than design. We recommend the reader look again at the descriptions of PMS and GMIS in Chapter 5 to see how the design strategy we have presented is made operational. We have, of course, glibly evaded technical problems and must acknowledge that DSS often require state-of-the-art software and hardware and tenacious, creative programmers. However, the key *strategic* issues for making most effective use of technical skills concern the decision process and the manager's task. The prime need is to identify the criteria for design. This means that:

1.   The predesign cycle requires immense effort.[7]

2.   The managers' opinions and understanding of the decision situation are a major input to the design process.

---

[7]In Chapter 7, on the implementation of DSS, we discuss entry in more detail and estimate that it may take up as much as 70 percent of the elapsed time for a project.

3.   The design team needs to understand, in substantial detail, both the existing decision process and potential ways of improving it.

4.   The DSS design must be evolutionary.

Much of the strategy we present is an approach to implementation, to meshing the formal system into its context. Figure 6-5 summarizes the strategy. Its key features are:

1.   The use of *decision research* (the term is from Stabell, 1977) to describe the decision process, define key decisions, and identify areas for decision support.

FIGURE 6-5   The Design Cycle

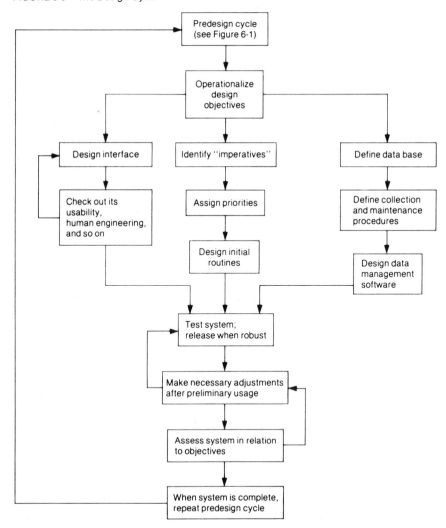

2.   The use of *normative models* to define multiple design alternatives and to help position a DSS in terms of degree of change, payoffs, and likely implementation problems.

3.   The focus on *system usage and objectives* as determining structure and technical design.

4.   The *separation of interface and imperatives* to allow flexibility and evolution.

5.   The *inseparability of design and implementation.*

This last issue is the subject of Chapter 7.

IMPLEMENTATION:
THE MANAGEMENT
OF ORGANIZATIONAL CHANGE[1]

SEVEN

INTRODUCTION

Managers have increasingly criticized computer professionals for their relative inability to deliver systems that meet users' real *needs* and that are on time and cost effective. They point to innumerable instances of models and systems being built but never used. The reasons for this failure in implementation seem rarely to be technical. The systems "work" but are either of little value to managers or awkward to use in regular operations.

In the good times of the 1960s, when all aspects of the computer field were growing at a bewildering but exciting pace, the issue of implementation was easily brushed aside. Companies were involved in many new ventures in information systems development that were avowedly experimental, at the same time that they were wrestling with the mysteries of third-generation hardware and operating systems. Their reach constantly exceeded their grasp and it was no surprise to them that many systems had to be abandoned. The failures could be expensive but so long as the organization was getting some return from the overall portfolio of computer applications, this was tolerated. However, managers now clearly see that the implementation rate for computer projects has always been low and that even the most skilled technicians often cannot deliver systems that are useful to the customers who pay the bill.

This chapter discusses strategies for implementation. These apply to information systems and models in general and not just to DSS. However, for a system that automates a well-defined procedure with few organizational interdependencies, *design* is the key issue; for a DSS, which explicitly focuses on management processes and which aims at changing procedures and concepts, *implementation* may be far more complex than the formal design process. As we have emphasized, the "system" is not an artefact but a set of computer routines that must be meshed into the organizational, political, and behavioral context.

The five disciplines defined in Chapter 2 have very differing perspectives on implementation; these differences reinforce the critical need when developing a DSS

---

[1]This chapter draws heavily on prior publications and research projects in which the authors were involved. See, especially, Keen (1974, 1975), Ginzberg (1975), and Alter (1975). Keen's *Implementation Research in MIS and OR/MS: Description versus Prescription* (1977) summarizes work on implementation over the past 5 years.

to use all the disciplines rather than adopt a single perspective. Obviously, in retrospect, the most technical specialities of computer science and management science simply overlooked the question of implementation, focusing instead on their missionary purpose of developing techniques independent of their effective use. Much of the recent research on implementation in management science consciously draws on organizational theory and on managers' insights in a way entirely lacking even a few years ago (see, for example, A. S. Bean et al., 1973).

Computer Science

Computer science views techniques as ends rather than means. Thus, a new generalized data-base management system is considered a piece of software that potentially extends the ability of information systems designers to produce new and better applications; it is explicitly designed, however, to be independent of particular applications, and the designer's responsibility excludes most aspects of implementation. One of the most striking examples of this emphasis is OS/360, the operating system for the third-generation IBM/360 series of computers, introduced in the mid-1960s. For most programmers, OS/360 was complex, labyrinthian, infuriating, clumsy, and perilous to use. Its designers had built OS/360 from their own very technical perspective and initially ignored issues of human engineering.[2] Since then, computer science has become much more sensitive to these questions, which imply ease of learning and use and compatibility with current procedures. Many computer scientists, for example, are now trying to develop "natural" programming languages and software systems to "humanize" the interface. At the same time, this work continues to emphasize design rather than the process of implementation.

Management Science

As in the case of computer science, management science has traditionally ignored most issues of implementation. In fact, the standard refrain of research on implementation is an attack on the management science profession for its damaging indifference to the decisionmaker's prime concern—the *use* of the model rather than the model itself. The major journals generally discuss techniques only; for example, G. L. Urban (1974) points out that only 3 percent of the 150 articles in *Management Science: Applications* between January 1971 and June 1973 represented a situation where something had been implemented in an organization.[3] Many management scientists tend to stress abstract theorems and algorithms rather than applications: their professional identity and peer approval come from developing the *best* models—"best" here essentially means the most elegant, most powerful, and most complex. That managers will be more satisfied with a small, perhaps even incomplete, model that is good enough for their purposes is hard for them to see.

---

[2]Brooks (1975) draws many useful salutary conclusions from his experience as the leader of this project, which can at best be viewed as overnarrow in its focus. Brooks' book is an excellent introduction to the effective design of complex software projects.

[3]Urban also points out that the word implementation does not even appear in indexes to OR/MS publications before 1970.

That said, the management science profession includes many highly effective implementors. We are gradually culling the fruits of their experience and the addition of the *Interfaces* journal to the Institute of Management Science publications provides a forum for discussing implementation.[4] Also, the fusion of management scientists and behavioral researchers has produced case studies and applied research over the past 3 years that are both descriptively insightful and valuable in their direct lessons for would-be implementors. (This research will be described in a separate section of this chapter.) One of the key conclusions is that there is a need for a type of management scientist who will not behave just as a technician nor assume that the responsibility for implementation is the client's.

Behavioral Science

Behaviorally oriented practitioners and researchers in the computer field have always made implementation their prime focus. Until recently they have been few in number and in some cases have been on the edges of the field, with insufficient understanding of the technology to do more than criticize from a distance. Their contribution to the development of more effective uses of computer-based systems has increased rapidly, largely due to their *explicit* concern with implementation at a time when both managers and practitioners have recognized this as the weakest aspect of systems development efforts. The main focus of the behavioral approach is on the *context* of an information system. It thus draws attention to important influences on the implementation process that are easily overlooked. The design tradition focuses on the system itself; the behavioral perspective stresses the context that constrains design and delivery.

Data Processing Professionals

Managers in electronic data processing (EDP) have always been painfully aware that their staff are famous for their inability to estimate the costs and time needed to implement a new system. Even seasoned professionals admit that their rule of thumb for making estimates is: calculate as precisely as you can and then double everything—and even then it will be 50 percent too low. Large MIS projects often involve teams of over a dozen programmers and analysts for about a 2-year period; other departments within the organization may at the same time be heavily involved in collecting data, creating new master files, and so forth. Because of this, the EDP manager has mainly viewed implementation in terms of project management; the best textbooks on MIS take this approach and there have been many ef-

---

[4]*Interfaces* also seems to provide a release valve for individuals frustrated by the general indifference to the implementation issue for researchers and even management scientists working in organizations. The danger here is that the writers and readers of *Management Science* and *Interfaces* may become even further separated, with those concerned with theorems never needing to encounter an article on applications and with those primarily interested in implementation being similarly shielded from conceptual analysis. Managers complain of the "two culture" problem (see, for example, Grayson, 1973) between themselves and OR/MS; encouraging two cultures *within* the latter does not seem a useful development.

forts by consulting groups to package techniques for measuring programmer productivity, reporting progress, documentation, and so on.[5] The frequency with which new variations on these techniques appear suggests that they have not been too effective. Perhaps, too, the project management approach can work only in particular circumstances, such as the design and delivery of standard transaction-processing applications in organizations with substantial experience with systems development. As will be shown later in this chapter, research on implementation of one-shot OR/MS models suggests that the highly structured, depersonalized techniques necessary for project management (which are very effective in shipbuilding, engineering applications, and so on) are totally unsuited to the uncertainties, risks, and complexities of innovative information systems.[6] Such systems are an invention that has not existed before and the system-builders can honestly not forecast how they will turn out. This has immense implications for DSS and means that the design, implementation, and evaluation steps must be closely interwoven. While we still can draw on the experience of the EDP professional in this respect, the project management approach to implementation seems to have relatively low value for DSS development.

Management

Technical specialists are often more concerned with an information system as a product than as a service to the client who is financing it and who needs to be able to use it. For example, the pages of *Management Science* are full of "elegant" models that were never used but that impress because of their structure, new algorithms, or so forth. The systems analyst in an EDP application, although obviously concerned that the system be a success, may have as a personal priority the technical quality of the system—he or she may resist pressures to do a "quick-and-dirty" job, and insist on tightening up the code, generating a more efficient search routine, and so on.

Management is rarely concerned with "elegance," technical virtuosity, or tight code. They want "results," which in practice means something they feel is useful (not something the specialist feels *ought* to be useful to them) and which is delivered at the time they need it. To an extent, they have been lonely voices in the wilderness, crying out for the primacy of implementation over design. They complain that most computer specialists do not understand or relate to management's needs and decision processes, that they lack a business focus, and that the computer has been a source of trouble rather than support. Of course, many of the specialists

---

[5]These techniques are most effective when they address the issue of programmer efficiency. They rarely, however, improve the process of project initiation, system definition, and institutionalization of the system. These activities are generally not structured and involve close interaction with other units of the organization, bargaining, and politics.

[6]For example, project management techniques are effective only when the component activities can be precisely identified, reliable time estimates derived, and the interconnections among subtasks defined. This is reasonably simple if a systems development effort is essentially one of software engineering, as in many standard data processing applications, but it is generally infeasible for R & D projects such as a DSS.

counter this: they feel that managers have rarely bothered to clarify what it is they want and that they simply do not understand, even in broad terms, the nature and constraints of the technology.

Our choice of the words *decision support system* to describe the type of information system we feel most needs to be added to those currently in use in organizations was deliberate. The system is to *support* the managers in their ongoing decisionmaking. It will only be used by them when they feel it is useful (unlike the payroll system or the sales reporting system that they simply have to use). The relative failure of management scientists and MIS personnel to have the millennial impact on organizations that they glowingly predicted certainly seems due to their lack of attention to what managers' needs, attitudes, and abilities are and how they can best be supported. Far too few of them understand managers; if they make the effort to do so, they are much more likely to become effective implementors rather than just designers. In Chapter 3 we discussed the decisionmaking process in detail and that chapter is a key section of this book. While managers may have no clear ideas on *how* to implement information systems, two things are clear:

1. Implementation is their first concern.

2. The manager's reality is the one in which implementation takes place; the technology to be used must be adapted to that context and not imposed on it.

The discussion above highlights some issues in implementation but does not provide any answers to what is a very complex problem. Perhaps, though, the critical first step is to recognize that implementation *is* the purpose of a project. The point should be obvious, but if a designer regards implementation as the responsibility of the client, then she or he is in fact designing an artefact without considering the organizational context, the nature of its use and users, and the key factors that will hinder or help its introduction. Our chapter on the design of DSS has already covered many topics relevant to implementation and explicitly argues that design and implementation are inseparable—in Chapter 8 we similarly point out that evaluation of the outcome of a project is also an integral part of the full design-implementation cycle. With this caveat in mind, we can now review what we know about effective implementation.

THE CONVENTIONAL WISDOM ON IMPLEMENTATION

Empirical studies of implementation fall into fairly distinct categories that reflect equally distinct viewpoints on what variables most influence the likelihood of successful implementation (the discussion below is mainly drawn from M. J. Ginzberg, 1975). The earliest approach comes from the "wise old men." These are, generally speaking, practitioners who have been in the computer field since the "Dark Ages" (or "Golden Age," depending on one's affection for machine-language debugging) of first-generation hardware. From their broad experience, they distill general principles for implementation. The value of their argument obviously comes from its firm roots in reality; one of the main difficulties in studying implementation from any viewpoint is that we lack a broad perspective and large number of detailed case studies. The wise old men are usually very prescriptive in their approach; unlike behaviorally oriented academics, they are interested not in developing comprehensive descriptive models but in telling us *how* to go about implementation. However, a characteristic of their approach is that they often define what one should do as being the opposite of what was done in projects that failed.

An excellent and influential example of the wise old men school is R. L. Ackoff. His article "Unsuccessful Case Studies and Why" (1960) examines a number of OR implementation efforts and concludes that there were three common patterns that led to failure:

1. The personnel who were interested in the project and had enough influence within the organization to facilitate its progress often left or were transferred, so that there was a lack of continuity and, more critically, a lack of a power base.

2. The projects lacked top management support.

3. Staff personnel often obstructed the project in the interests of their own political position.

The common thread in the unsuccessful situations was the fact that the operations researcher did not have the power needed for successful implementation.

Ackoff defines a strategy for getting this power, with the unstated and untested implication that this will reverse the situation:

1. Make sure that you have a formal contract that you can break.

2. Make sure that you report only to someone in the organization who has the power and seniority to force cooperation from relevant personnel.

3. Complain loudly!

4. Never do work for free.

Ackoff's arguments are compelling and they are representative of the current conventional wisdom. However, other wise old men, with different biases, similarly look at failures but, because they identify different causes for the lack of success, define normative approaches to implementation that are in direct conflict with other wise old men. For example, C. Argyris (who comes from a very different tradition than Ackoff) argues almost in the opposite direction (1970, 1971). His experience suggests that most implementation failures are caused because the management scientists' intervention is a threat to the members of the organization; their impersonal, highly rational approach is an intrusion into the present equilibrium, and they come backed by the power base of top management with an explicit mandate for change. They are often insensitive to interpersonal issues. Argyris argues that management scientists must develop interpersonal competence and play down, or even avoid, the threatening use of power.[7] This is, of course, the opposite of Ackoff's recommendations.

---

[7]Argyris and Ackoff's articles are examples of the failure literature in studies of implementation (see, for more details, Keen, *Implementation Research in MIS and OR/MS: Description versus Prescription*, 1977). This category of study was popular in the early efforts of researchers to raise the consciousness of OR/MS and draw attention to the reality—that far more models and systems are built than are used. The failure study is still popular, but it provides little real evidence and—as is clear here—it encourages generalization from very limited data.

We have discussed these two wise old men in some detail because they highlight one of the major difficulties in studying implementation—the development of general principles from specific instances. A main reason for focusing on failures in implementation is that successes are generally uneventful, while one can often, in retrospect, identify why a project failed—and, of course, seize on that and promise to oneself to take the opposite approach next time. As we shall see later in this chapter, many recent researchers argue that there are *no* absolute general principles; that both Ackoff and Argyris are correct but that their argument applies only to specific types of situations. For example, P. G. W. Keen (1975a, p. 12) suggests that the main basis for an implementation strategy is the adoption of a clinical approach that enables one to examine the situation as a whole, in order to identify the key contextual forces and constraints; the "right" strategy for implementation depends on the situation and Ackoff's and Argyris' prescriptions may be perfectly or disastrously matched to a particular context.

There is a second category of implementation study that until recently dominated much of the academic research on implementation. This is the "factor" approach, which surveys large samples of implementation efforts and tries to define the general factors that seem to be associated with successful outcomes. The surveys are obviously descriptive in intent and general in scope. Factor researchers argue that we simply do not know what matters in implementation and that we cannot develop better techniques until we have broad maps and signposts. Most managers and many practitioners will agree in principle with this. However, it seems very probable from the results thus far that the factor approach is a will-o'-the-wisp. As with the wise old men, it has become clear that there are no absolute factors that "explain" implementation. For example, Ginzberg (1975) dissects 14 factor studies, all of which are extensive, well-researched, and, in their way, insightful. Each tries to answer the deceptively simple question: What are the factors that enhance the likelihood that an implementation effort will be successful? The 14 papers identify 140 distinct factors reported as having a significant correlation with success. Of these, only 15 (11 percent) appear in 3 or more of the 14 studies, and 102 (73 percent) appear in only 1 study. Table 7-1 shows the breakdown of the 140 factors:

TABLE 7-1   Factors that Enhance the Likelihood
of Implementation Success as Reported in 14 Studies

No. of Factors	Percentage	No. of Reports Factor Appeared in
102	73	1
23	16	2
12	9	3
2	1	4*
1	0.7	5†

Source: Ginzberg, 1974, pp. 51–68.

---

*The factors were: "well-defined, measurable objectives" and "complexity of techniques and models."

†The factor was: "top management support."

Thus only three factors appear to have had any broad empirical exploration. In some cases, factors found to correlate with particular patterns of success or failure in implementation are hard to interpret. For example, one researcher found "well-defined, measurable objectives" to be of substantial impact while another study reported it as having no discernable influence according to any of the four measures of "success" employed. It was found to have a moderate effect in yet another study, and in a very ambitious study, a very large impact. This lack of consensus is not at all unusual in an immature field of research (or in mature ones, as the recent history of economics indicates) but, of course, it hinders the development of prescriptive techniques.

The factor approach, the main body of research in implementation, is less than the sum of its parts. It has helped clarify *some* of the clusters of variables relevant to implementation (although without throwing much light on their interrelations and on the dynamics of the implementation *process*). For example, the McKinsey study "Unlocking the Computer's Profit Potential" (1968), which surveyed 36 companies in 13 industries in the United States and Europe, first pointed up the likely importance of top level support and of operating management's involvement in an implementation effort. A. H. Rubenstein et al. (1967) similarly drew attention to the importance of the stage in the life cycle of OR/MS activity that the organization is moving through for determining the type of project that should be undertaken and the organizational constraints that the cycle imposes. Nonetheless, when we try to synthesize a conventional wisdom from all this research, little emerges. At best, we can conclude that the factors below are the only ones that have been plausibly shown in a range of studies and settings to have substantial impact on the likelihood of success:

Top management support.

A clear felt need by the client.

An immediate, visible problem to work on.

Early commitment by the user and conscious staff involvement.

A well-institutionalized OR/MS or MIS group.

Some of these may be only "hygiene" factors (see F. Herzberg, 1959); for example, without top management support a project faces major difficulties, but having that support may be of little direct help. Nonetheless, the conclusion to be drawn from both the wise old men and the factor research is not so much that we lack any basis for a conventional wisdom as that there are obviously very few absolutes. It is this fact that makes it so hard to study implementation and learn better ways of increasing the chances of success. The contradictions Ginzberg found in the 14 studies suggest that implementation is a *contingent* process, meaning that the characteristics of the *situation* most determine the approach the implementor should take.

While many of the issues highlighted by the wise old men and the factor researchers are important mainly to theoreticians and academics, they are in the long run equally relevant for practitioners. The most obvious point is that we just do not understand the *dynamics* of implementation. This is really an extraordinary fact; implementation is the avowed purpose of a large number of highly skilled and experienced professionals in the computer field, but while many of them are certainly successful implementors, they seem unable to pin down any general principles underlying their successes. Hordes of researchers have analyzed millions of questionnaire responses and the best they can conclude is that top management support is essential. If we assume that the practitioners are competent and the researchers intelligent, then we must suggest either that implementation is impossibly difficult or that there are some key barriers to implementation that arise from the nature of the technology itself or the personality, training, and behavior of the implementor and/or the client. Some professionals do feel that implementation is largely a matter of some intuitive skill, that it is the management of unanticipated consequences and all one can do is to react to problems as they arise. They feel that the best approach to implementation is to be technically competent and do one's best. Obviously, this view—which empirically has much to support it—reinforces the traditional technically based attitudes of management science and computer science.

A number of practitioners and researchers have focused on the second of the two possibilities, that the technology or the people involved in computer projects impede implementation. Clearly, the technology has been a barrier in many instances. Managers do not understand it and may even feel actively threatened by it. While computer specialists may feel that the particular methodologies they propose are self-evidently correct, it is hard to argue that a manager should accept that on trust. There have been too many spectacular failures in the technology to justify that view. It seems unlikely, however, that lack of understanding is the critical barrier; managers listen to the recommendations of their R & D specialists, even where they do not follow the technical details and implications.

Many well-known figures in the MIS area have suggested that the weak link in implementation is the lack of education—education of managers in analytic methods and management scientists in general management. R. E. D. Woolsey, whose amusing and barbed articles "All Around the Model" were a regular feature in *Interfaces* until recently, feels that the OR/MS experts who lack practical, real world experience should even offer their services at no fee in order to get that vital training. H. M. Wagner, in "The ABC's [achievements, beliefs, and content] of OR" (1971) feels that many problems in implementation are caused by weaknesses in OR/MS education, which generally lacks any focus on applications. The strongest argument in favor of resolving the implementation problem through education is C. J. Grayson's "Management Science and Business Practice" (1973). This article seems, frankly, wrong in almost all its conclusions but it raises, very clearly indeed, the central issue of the difference between the manager and the management scientist. Grayson recalls C. P. Snow's famous dictum about the two cultures of science and the humanities: "Managers and management scientists are operating in two separate cultures, each with its own goals, languages and methods. Effective cooperation—even communication—between the two is just about minimal" (Grayson, 1973, p. 41). Grayson bases this pessimistic viewpoint on his experiences as chairman of the Federal Price Commission; he expected to be able to make substantial use of management science techniques—the article is a somewhat embittered summary of his disillusionment. He feels very strongly that the real cause of the implementation problem is what C. W. Churchman and A. H. Schainblatt pointed to in 1965, the lack of "mutual understanding" between manager and scientist.[8] Grayson concludes that a major educational effort is needed to move them toward a closer common ground.

---

[8]This important article underlies much of the research on cognitive style in OR/MS. See also Keen (1977b).

A major difficulty with Grayson's argument is that while it may be true that the difference between the two groups causes problems, that same difference is what makes each of them distinctive. The skills and training of the manager are very different from those of the management scientist or EDP professional—the latter are specialists and they are hired to provide a particular and unusual approach to problems. It seems very inefficient (and likely to be ineffectual) to try to educate each to be like the other. Nonetheless, Grayson's point that there are two separate and potentially hostile parties involved in the implementation of an information system or model is a critical one. The research on cognitive style discussed in Chapter 3 focuses on this barrier to implementation.

Apart from their different styles, the computer professional and the manager often have entirely different criteria for a project; the designer will tend to value technique and formal quality and the manager will look for "usefulness." Because both of them are successful and competent in their own sphere, they easily project their own logic onto the situation and assume that what is self-evident to themselves is equally so to any other reasonable person. MIS personnel are now much less likely than before to act as if they were missionaries bringing enlightenment to the heathen, but Grayson's main argument seems valid—each party approaches implementation from his or her own justifiable and specialized viewpoint and may simply not be aware of just how different are the other's needs, attitudes, and assumptions.

In Chapter 3 we stressed the importance of understanding how managers make decisions; this may be very different from how technical personnel think they *ought* to make them. Many analytic specialists, partly because of their training and partly because of personality variables and preferences, are far too ignorant of how managers operate. While they should, of course, maintain a normative focus—after all, one of their explicit purposes is to help improve the decisionmaking process in organizations—they need to know where they start from and that is the world of the *manager*. By adopting a decision-centered, diagnostic approach, they have a much better chance of matching techniques to context. Argyris' (1970, 1971) attack on MIS and related disciplines is perhaps unfair, but he highlights the fact that analytic specialists quite simply scare many people—they operate in an alien fashion, are outsiders, and think and feel in different terms. Fairly obviously, this is not the basis for successful implementation since the specialists may not understand the organizational context in which they act and they lack a relationship either of trust or of understanding that can lead to joint goal setting, cooperation, and mutual appreciation.

Given that the manager and the scientist are different, successful implementation must involve both a recognition of that fact and the development of a conscious strategy for managing the implementation process. The strategy we recommend does *not* assume that the relationship should be free of conflict or, unlike Grayson, that the differences need to be eliminated. However, the implementor, who is in most cases also the system designer, must take responsibility for:

1.   Clarifying the differences—personal, political, cognitive, and so forth—among the parties and assessing the extent to which they constrain the direction of the design and implementation effort.

2.   Recognizing that any innovative information system is a change program and that the organization has an existing equilibrium that will

be disturbed by the introduction of the system. There will be resistance to change; generally, computer professionals view such resistance as pathological but it is very often a reasonable response from a system in steady state whose members want to avoid the upheaval and effort—and immense risk—of change.

Implementation is a *process*. This cannot be stressed too much. One reason the factor studies have not found any general factors that affect implementation is almost certainly because the dynamics of the process swamp particular structural aspects of the situation. For example, it may well be that top management support is a critical facilitator in implementation because it provides a power base, credibility, and momentum for action. However, the *behavior* of the parties in the implementation can either erode or build on this support. What determines the quality of the outcome is the designer's ability to identify the key constraints in the situation, to then match the formal technology to those constraints, and to work with the people to whom they apply. This is a complex process and very few rules can confidently be applied.

IMPLEMENTATION AS A PROCESS OF SOCIAL CHANGE

We often fairly glibly talk about implementation as an organizational change process and the consultant as a change agent, without pausing to examine the implications of interpreting that literally. There has been an immense variety of work throughout the social sciences on the dynamics of planned change and this work shows a remarkable unity, whether its specific topic is the training of Benedictine novices (E. Erikson, 1958), brainwashing of POW's in Korea (E. H. Schein, 1961), organization change (W. G. Bennis, 1965), or group dynamics (D. Cartwright, 1951). On the whole, work on planned change has ignored the technical and technological aspects of social change, but its insights still hold extremely well in the world of MIS and DSS. In fact, a number of researchers and practitioners have adopted this perspective on implementation over the past few years. From the way we have set up the wise old men and factor research as straw men, the reader can deduce that we feel this third approach to implementation is by far the most useful.

The most basic framework for discussing behavioral and organizational change is K. Lewin's (1952; expanded by Schein, 1961), which views change as a three-stage process (see Figure 7-1). Each of these stages must be worked through for a change program to be effective. Schein (1961, p. 109) defines the stages as follows:

1. *Unfreezing:* an alteration of the forces acting on the individual such that his stable equilibrium is disturbed sufficiently to motivate him and make him ready to change; this can be accomplished either by increasing the pressure to change or by reducing some of the threats or resistances to change . . .

2. *Moving:* the presentation of a direction of change and the actual process of learning new attitudes . . .

3. *Refreezing:* the integration of the changed attitudes into the rest of the personality and/or into ongoing significant emotional relationships.

FIGURE 7-1   The Lewin-Schein Model of Change

Schein's description maps well onto implementation ("implementation" here includes all three stages, of course; although the technical tradition views the middle stage, which specifically involves the design of the change program, as equivalent to implementation and considers the responsibility for the preceding and succeeding processes as being the organization's, not the designer's). The unfreezing stage explains much of our conventional wisdom. For example, "top management support," "a felt need by the client," and "an immediate, visible problem to work on," factors that seem to facilitate implementation, all relate to the need that there be motivation and momentum for change. On the other hand, S. A. Alter reports, in his detailed study of over 50 DSS (1975), that systems that were sold to the user by the technical group were rarely successful. Change needs to be self-motivated and the client-system must take responsibility for and be committed to the change program.

"Resistance to change" reflects a lack of unfreezing; such resistance is often assumed by the analyst who encounters it to be a pathological rejection of "truth." The Lewin-Schein model highlights the fact that this resistance may be a reasonable response from a system in equilibrium that feels no motivation to adjust. The currency of the computer profession is change and analytic specialists often work from the viewpoint that it is generally desirable in itself. Since, however, change programs are almost certain to be ineffectual unless the unfreezing stage has been worked through, the systems developer *must* take on, as part of his or her function, the creation of a climate for change. Sometimes this climate builds itself—for example, an urgent problem involving substantial cost or profits can unfreeze a manager very quickly.

A frozen system will be homeostatic; once unfrozen, however, that system *must* change, must find a new equilibrium. By working to unfreeze the organization, the implementor can coopt its energy and momentum. In marketing terms, one cannot sell change but must make the consumer want to buy; the selling effort must focus on building a "felt need" for which we happen to have the solution.

The refreezing stage explains many semisuccesses in computer applications, projects that have an apparently successful outcome but that lose impetus and sink into oblivion when their sponsor or designer leaves the scene. The system in that situation is not self-sustaining but maintained by the enthusiasm and effort of a single individual. Change needs to be institutionalized by the building of a new and stable equilibrium that supports the change. Again, there are clear implications for building systems such as DSS, which are intended for more than one-shot use—the change must be truly "complete" and the system must be embedded in the organization. This may require training, the assignment of a systems "manager" within the user department, or even new operating procedures. In particular, the change is not complete if the DSS is not consonant with the organization's control and reward systems. Alter, for example, reports that many of the systems he examined had difficulties obtaining the necessary input data if that data were not processed routinely by the department responsible.

The dynamics of the Lewin-Schein model are complex and only casual examples have been given here. R. E. Sorensen and D. E. Zand (1973) used the model in a study of 280 management science projects. Their results suggest that the framework has substantial explanatory power and that the refreezing stage seems most critical in explaining implementation success. Ginzberg's study reinforces these conclusions.

A Strategy for Managing Change

Regardless of its value as a basic paradigm, the Lewin-Schein model lacks detail. D. A. Kolb and A. L. Frohman's (1970) model of the consulting process in organizational development extends it and provides a rich, normative base. [For example, G. L. Urban uses the Kolb-Frohman model in his own implementation of marketing models; his paper "Building Models for Decision Makers" (1974) discusses it in substantial detail and relates it directly to the technical minutiae of a modeling project.]

Like Lewin and Schein, Kolb and Frohman argue that effective organizational change involves working through a series of stages, presented in terms of the consultant's actions. Figure 7-2 shows the Kolb-Frohman model and Urban's reformulation of it in the context of data-based marketing models used as part of a DSS. While systems developers in a company are often internal staff specialists, from a line manager's viewpoint they are generally *outside* consultants and their strategies for action need to recognize this. Action, of course, is not implementation, any more than getting a model up-and-running guarantees its use. The central action stage must be preceded by the establishment of a contract for the venture (this is an elaboration of unfreezing) and followed by evaluation and termination, where the system is linked into the ongoing organizational activities.

Scouting is the stage least directly relevant to implementation (although certainly relevant to consulting in the MIS/DSS area). It involves matching the capabilities of the consultant with the needs of the client-organization. The consultant must avoid predefining the problem in terms of her or his favorite methodologies. Some technical specialists too often assume that *any* problem is solved by their favorite technique.

Entry involves ensuring legitimacy for action: defining the problem situation, the nature of a solution, the criteria for evaluation, and the allocation of responsibilities and resources, even if only at a general level. DSS developers should define their role as being essentially clinical and facilitative, building a climate and commitment for change. Entry requires subtle skills and, in many instances, far more time and effort than any other aspect of implementation. Far too often, analysts respond to the pressure for visible results and focus on formalizing the system, leaving "people" issues to be sorted out later. However, most of the critical decisions are made at entry, particularly in complex projects that involve an innovative DSS with many inputs, users, and applications. Moreover, it is at entry that the client's expectations are set; to some extent implementation *is* the management of expectations—many failures occur not because a "good" system was not delivered, but because the

FIGURE 7-2   *Kolb-Frohman Model of Change and Urban's Re-statement of It in the Context of Marketing Systems. (Priors are preliminary assessments that will be revised as new information becomes available.)*

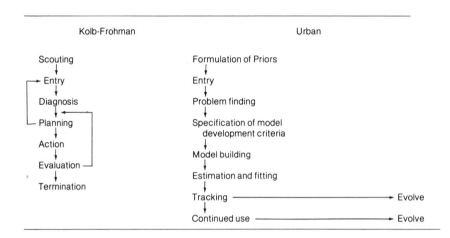

right one was not or because the user had excessively high expectations that led him or her to enthusiastically support the effort but that could never be met in practice.

H. C. Lucas, Jr., and R. B. Plimpton (1972) provide a case study of how the entry stage should be managed. They describe a technically simple MIS built for the United Farm Workers Union (the simplicity of the system meant, of course, that action was brief and easily handled). Lucas and his co-workers diagnosed the state of the client-system and found that the long-service, older, professional core of the UFW would need careful unfreezing—that while they might not actively resist the change in operations and style implicit in the system, they were clearly not motivated to accept it. The MIS team arranged a retreat at which they presented a simple design plan with the statement that they would feel unhappy if at least half the plan were not rejected and redefined by the UFW personnel. In this way, the criticisms, restatements, and definitions provided by the UFW group shifted the change program from being externally brought in toward being self-motivated and under their own control and initiation. As a tactic for unfreezing, this approach seems generally valuable.[9] Urban (1974) similarly designed a simple "Mod 1" model for a family planning agency.[10] This model was overgeneral and incomplete, but by

[9]It was used by Lucas and his co-workers only after the project came close to collapsing. The group had acted up to then as outside experts, administering questionnaires and making formalized proposals. They were surprised when a key meeting they had scheduled was cancelled and it became clear that the union workers viewed them as intrusive and unresponsive. At this point, Lucas and his team began again.

[10]Urban's article, "A Model for the Management of a Family Planning System" (1974), richly illustrates how Kolb and Frohman's behavioral model can be translated to a technical context. He spent substantial effort on entry and on termination; the actual

getting the user group to determine whether the errors in output were due to faults in the model or to some aspect of the wider environment that the user group had not identified, Urban threw the responsibility for developing a better model onto the users, committing and involving them.

The following list of issues to be resolved in entry is synthesized from a range of empirical studies, several of which explicitly used the implementation strategy implied by the Kolb-Frohman model. Successful entry requires:

1.   A felt need.

    a.   The implementor must make sure that the problem to be worked on is visible and seen as relevant.

    b.   The implementor must make sure that the client has a motive and commitment for action.

2.   Definition of goals in operational terms.

    a.   What are the criteria for "success"?

    b.   What are the priorities and trade-offs?

    c.   What "key indicators" can be used to measure progress and accomplishment?

3.   A contract for change. This involves a "deal" between designer and client that establishes:

    a.   "Trust"—personal, professional, or political.

    b.   Mutual understanding.

    c.   Mutual respect for each other's style, investment, and needs.

    d.   Realistic, mutual expectations.

4.   Diagnosis and resolution of resistance to change. This involves:

    a.   Including *users* as well as the *client* in implementation. (Designers often ignore the *secondary* users, groups who are indirectly affected by the system, such as the people responsible for collecting certain input data.)

    b.   Recognizing that resistance is a signal needing response, not a pathology to be eliminated by fiat, power, or endplays.

5.   Initial allocation of resources and responsibilities. This involves:

    a.   Meaningful user involvement.

    b.   The development of a team.

---

building of the model required only a few days but entry involved several months. A rough rule of thumb, based on the authors' experience, is that 70 percent of the elapsed time for a DSS is likely to be spent on entry.

This list is arid shorthand for a complex process (see Ginzberg, 1975, and Urban, 1974, for further discussion of entry). The characteristics and behavior necessary in the implementor for the entry process to be successful correspond closely to Schein's definition of a "process consultant" who must know "how to diagnose and establish helping relationships," who is an expert at getting a feel for a situation while at the same time being able to get people working together and to make goals and procedures operational.

One formal issue, which obviously must be resolved in entry, is the question of who pays for the system. We recommend that, where possible, the user should bear the major costs of development, if only because this certainly ensures commitment and joint responsibility. Many companies have well-established policies for "charging out" development costs. It may be that these should be used for EDP projects where the time and level of effort required for implementation can be accurately predicted, but for an evolutionary venture that is also an invention, this may be unsuitable. In any case, the question of paying for all or part of the costs must be dealt with at the entry stage.

The entry stage also provides the basis for evaluation. In many projects no real definition of or criteria for evaluating success is ever made. The venture is justified on the basis of the standard polite fictions of saving x dollars on clerical personnel and increasing the work load by y percent. The *real* impetus for the project may remain a hidden agenda—the sponsor's belief that the system will lead to "better" decisionmaking. After the event, when the development costs and time are their customary large fraction over budget, it is too late to open up the hidden agenda and argue that the system is a "success." Evaluation of a completed project can really be made meaningful only by formalizing—*before* the system is even designed—a "deal" or "contract" that includes some definition for success; this would require specifying "key indicators," variables that the consultant and client agree can be used as surrogate measures for "better decisionmaking." Evaluation cannot be an expost facto audit. The key indicators provide a basis for monitoring the progress of the implementation effort and identifying when the system is complete. For example, Ginzberg (1975) identified a number of cases where, even after the event, the designer and user had very different perceptions of the aims for the system and the degree to which it was successful. "Success" is contingent on intent, and the responsibility of the system developer is to ensure that there is joint resolution of the contingency. M. Radnor et al. (1970), whose approach to implementation is much more analytic and technical than ours, argue in a similar direction: they point to the relative difficulty of measuring the results of OR/MS activities and strongly suggest that the predesign stage (approximating entry) is where the project evaluation criteria must be established. Only then can nonoperational goals be formalized and any incongruence between the client and designer, in terms of goals and expectations, be resolved. As we discussed in Chapter 6, entry and the predesign cycle of decision analysis are inseparably linked.

Chapter 8 discusses evaluation in more detail. It is worth stressing here that a DSS generally has a qualitative impact on the decision process or task; it may or may not directly reduce costs and it can be difficult to identify the direct impact of the system on profits and performance. It is therefore critical to pin down the criteria for evaluation at entry. In the PMS case, this was not done and while the system was in the end a success, its evolution and political fortunes were at times badly damaged by that fact. Its critics pointed to the costs of the DSS, its relatively low initial usage, and that it did not lead to the savings in personnel promised in the original proposal. The defenders of PMS inevitably sounded defensive in their claims that, while all this was true, the system seemed to be improving the overall quality of analysis by the portfolio managers and the performance of the department.

The diagnosis, planning, and action stages (see Figure 7-2) essentially correspond to the design process discussed in Chapter 6. The termination stage applies perhaps more to DSS than to almost any other type of information system or model. For example, an inventory ordering system is complete when it generates correct and complete answers and when its users have been adequately trained. With a DSS such as Brandaid or PMS, early use of the "operational" system will be fairly exploratory and it will take time for it to be integrated into its organizational context. This refreezing obviously requires the implementor to nurture the system; the DSS is "complete" only when it is self-sustaining. Ginzberg's finding, cited earlier, that designers and users often differ in their view of how successful a system is, reflects a general tendency to overlook the importance of termination. The DSS, up to that point, has been an R & D venture; now it is "operational" and if the designer leaves the scene he or she may feel it is a success. However, exposed to the stresses of everyday organizational life, the system too often turns out to be organizationally infeasible—it is *not* complete and the designer needs to remain to help in this key final stage of evolution and integration.

EXAMPLES OF DSS IMPLEMENTATION

Most of the DSS we have studied were relatively well implemented. (Of course, the failures are undocumented and memory of them suppressed.) There are several factors that may explain this:

1. Many of the DSS we have examined have been initiated by the user department, either by a staff specialist or a senior manager. This means there is already a "felt need" and momentum for change.

2. The user group played a leading role in the design and implementation process; the consultant-designer interacted closely with them, especially in the decision analysis stage; this led to joint commitment and to a facilitative relationship.

3. The DSS designers have—so far—invariably been knowledgeable about the manager's functional area.

These factors may well have been fortuitous. So far, DSS implementors have "skimmed the market" and taken on only interesting projects where managers are actively supportive and the organization competent.

Several DSS (including PMS and Brandaid) have been implemented in more than one organization. A common pattern in the evolving learning and strategy of the system developer has been to ensure that the DSS is owned by the organization and not the consultant. The first time each system was implemented, there was no single person in the user department identified with and responsible for the system. This made termination very difficult; no organizational linkage and "home" for the DSS had been created during implementation. For example, there was no manager of the system who could take charge of education and coordinate the further evolution of the DSS. In those two instances, the next time the (in this case, external) consultant negotiated a proposal to implement this or a similar system, he insisted—during entry—that the organization assign a system manager, generally drawn from among the potential users [that is, a portfolio manager or senior research analyst (PMS) or a brand manager or senior marketing staff member (Brandaid)]. This development is fully consistent with the Kolb-Frohman paradigm. It makes sure the DSS belongs to the organization. It facilitates institutionalization of the system and encourages the user group to take part in design and evolution.

One DSS, the Venture Analysis System (VAS) was implemented in three settings, two in the same organization. (This example is heavily disguised to protect confidentiality.) VAS is an interactive system with a fairly large data base on real estate and underwriting investments. It is used to plan new investments such as re-insurance and mortgaging and short-term borrowing. The first implementation of the system (VAS-A) followed an all too familiar pattern. Technical problems with a new graphics terminal delayed the system by more than a year. Its original sponsor had left the company by then. The costs of development were almost double the estimate and even after the system was operational there were software glitches. Top management ordered a detailed evaluation of VAS; supporters of the system justified it by arguing that it was the first step toward professional management and exploitation of quantitative methods and such it had to be taken on faith. Several users viewed VAS as indispensable.

VAS is still in use in this organization, 4 years after its inception. At least two managers were fired, partly as a result of the costs and political infighting it generated, and one senior executive has publicly stated he intends to get the system removed. The consultant who implemented VAS no longer deals with this organization. He accepts that most of the problems the system encountered could have been avoided. He feels he paid far too little attention to training and handing over the system to the user department. VAS was not well understood by most of the managers and their overall attitude was defensive.

The second installation of this DSS (VAS-B) also encountered many technical problems. VAS had been extended to handle additional types of investment (commodities and commercial paper) and to use minicomputers as the "front end" to the company's large-scale IBM 370. It was also well behind schedule. Nonetheless, the implementation was far less difficult. The consultant had emphasized the risks VAS-B involved (in the first situation he had glossed over many of these since both he and the internal sponsor of the DSS were anxious to sell its merits to the senior management). Management accepted the fact that the system would require several years of usage before its benefits could be fully evaluated. The assistant vice-president for financial planning took charge of VAS-B, scheduling regular seminars and feedback sessions with the system users and coordinating the development of additional reports and analytic routines. While it took at least 18 months before all the problems and complaints were resolved, there was a remarkable lack of strain. The assistant vice-president stated on several occasions that the company was fully committed to VAS-B and regarded it as a long-term *investment.*

The third installation (VAS-C) went one step further. There were few technical problems to be dealt with so that all the parties involved were able to concentrate their efforts on implementation. A manager for the VAS-C system was appointed with complete responsibility for it (including a budget and job description). Substantial attention was paid to introducing the system to the managers. A staff specialist acted as an "integrating agent," helping to sell VAS-C to the managers in the company. In some cases, he would act as a "chauffeur," working with the manager at the computer terminal, typing in commands for him, and offering advice and interpretation.[11]

An important aspect of the VAS experiences was the rather belated recognition by the consultant that his decision needed to be complemented by an explicit implementation strategy that reduced his own visibility and responsibility for the system. One of the main roles of the system manager–coordinator in VAS-B and VAS-C was to act as an integrator and to provide meaningful training. In VAS-A, education was formal and tacked on late in implementation. In the other two situations, it was far more pervasive, with, for example, regular workshops at which users were able to gripe (at the system manager) and compare notes on VAS—after a while, some managers began to describe new uses of the system or clever tricks they had developed.

The consultant-designer of VAS has built several other DSS. He now emphasizes to clients the elusive issues of entry and termination. In one instance, he turned down a profitable and interesting contract when it became apparent that the organization was unwilling to allocate a manager's time to implementing the DSS. He felt that this reflected a lack of real commitment and understanding of the experimental nature of the venture. Interestingly, the organization contacted him within a few weeks and agreed to his request.

The GADS system (see Chapter 5) is a prototype DSS used for several one-shot decisions; it has never been institutionalized in any organization. Nonetheless, the experiments using GADS carried out by the IBM Research Laboratory, San Jose, California, have produced several results of direct relevance to implementation. B. F. Grace (1975), for example, has focused on training users. She concludes that most managers or professionals have a "low tolerance for training" and generally do not expect to use a computer terminal directly (this seems to reflect a fear of making mistakes and an association of the terminal with typing). The IBM group made frequent use of a chauffeur, a skilled intermediary who knew the system in great detail. This "integrating agent" (see J. Bennett, 1976) acted as (1) an *exegetist* who explained the DSS to the user, (2) a *crusader* who "sold" the system, largely through personal enthusiasm, (3) a *confidant* who built up the users' self-confidence and acted as an advisor, and (4) a *teacher* who provided personalized instruction.

Much of the integrating agent's activities relate to the entry and termination stages.[12] Experience with GADS, VAS, and PMS demonstrates the immense leverage of such an integrator in introducing technically based change in an organiza-

---

[11]Keen (1976) argues that a DSS designed to aid senior managers may require a skilled intermediary who, among other activities, can quickly modify or extend the data structures or analytic routines, that whereas a system such as PMS is built around a reasonably stable task, a DSS for corporate planning is far more *ad hoc*. Flexible software languages such as APL or the GMIS virtual machine system (see Donovan and Madnick, 1976, and Chapter 5) are necessary for the system to be responsive to situational needs. Most of the DSS discussed in this book were designed to support middle-level managers; for such "institutional" DSS, an intermediary is not always needed, but he or she may be essential for *ad hoc* systems.

[12]It must be admitted that such an integrating agent is not at all easy to find! The mixture of technical, interpersonal, and business experience required is more likely to be found in a senior manager than in a relatively junior staff specialist.

tion. Also, integrators are far more likely to be needed for a DSS than for most other types of information systems, in that usage is self-paced, and largely self-initiated and self-directed. While the implementor can provide specific instructions (probably in a formal manual) for using an inventory reporting system, the semi-structured tasks for which DSS are intended preclude such predefinition.

A CLINICAL APPROACH TO IMPLEMENTATION

The integrating agent is obviously a facilitator of organizational change. The whole process of implementation requires this facilitation, which is, in many respects, based on opportunism. Since there seem to be no absolute rules for successful implementation, the change agent must above all be able to *diagnose* the situation and identify the factors relevant to this particular venture. For example, if there have been previous political crises about who controls the computer resource or about large expenditures on a system in trouble, then these historical factors will influence the natural outcome of any new implementation effort (probably in a direction that hinders success). A clinical approach is needed both because this sort of factor is not easily apparent and will require some ferreting out and because there will be a huge variety of such variables, some of which will exert substantial pressure and some of which will be of only minor relevance. Furthermore, the same factor may be critical in one situation and unimportant in another. The responsibility for sorting out what is happening has to be taken by the implementor. The consequences of not doing so can be large and painful.

Outsiders who remain outsiders can rarely be effective clinicians. They have no sense of "background" features, the historical, political, and personal issues that are rarely discussed but obvious to insiders. They lack perspective and in many instances will get a very one-sided view of the situation simply because their main source of information is a particular manager or group whose opinions they cannot easily validate.

Effective implementors build trust; they become insiders. They can accomplish this by being technically useful, personally credible, or because of their obvious understanding of the organization and of the managers' needs and processes. They *must* be good listeners. Much of the value of descriptive analysis of decision processes (see Chapter 6) is to help implementors build up a clear and complete picture of the situation, to empathize with the users of the DSS and to build links with them. Far too often, designers trained in the technical tradition deliberately isolate themselves from managers and narrow their focus. This is especially true in relation to political issues. As M. K. Starr points out in "The Politics of Management Science" (1971), the analytic view of truth is "0,1" while the manager's "truth" always has a political context; Starr further argues that the analyst must also be a political scientist who includes managerial attitudes in the choice of a solution, an argument parallel to the one made here.[13] Starr's example is especially relevant in that some systems designers consciously choose to ignore political forces even

---

[13]Although Wildavsky (1964) deals with federal budgeting, his arguments seem equally relevant to the implementation of computer-based decision aids. He emphasizes the need for political as well as economic rationality. See also Keen and Gerson (1977).

though they are readily apparent. C. F. Gibson and J. S. Hammond (1974) provide a fairly typical example of this. They describe a large-scale project in the corporate planning department of a major manufacturing company. Progress during the first 3 months was excellent and the staff viewed it as a very effective venture. It was, however, abruptly terminated. The model built by the staff was technically well designed and the logistical problems were handled well. The economic issues involved were understood by both the design group and the planning staff. Moreover, the operational characteristics of the model were clearly suited to the planners and analysts who used its outputs in preparing their recommendations. Their report was skillfully presented and, indeed, very well received by Mr. Cabot, the vice-president who had commissioned the model. Despite all this, the implementation effort had no impact on top management's decisions except to arouse their anger. Unfortunately, Mr. Cabot had aspirations for succeeding to the recently vacated presidency of the company and was using the modeling project, *as the design team was almost gleefully aware*, as a way to "preempt other departments in the planning process and later to shine in front of the board" by presenting the very impressive results of the model. He was shot down and the corporate planning department bore the brunt of his dismay and top management's irritation.

The key symptoms in this project, what Gibson and Hammond call the informal social contingencies, were known and ignored. The design group presumably had not thought through the direct relevance of such outside, nontechnical forces for their own actions. The political dimension is not *always* relevant to an implementation effort, but here it was, and the design team should have recognized it as being so. To explain the failure of the project as being due to nonrational "politics" is not to excuse it. The lack of a clinical definition of their role led the designers into a venture they could not control and the outcome was once again one of unanticipated consequences.

Of course, political undercurrents in an organization are not easy to pick out at times. In particular, hidden agendas are intendedly secret. This fact reinforces the need for a clinical perspective. Gibson points out, in a study of a large-scale project in a bank (1975), that the analyst will generally be given an overrationalized explanation of organizational practices and that the researcher (implicitly, too, the practitioner) must consciously try to dig beneath the surface.[14]

CONCLUSION: THE ROLE OF THE IMPLEMENTOR

A role is mainly a set of expectations about how to behave. In general, the expectations of graduating OR or MIS specialists have been that their role should be that of a technician, or that any difficulties they encounter with the managers who use the tools they provide come from the managers' inadequacies, not theirs. In the case of DSS this is a particularly damaging view. What has been presented in this chapter is an outline for a more effective role. It really requires little new knowledge, only small adjustments of attitude that lead to large changes in outcome. The role of "facilitator" and manager of change is in some ways an easier one than that of the

---

[14]The "action research" strategy he recommends seems especially useful at the entry stage. It is diagnostic and involves the outsider working hard to become a trusted insider.

much-beleagured, ever-struggling expert in an alien land. This does not argue against technical ability; indeed the argument here takes technical skill as a given. However, techniques are a means, not an end, and must be matched to context.

We conclude this argument with a convenient, though arbitrary dichotomy, between technician and implementor (see Table 7-2).

Table 7-2 is largely self-explanatory. The technician's role is an isolated one, strongly centered around expertise. This view of change as a process of "diffusion of innovation" is that of NASA; potential users are kept informed of new developments and techniques with the assumption that they will recognize their value and adopt them.

Implementation will never be easy. A complex DSS is an invention. It has never existed before and we have very few guidelines for building it. Now that the "easy" triumphs have been accomplished—the automation of payrolls and accounts receivable—future innovations, especially in the DSS area, will involve mainly qualitative improvements in decisionmaking that will demand substantial adjustments in the behavior and attitudes of the system users. A DSS can never be just plugged in. In all the examples we have quoted in this book, the design and implementation process was lengthy, involved many adjustments and negotiations, and demanded a flexible, evolutionary strategy. While the issues we have discussed in this chapter apply to EDP, OR, MIS, and, in fact, to any technologically based innovation in organizations, they are critically relevant in implementing DSS. Perhaps the most important single implication is the potential impact that the designer personally can have if and only if she or he adopts the role we have suggested, that of a clinical, facilitative change agent. In many discussions with outstanding practitioners—the same ones who say that they cannot articulate any general principles for implementation—this aspect of their behavior is most obvious. They regard themselves as there to help managers, and understand and em-

TABLE 7-2   Distinctions between Technicians
and Implementors

	Technicians	Implementors
Locus of effort	Design	Entry, evaluation, termination
Output	Product	Service
Attitude toward change process	Diffusion of innovation	Process consultant, change agent
Main skill areas	Knowledge and techniques	Diagnosis, facilitation, and techniques
Assumptions about the decision process	Prescriptive, analytic	Descriptive
Slogan	"Have technique, will travel"	"It all depends . . ."

pathize with them even where they aim at changing the ways in which the managers operate. In describing particular implementations, they generally start off with some statement such as, "What you have to understand is that a couple of years ago. . . ." They have a very subtle sense of the background features, the contingencies of the situation, and spend much time ensuring they themselves are well linked into the organizational context.

Implementation requires a *strategy*—enthusiasm and skill in design are not enough. The main reason we have so little insight into effective implementation is that it is clearly a contingent process. For this reason, the system developer must be a good clinician, needing the following skills:

1. An understanding of the manager's world and perspective; this essentially requires a descriptive insight into the decision process.

2. "Process consultancy"; this involves the ability to facilitate change and build credibility with managers.

3. Broad organizational knowledge; this involves the ability to synthesize the elements of the Leavitt "diamond"—task, technology, people, and structure (see H. A. Leavitt, 1965).

The paradigm of implementation as a social change process is a robust one that several practitioners have explicitly used with great effect. It provides a general but precise strategy that focuses on the key factors that very often determine the success of a system:

1. Mutual commitment and realistic expectations by designers, sponsors, and users.

2. Recognizing and resolving resistance to change.

3. Institutionalizing the completed system.

These issues are relevant to implementation of information systems in general, but are especially important for DSS, in that these systems explicitly aim at some degree of organizational change since they focus on the *effectiveness* of decisionmaking. Efficiency generally involves more economical ways of doing the same thing; effectiveness involves learning, adaptation, and rethinking.

The main difference between the technical tradition and the social change paradigm is that the latter emphasizes the beginning and ending stages in implementation when "nothing" happens. No code is written, no test runs are made; instead there is a lot of talk and mutual assessment of motives, assumptions, and intentions. The formal design of the system is meshed into its context.

Implementation is the soft underbelly of information system development. We cannot stress too much how critical it is for the developers of a DSS to consciously view themselves as change agents and to make sure they understand the social reality in which they act. In this brief chapter we have space only to touch briefly on this issue. It is critical and we recommend that all managers and practitioners review their own understanding of the implementation process and their skills as facilitators of change. Ineffectual implementation of the "right" design is an inexcusable waste of energy, resources, and personal credibility.

EIGHT

INTRODUCTION

Evaluation is perhaps the most difficult aspect of DSS development, especially since such systems are evolutionary in nature and generally lack neatly defined completion dates.[1] As P. Andreoli and J. Steadman (1975) point out in their discussion of PMS, it may take several years before a DSS is fully in place and a complete evaluation meaningful. Moreover, as with most types of computer projects, there is all too often a reluctance to take time to review what took place and a pressure to move on to the next crisis. Turnover of personnel may also result in few of the original design team remaining when the system is "complete."

Some of these problems are unavoidable; others can be overcome if the critical importance of evaluation and the methods by which it can be accomplished are recognized. The decision-centered approach to design and the implementation strategies presented in the preceding two chapters *require* a formal evaluation methodology. A DSS aims at "improving" decisionmaking; successful completion thus depends on:

1. A prior definition of "improvement."

2. A means of monitoring progress toward the predefined goal.

3. A formal review process to determine when the system is complete.

All three of these are, of course, aspects of implementation as much as of evaluation; they correspond to the entry, evaluation (here equivalent to monitoring), and termination stages in the Kolb-Frohman model (see Figure 7-2). In this chapter, we will focus on the *methodological* aspects of implementation/evaluation and in particular on the definition of "key indicators" (criteria for assessing improvement) and on the type of data to be collected for evaluation. We present a "smorgasbord" of methods; no one criterion is likely to be sufficient to evaluate a DSS.

The key to successful evaluation is an explicit *prior* plan, developed during the entry stage. This plan states, often only in broad outline, what is to be ac-

---

[1]See Urban, "Building Models for Decision Makers" (1974), and Keen, "Computer-based Decision Aids: The Evaluation Problem" (1975). It is worth noting that all of the systems described in Chapter 5 evolved through use and experience; choosing *when* to evaluate them was as difficult as choosing *how*.

complished; of course, making the more qualitative or contentious goals operational can be hard but it is essential. If we cannot specify *exactly* why we want to build a system and what *changes* it should lead to, there is a real question as to whether we should proceed and strong doubt about a successful outcome.

A second key requirement is that the project be kept to a manageable size. The elapsed time should be short (we suggest a maximum of a year, if possible). Whatever the overall length, the time between major visible events that are to be reported to senior management (the completion of phase 1, the delivery of specified outputs, and so forth) should be about 3 months. These suggestions are, obviously, a little arbitrary, but project length is a major constraint on evaluation (and on implementation in general; throughout this chapter, it should be assumed that our arguments apply to evaluation-within-implementation and implementation-as-controlled-by-evaluation). In a long project, members of the design team and the user group may leave for other jobs (S. A. Alter, 1975, cites turnover of key personnel as a major problem in his survey of DSS developments). In addition, the environment and the problem definition on which the design was based will change. It seems best to divide a system into self-contained phases, review accomplishment at the end of each stage, and use that evaluation to make any necessary adjustments and to define the next phase.

An effective evaluation strategy is the key to controlling the development process. We assert that the best way to build big systems is *not* to do so, but instead to start from a smaller and shorter implementation effort and *evolve* the big system.

Some of the issues for evaluation of DSS are the same as for any computer-based project. Others are very different. In particular, a DSS is designed to address a relatively unstructured problem with—by definition—no clear criteria for assessing performance or definition of *exactly* how the decision is to be supported. As a result, the effectiveness of the system largely depends on its *evolving* usage; the preliminary stages of decision analysis and construction of the initial DSS (with the constant involvement of the manager concerned) almost always result in a new level of awareness and understanding of the decision the DSS supports—and sometimes even a redefinition of the "real" problem. This learning is a central aspect of DSS development and usage. It can, in extreme cases, make the DSS obsolete. It is hard to calibrate and put a value on. It may also make evaluation extremely difficult, in that there may be no "final" system; the DSS dynamically evolves and becomes more effective as the users adjust to or exploit it. PMS, for example, initially was viewed by some skilled observers as a failure but after only a few more months of usage, others saw it as clearly successful. The system as an artefact had not changed but the system as a human-machine combination in an organizational context *had* changed. This experiential aspect of a DSS reinforces the need for evaluation as an ongoing monitoring rather than simple auditing.

Learning is qualitative and incremental. It may be apparent only through a manager's subjective opinion that she or he now has "a better grasp of the problem" and is able "to consider more alternatives." A system that evolves as the user learns (and that in itself facilitates such learning) is a *service* rather than a product. Products can generally be valued in terms of cost/benefit and rate of return analysis used for most capital investments. Thus, for example, evaluation of data processing projects tends to use cost/benefit criteria. The costs are often ones that can be "displaced," for example, the existing human costs (clerks) are replaced by (hopefully) lower computer costs. Such cost displacement is usually measurable and the payoff from the system easy to identify.

A DSS seldom provides substantial cost displacement. It is intended to *help—not replace—*managers and to improve their decisionmaking. Evaluation of DSS thus requires measuring change and, more particularly, "better" decisions. There can be no simple technique for doing this. We suggest a smorgasbord of eight methodologies to be matched to the specific situation. These involve examining:

1. *Decision outputs*

2. *Changes in the decision process*

3. *Changes in managers' concepts of the decision situation*

4. *Procedural changes*

5. *Classical cost/benefit analysis*

6. *Service measures*

7. *Managers' assessment of the system's value*

8. *Anecdotal evidence.*

Each of these eight methods cannot be used in detail in every evaluation process. Some are more important in a given situation than others, and, obviously, if a system is specifically intended to save hard dollars, then that is the *main* issue in evaluation; changes in the decision process, for example, while possibly beneficial, are irrelevant in deciding how well this system's *aims* have been accomplished. We maintain, however, that evaluation must use more than one technique, and that each one mentioned here should be tried, if only briefly, and rejected explicitly as a means of evaluation on solid grounds and not because it is awkward to use or because it suggests negative results from the DSS.

One of the main requirements in the entry stage is for the designers and user group to reach consensus on the set of evaluation methods to be selected from the smorgasbord. Each of these eight are examined below, with illustrations to clarify the key features.

DECISION OUTPUTS

The ideal measures for evaluating a system that aims at better decisions is, of course, the actual result of the decisions. For example, since PMS should help managers improve investment decisions, one could compare the yield and rate of return on their portfolios before and after the introduction of the system. Unfortunately this ideal measure is rarely meaningful. Even if the yield and return were higher, the improvement could be due to a variety of factors—the DSS, a rise in the overall stock market, or just a Hawthorne effect (where any new gimmick would, in this case, cause the managers to pay more attention to their portfolios). In practice, too, the system will *not* necessarily lead to dramatic improvements in decision output. It is naive to expect, for example, CIS (described in Chapter 5) to directly lead to product plans so much better than the ones before the DSS was introduced that any evaluation would conclude the system had *caused* the improvement. The plans involve many organizational interdependencies and environmental uncertainties; the decision process is complex and the outputs are not directly relatable to the quality of the decision process. Of course, wherever possible, one should evaluate changes in the decision output; they are the most striking evidence of improved decisionmaking *if* other environmental or organizational issues can be factored out.

With some types of DSS (for example, in cash management and certain production planning systems), it is possible to show a strong causal relationship between the DSS and improved decision outputs. However, with many of the more complex decisions in which a DSS can usefully be built, it seems unlikely to us that *any* planning aid, model, DSS, or organizational change program will cause immediate and large improvements, and hence it is foolhardy for a designer to encourage evaluation of a DSS on that criterion alone. We recommend in such cases that output measures be included in evaluation but never viewed as the dominant issue.

The laundry equipment case, described in Chapter 1, provides an example of how output measures could be used in evaluation (the system designer, one of the authors of this book, had not yet, alas, realized the breadth that evaluation should cover). The laundry equipment system was built as an experiment. One of the company's key decisions was how much product to make in a given month. Profits were very sensitive to inventory levels and profit margins were small (about $20 on a $150 appliance). Overproduction meant that products would have to be dumped at virtually no profit, while, of course, underproduction would lead to a loss of market share that would be hard to regain in the company's very competitive industry. The development of the monthly production plan thus reflected a classic conflict in such organizations; the marketing group wanted all products in all models in all warehouses while manufacturing aimed at one model—white, no extras, standard size.

The issue of evaluation arose only after the DSS had been successfully installed. The question to be answered was: Are the new plans, made with the aid of the DSS, better than the old ones? "Better" decisions could be measured in terms of several variables: (1) increased profits; (2) lower inventory levels, with the same degree of service; (3) fewer backorders; and (4) less inventory on hand at model changeover time. The obvious difficulty is that many factors other than the DSS affect these variables—competitive actions, economic trends, a new model design that catches on with the public, and so on.

Had we followed our present prescription for implementation and during the entry stage defined key indicators for evaluation, this problem would have been immensely reduced. We would have had a list of the changes in output (for example, inventory levels) that the parties involved would accept as circumstantial evidence of "better" decisions. Historical data for each factor on the list would have been collected, over a period long enough to place any short-term fluctuations in perspective. Actually, in the laundry equipment case, data on inventory levels (as a percent of sales) and backorders had been gathered for the 3 years prior to the introduction of the DSS and were updated as part of the monitoring of the use of the system over the following years. There was a clear improvement in these levels, which *implied* that the DSS had indeed improved the quality of the production plans. The change in output was not proof, but reasonable evidence in favor of the system. It needed to be complemented by other evaluation measures and, of course, it would have been far more striking and convincing if defined in terms of key indicators rather than identified after the event.

CHANGES IN THE DECISION PROCESS

A second approach to evaluation is to look at changes in the way decisions are made. This is done irrespective of the *output* of the decision, the argument being that better decisions will occur if the process by which they are reached is improved. There can be no proof that the new method of arriving at a decision is better; the test is then one of plausibility—do the sponsors of the system accept that this is a more effective process than the original decisionmaking activity?

The laundry equipment system led to major changes in how the production plan was generated. Regardless of the improvements in inventory levels and back-orders, a strong case could be—and was—made that better decisions were now being made because of the clear improvement in the decision *process.* The former process had an implicit satisficing rule: the first acceptable solution to be obtained was implemented. "Acceptable" was defined as a solution that the marketing and production groups could live with. Using the DSS, the managers invariably went beyond this first solution and examined additional alternatives. Sometimes these tested the sensitivity of earlier solutions to minor changes in decision variables, but more often they were exploratory—investigation of "interesting" alternatives or il-lustrations by either the marketing or production groups of some line of argument (or counterargument). The DSS reduced the cost of considering one more alter-native from several days of detailed hand computation to a few minutes and as a result encouraged far more wide-ranging search. Obviously, analysis of more alter-natives does not necessarily mean better decisions, but this change in the decision process was clearly both caused by the DSS and likely to improve the quality of the production plans.

This strategy for evaluation is made much more convincing if the decision-centered approach to design presented in Chapter 6 is used. This explicitly includes a normative model that defines a "better" decision process. At the end of the design/implementation stage, a new *descriptive* model can be developed and com-pared with the normative one. The comparison should show very clearly if different types of information and analysis are now used, response time improved, calcula-tions and search more consistent, and so forth. Of course, it is the a priori definition of the normative model that makes such evidence most meaningful.

In the laundry equipment case, there was no predefined normative model; the comparison was between two descriptive models—before and after the introduction of the DSS. However, whichever approach is used, this mode of evaluation re-quires, above all, insight into how decisions are made, and the methodologies in-volved are those of the behavioral rather than the technical sciences.

Since changes in the decision process are generally a central issue in DSS development, we need to extend and refine techniques for measuring them. One ef-fective approach has been the use of "traces." Much of the description of PMS in Chapter 5 is based on traces made by C. B. Stabell, M. J. Ginzberg, and Andreoli and Steadman. All interactions with the DSS at the terminal are recorded and saved by the computer on a disk file. These indicate the identity of the user, the date and time, and the function used (LIST, HISTO). A trace is recorded for every input re-quest. Special programs were written to analyze the traces, which now amount to 5 years of detailed data on PMS. Stabell (1974) used them to examine individual dif-ferences in system usage and Andreoli and Steadman (1975) to study the evolution of the system. In addition, the managers of the Great Eastern Bank have used them periodically to monitor the status of their system; for example, after a series of seminars had been provided for the portfolio managers to encourage the use of PMS in account reviews, the traces provided a detailed indication of their impact.

Traces provide access to the decision process in a way, and to a depth, that has not been available before. The software and computer overhead required to record them are inexpensive. However, it seems essential not to implement them without informing users that they exist—traces are a form of surveillance and it would be an invasion of privacy to generate them in secret. Even when used openly, there can be other problems in this area; individuals may be unwilling to try out a DSS if they feel their mistakes are being monitored. Nonetheless, traces are one of the most powerful methodologies so far developed for the evaluation of the qualitative impact of DSS.

CHANGES IN MANAGERS' CONCEPTS OF THE DECISION PROCESS

Looking at the decision process involves a focus on "observables," such as the choice of information, the number of alternatives considered, and so on. What goes on in the manager's mind may be more important but is obviously far more difficult to access. The growing interest in cognitive processes within MIS research reflects the relevance of an understanding of human information processing for the development of computer-based information tools. A main reason for providing a DSS is to extend managers' "bounded rationality" in tasks that involve complexity of information and concepts. The DSS is partly a system for learning—better decision-making should result from better understanding, richer insights, and more extensive assessment and synthesis of data. We need to be able to monitor and evaluate such learning. This so far has been close to impossible. The methodologies available are clumsy and the results they generate not too convincing. Further research, however, should improve them.

Several researchers have examined cognitive processes in relation to DSS. Stabell (1974) used complexity theory (see Chapter 3) to study the information sources used by the portfolio managers of the Big Western Bank. He employed a structured interview technique together with the Kelly Role Repertoire test, a variant of the Q-test methodology widely used in social psychological research.[2] Stabell's study was a research project but his conclusions indicate the value of this approach for evaluation of a DSS. The normative model underlying the design of PMS emphasizes financial portfolio theory (see Chapter 5) in which diversification is a key concept. Stabell found that, even after the introduction of the DSS, the managers had an extremely weak idea of diversification and that in fact the system was used in a security-oriented and not portfolio-centered mode of analysis. His evaluation had no direct impact on the Big Western Bank, but it did influence the

---

[2]Kelly's theory of personal constructs argues that a "person's processes are psychologically channelled by the ways in which he anticipates events" and that "each person characteristically evolves, for his convenience in anticipating events, a construct system embracing arousal relationships between constructs" (see Kelly, 1955, p. 46). Such constructs are dichotomous and bipolar (for example, concrete versus abstract or black versus white). Stabell's methodology identified the categories managers use to distinguish among information sources and to describe portfolios.

design and implementation strategy for the Great Eastern Bank's version of PMS; his methodology would help Great Eastern monitor the ongoing evolution of the system and of the managers' learning.

Extension of approaches such as Stabell's will require simple diagnostic techniques for capturing managers' concepts and learning. These will be developed by researchers (see R. T. Keim and R. H. Kilmann, 1975, for examples of such a project[3]). At present, the use of such techniques in real world applications is close to zero.[4] Despite this, any implementor can—and should—try to capture these cognitive processes, if only through questionnaires. As with all the methodologies in our smorgasbord, the key need is to measure the situation before and after the DSS, as realistically as possible, and to use the normative model of better decisionmaking as the basis for assessment.

Other aspects of learning are easier to identify, for example, knowledge, perceived understanding, new insights, and so forth. The development of a DSS focuses the efforts of intelligent people on the need to improve a key decision. That process often clarifies the underlying structure of the problem and can be in itself a rewarding intellectual effort. For example, the initial discussions of PMS pointed up the logic of formal portfolio theory and of such concepts as diversification. As a result, one of the main aims of the system was to extend this learning and encourage managers to deepen their analysis and understanding (Stabell's results, of course, suggest that this goal was not readily met in the early stages of use).

To the extent that learning *is* an objective in any DSS development, it is relevant to evaluation. Unfortunately, measurement techniques for this are close to nonexistent (they are not much more available for evaluating the long-term impact of graduate school curricula on students). In general, though, managers are sensitive to this question and if asked can give a fair assessment of how much the DSS has helped them understand the decision or its context. The case study cited in the discussion of Projector in Chapter 5 provides an example of this. In his evaluation of the system, the main benefits identified by the president of Acrofab were the learning and insights that the system stimulated (of course, it is very difficult to say how much it is worth paying for these benefits).

In addition to changing decision processes and stimulating learning, a DSS often helps change attitudes such as those toward the users' tasks and the use of analytic tools and toward other units of the organization. In the case of Brandaid (see Chapter 5), several organizations decided to implement the system not so much because it would necessarily lead to better decisions but as part of a long-term plan to get the marketing managers to make fuller use of quantitative methods, where suitable, and of existing information sources. (For example, in one company Brandaid was complemented by the development of an on-line information retrieval system linked to a large-scale data bank.) Obviously, in such instances evaluation of the system should center on changes in attitudes (and on learning).

---

[3]Kilmann and McKelvey's (1974) MAPS (Multivariate Analysis Participation and Structure) technology is a questionnaire-based methodology that clusters and matches tasks and people on the basis of attitudinal and cognitive preferences.

[4]One reason for this is organizational resistance to research. "Evaluation" of a system is often reasonably enough viewed as evaluation of its users. The types of instruments discussed here must be made meaningful to their subjects and relevant to their work before they can be integrated into the formal evaluation process.

Attitude changes are relatively easy to measure. Much of the factor research described in Chapter 7 makes use of Likert scales, which are questionnaires that ask respondents to indicate their degree of agreement with such statements as, "The XYZ system has helped me examine more alternatives in my decisionmaking"; a five- or seven-point scale is generally used, with a 1 indicating "completely disagree" and 5 (or 7) "completely agree." Such questionnaires are easy to administer and to analyze.[5] The only danger is that managers may find them intrusive or meaningless. However, this problem should not arise if system developers have from the start stressed the importance of evaluation as part of the implementation process.

Changes in concepts, learning, and attitude, even if measureable, may be hard to place a value on. In many cases they so clearly influence the likely quality of decisions that they *must* be the central focus in evaluation, however difficult this may be. This is not a task that computer specialists and managers have traditionally undertaken. The training and tools for it are lacking; developing them must be a priority for research. It has been clear to us in revisiting the Great Eastern Bank on an annual basis that the users of PMS often value it—and find it exciting—mainly because it has given them new ideas and insights. They now (1977) speak with enthusiasm of getting together for bull sessions where they play with "way out" approaches to thinking about investment decisions. This is exactly the sort of learning that a DSS can provide. It is valuable and therefore should be explicitly evaluated. In practice, however, Great Eastern's management has never systematically collected this information. The portfolio managers regard it as interesting but have not assessed it. They view our focus on it as typical of ivory tower academics. We feel strongly that learning is often not a by-product of a DSS but a valuable and primary contribution it can make. We recognize both that organizations do not, on the whole, share this opinion and that they will (and should) do so only when the tools are available to make it a precise and operationalized aspect of the evaluation process.[6]

PROCEDURAL CHANGES

The first three components of our smorgasbord focus specifically on the elusive issue of decision quality. The other five address this question more indirectly but examine broader areas of concern. For example, procedural changes refer to those activities within the decision process that are in some sense physical, such as the mechanical procedures and the use of such resources as people, machines, and paper. These need to be distinguished from information, analysis, and learning, the

---

[5]The degree to which such measures of attitude reflect actual *behavior* is, however, unclear.

[6]For example, Andreoli and Steadman (1975), when discussing PMS, point out that users did not feel the DSS had influenced their decisionmaking, which they defined in terms of the *choice* of a decision, not the full problem-solving cycle of intelligence, design, and choice. Many managers find it hard to relate to the idea that a DSS may help them clarify the implications of their own assumptions, build a concept of their environment, or formalize their sequence of analysis. This type of learning is also not easily identified, which, of course, makes it difficult to evaluate.

mental components of the process. The distinction is partly between effectiveness and efficiency. Better decisions should be more effective decisions. These are to be obtained by improving the content of the decision process and not the physical procedures.

Procedural changes are observable and can generally be assessed more easily than changes in decisionmaking. For this reason it is too often tempting to emphasize them in evaluation. While they *can* be important, they are not necessarily so. For example, the laundry equipment DSS led to three changes in procedures:

1. Time: The decision process moved from 5 1/2 days of meetings with at least two of the managers involved to 1/2 day with all three, saving 10 man-days per month of upper-middle-management time. As such, this is a small gain in efficiency, worth noting but not worth building the DSS for. Of course, if the managers were to use the time released by the system to solve some other other important new problem, then, arguably, their effectiveness has increased.

2. Human resources: The new decision process freed clerical support personnel for other tasks.

3. Computer resources: Large amounts of time spent printing voluminous computer reports were saved. Of course, this has to be offset against the new charges for conversational support.

These changes are easy to identify but in no way justify the time and effort required to develop the DSS. In this situation, and in most similar semistructured tasks, it would be a strategic mistake to allow the success of the system to be mainly measured in these terms. In structured tasks, on the other hand, especially for operational control, procedural changes may be very valuable; for example, the main impact of EDP has been in exactly this area. Because procedural changes are easy to observe, they are far too often included in evaluation instead of the other more elusive and qualitative components of the smorgasbord.

COST/BENEFIT ANALYSIS

All the types of change we have examined so far in this discussion of the smorgasbord involve costs as well as benefits. Some of these are obvious and easily monitored: salaries, computer resources, and clerical support, for example. Others are less quantifiable, such as time and commitment of managers, and some are hidden, such as the psychological cost of change, the disruption of the organization's equilibrium, and so forth. These "soft" costs are not easily converted into hard dollars but it may be highly misleading to exclude them. Cost/benefit analysis, which on the surface seems an exact and logical method of accounting, is in practice an imprecise art.[7] In any case, the "relevant" costs should be defined as broadly as

---

[7]This is only partly because many of the most relevant items are hard to quantify: political and organizational costs and intangible benefits, for example. More importantly, cost/benefit analysis often requires computations that are too complex to be practicable, so that surrogates and approximations are used instead. These are easily challenged by other interested parties; this tool of economic rationality may thus con-

possible, preferably by a disinterested party, and tracked carefully over the length of the implementation of the project. Intangible costs and benefits *must* be included in this analysis; if they cannot be assessed directly, it is often possible to identify a surrogate transfer price by asking managers how much they would pay to gain the benefit or eliminate the cost.

In the early 1960s cost/benefit analysis became an evangelical movement in many circles. It has proved ineffectual in most areas of public policy (for example, education, health, and government) largely because the intangible factors can rarely be satisfactorily converted to a dollar equivalent. For example, cost/benefit analysis in medicine requires placing a value on human life. A common measure for this has been estimated life earnings, discounted at a specified interest rate. As I. R. Hoos (1972) points out in her scathing attack on the cost/benefit approach, the resulting figures imply that a 21-year-old male is "worth" two baby boys or three baby girls.[8]

The logic of cost/benefit analysis is compelling and the method is well worth using, but only if it is complemented by other modes of evaluation and soft costs and benefits are not artificially translated into dollar equivalents. The process of *identifying* costs is in itself valuable. If approximate values can be attached to them, it may then be useful to look at the percentage of improvement required for a decision to provide a payoff. For example, if a DSS such as that used in the laundry equipment case involves a tangible cost of $300,000 with tangible benefits of $100,000 (from improved procedures), then there is a residual cost of $200,000. It should be easy to calculate how great an improvement in inventory levels or stockouts would be needed to cover this $200,000. If the figure is high (say, 70 percent improvement in existing inventory levels), it is very unlikely that the DSS can generate sufficient savings to justify its cost. On the other hand, if a very small (less than 5 percent) percentage improvement in the inventory levels will yield several million dollars savings, then one may feel more comfortable that the balance of the costs can be recovered through the use of the DSS.

Cost/benefit analysis is often used to justify a proposal for a computer system. The sponsor will promise huge savings from procedural changes, understate tangible costs, and ignore intangible ones. After the event, when the promised savings do not materialize, it is too late to justify the venture in terms of intangible benefits such as improved communication. (The initial implementation of PMS suffered from this problem. The system designers focused on "hard" costs and benefits even though in fact the main impetus for the venture was their belief that it would

flict with political rationality. Wildavsky (1964) makes a convincing case that such techniques are ineffectual and even undesirable for handling large-scale innovative programs that involve multiple interest groups. (PMS was, of course, exactly such a program.) The cost/benefit approach may thus be of most use for small-scale development projects that do not involve crossing departmental boundaries.

[8]Hoos' dissection of systems analysis is essential reading for anyone concerned with "rationalizing" organizational procedures. A key implication of her analysis is that simple, logical techniques such as cost/benefit analysis are immensely appealing and intellectually arguable but their very simplicity ignores political, ethical, and computational constraints.

result in many soft benefits such as improved decision processes.) Cost/benefit analysis of a DSS is most meaningful if the intangible factors are explicitly identified during the entry stage, quantified if possible but not excluded if quantification is infeasible. The key indicators in the implementation strategy presented in Chapter 7 are a direct effort to deal with the extremely difficult problem of intangible benefits. In some situations, where costs are all tangible and benefits qualitative, cost/benefit analysis is virtually meaningless and the evaluation process must focus on changes in outputs, the decision process, and managers' learning.

SERVICE MEASURES

Defining a DSS as a service rather than a product implies some broad criteria for measuring the quality of the system from the users' perspective. These include:

1.   Responsiveness of the system.

2.   Availability and convenience of access.

3.   Reliability.

4.   Quality of system support, such as documentation, and training.

These dimensions may be ignored if not raised explicitly. The service focus ensures that they will be included in the monitoring and evaluation process. While they may not be of particular importance in the initial justification of a project, they help significantly in fine tuning the operational system and suggesting where modifications or extensions are needed. For example, the Big Western Bank version of PMS overloaded the central computer and frequently led to frustrating crashes and slow response time. This poor quality of service was a critical weakness that undermined the value and credibility of the DSS. The system was not "complete" until these service issues had been resolved. They required frequent monitoring within the overall evaluation process.

MANAGERS' ASSESSMENT OF THE SYSTEM'S VALUE

Our discussion of cost/benefit analysis pointed out the difficulty of quantifying benefits. One effective way of defining value is simply to ask the managers. They frequently have a very shrewd sense of what a resource or service is "worth." Their perceptions can be gathered at regular intervals over the lifetime of a project, either through questionnaires or structured interviews. If their intuitions differ from the "facts" implied by other components of the evaluation smorgasbord, the process of unravelling the differences can yield useful insights. This was particularly true in the case of PMS. The formal cost/benefit evaluation strongly suggested that the Big Western Bank system was a failure, but many of the *managers* argued that the system was of great value to them despite the computer crashes and lack of reliability. It became apparent that PMS was a major marketing tool, an aspect of the system that had been viewed by the designers as secondary to its value as a support to the investment decision.

ANECDOTAL EVIDENCE

A DSS is a dynamic and complex invention. It often stimulates unexpected side benefits—and occasionally crises. Its impact is hard to predict and serendipity frequently plays a central part in its evolution. Because of this, it is useful to supplement the formal evaluation process by "anecdotal" evidence such as insights, examples, opinions, and events collected by a skilled observer. This can help flesh out the picture implied by the formal measures and often draws together useful information that would otherwise go unnoticed. C. F. Gibson (1975) has summarized this as an action research approach to implementation and gives several examples of how this informal evaluation aided the development of a computer system.[9] By gaining trust and credibility—the key requirements for becoming an insider—and by having a long enough period of time over which to observe, Gibson was able to identify many key factors not recognized by the design team. He acted as an intermediary between designers and users, monitoring the situational development of the system.

In several of the DSS projects described in Chapter 5, researchers studying the system acted in effect as evaluators gathering anecdotal data (Andreoli and Steadman's were collected after the implementation but indicate the useful insights obtained from this process). We have found two approaches to be most practicable. The first is to be present in formal and informal situations for continuous periods of time—to become, in effect, an insider. The continuity makes it possible for the observer to sample the moods of individuals and the overall climate. Ginzberg kept a diary of the implementation of a DSS. Another method is more random, involving in-depth interviews, often tape-recorded, and periodic observations. Both of these methods require a trusted, neutral, and skilled observer. The intent is to sample perceptions and feelings and to look for significant details; this is possible only if the members of the organization feel secure enough to trust the observer-interviewer.

CONCLUSION—THE EVALUATOR

Implicit in our discussion of the smorgasbord of evaluation methods is a definition of evaluation as a key and distinct task within the implementation process that may even require a full-time staff position. We feel very strongly that evaluation is a critical but largely neglected aspect of systems development and would recommend that any large organization involved in several concurrent DSS projects consider hiring an evaluator. The benefits can be immense; for example:

---

[9]Gibson points out that his strategy of building links with and becoming accepted by the various units involved in a system development effort is especially suited to academic research. He was seen by the organization as a disinterested observer, and individuals were willing to share their insights and concerns with him. Pettigrew (1976) reaches similar conclusions about his own position in his 1-year study of a major computer purchase decision.

Researchers often are anxious to obtain access to interesting projects; in return, it seems likely that they can provide the organization with valuable anecdotal evaluation. Obviously, the researchers must respect individual confidentiality. Both Gibson and Pettigrew comment on this need and suggest that the trust they built is essentially based on their making clear that they were not in any sense spies.

1. More complete and coherent definition of criteria for design and implementation.

2. Far better monitoring of the implementation process.

3. Gathering and analysis of information that would encourage learning from experience instead of repeating past mistakes and neglecting the lessons implicit in past triumphs.

Even if evaluation is not specifically assigned to a single individual or unit, the implementor is an evaluator and the strategy defined in Chapter 7 relies on effective monitoring and evaluation. The smorgasbord constitutes a rich set of methodologies to be matched to the specific situation. The key questions preceding and determining the selection of techniques are:

1. What are we trying to accomplish?

2. What are the criteria for determining our success or failure?

3. How will we know when the system is complete?

4. How can we determine if the effort was worth the cost?

It is worth mentioning that evaluation has increasingly been recognized as the weak link in most social change projects. Recently, for example, the Great Society programs initiated during President Johnson's administration have been reviewed by many of those who helped implement them. Almost without exception, the commentators have concluded that the main weakness of the venture was the absence of any consideration of criteria for evaluation (and inclusion in the budget of funds and personnel for evaluation). Increasingly, as a counterpoint to this failure, federal research projects for social programs require a separate evaluation unit and within a very few years we can expect to see full-time professional evaluators.

Our discussion of evaluation has been tentative and general. There has been very little discussion of evaluation in the MIS literature, except in terms of cost/benefit analysis. The smorgasbord we have defined can be used by an imaginative implementor to develop a personal specific evaluation package that aims at providing answers to the four questions listed above. Evaluation is vital; successful DSS development requires that it be given very high priority indeed. We must also admit that researchers at present care more about evaluation than do managers; researchers wish to learn lessons from existing DSS ventures but managers often feel that there can be time for assessment only when the system is fully in place—and by then they have no interest in "academic" review.

NINE

INTRODUCTION

The design and implementation of any DSS obviously takes place in a much wider context, which serves as both a constraint and an opportunity. This context is largely historical and involves:

1. The relative maturity of information systems usage within the organization.

2. The managers' attitudes to and experience with computer-based decision aids.

3. The relative influence, experience, and credibility of the designer.

Most of these factors are organizational. Some of them are fairly easy to recognize and take into account in developing a DSS. For example, we have stressed the importance of understanding the decisionmaker's viewpoint and procedures and the need to "unfreeze" the organization. However, many of these factors act as constraints on what an individual or group can accomplish. Lines of authority, predefined functional responsibilities, reporting relationships, and so on limit the discretion and influence of the systems developer. These background features must be recognized and any strategy for the *long-term* development of a DSS must consciously take them into account. One of the frustrations many readers of books such as this experience is that these wider constraints are generally brushed over and that the strategies provided for systems development *presume* that designers are masters of their fate. For instance, we argued earlier that it is best for the client in any DSS project to be charged for the development costs directly from his or her own budget, rather than using funds coming from a central R & D pool, since this is much more likely to ensure involvement and commitment. While this argument is valid, the DSS implementor, in the short term at least, has to live with whatever method is currently in use in the organization.

Many of the other background features relevant to long-term development of DSS are personal rather than organizational. In this final chapter one of our main aims is to sketch out a role and strategy for the effective DSS developer. We use the term *developer* rather than designer because we feel that one of the features that most distinguishes our approach from those of the traditional OR/MS/MIS fields is its emphasis on the manager rather than the technician. We expect, and later present limited, largely anecdotal evidence to support this view, that future DSS innovations will be initiated by managers and staff personnel in line units and that *they* will be the designers with the computer specialists acting as a (critical) supplier of the technical expertise required to support their efforts.

The whole computer field is still too young and fragmented for there to be many people in senior positions within organizations who have come up through the ranks of the computer profession. Nonetheless, in the past few years we have discerned broad trends in the careers of senior OR/MS/MIS specialists that are both encouraging and disturbing. For example, increasing numbers of operations research specialists have worked in the corporate planning area, building models for strategic decisions, and have thus been able to develop a good understanding of the organization's major functions and activities. They have been useful to top managers and have had to adopt a management rather than a technical focus. These individuals are now reaching senior levels in the organization and in many cases have integrated the use of computer and analytic techniques into executive planning and decisionmaking. By contrast, many equally able and even better paid MIS managers seem locked into a technical role; they have not been of direct value to *managers* and have not developed an understanding of the organization's key decision activities, so they are out on a limb—they are, in effect, unpromotable. They have reached the top of the computer function but cannot be transferred to a comparable level within other staff or line units because they simply do not know enough about the company's business and they lack management focus.

The career issue is an important one, closely linked to the main concerns of this chapter: the development of an effective long-term role and strategy. It is also linked to other aspects of personal and organizational growth over time—to the building of a climate in which DSS can take root and to the training and promotion of managers and staff specialists who can exploit the opportunities that climate will generate.

This final chapter is concerned with these long-term issues. Basically, we address it to the reader who has absorbed all the preceding arguments and now says: "Yes, I believe. What should I do?"

THE ORGANIZATIONAL REALITY

A number of researchers have identified an organizational life cycle effect (for example, R. L. Nolan, 1973, in relation to EDP, and M. Radnor and his co-workers, 1968, 1970, to OR/MS).[1] In general, the history of efforts to introduce computer systems or analytic models into organizations has followed a common pattern. The first stage is one of *missionary* work where energetic individuals try to build momentum. They take on projects with little centralized control or cost/benefit analysis, and their aim is simply to get something done, to build up a critical mass. In the early days of EDP, for example, this stage involved small groups of programmers working under a charismatic leader who placed minimal emphasis on dress, timeliness, and so on (to the chagrin of many people in other areas in the organization).

---

[1]The studies carried out by researchers at Northwestern University have provided rich insights into the evolution of OR/MS within organizations. Our arguments in this chapter draw heavily on them. See, for example, Bean et al. (1973), Neal and Radnor (1973), and Radnor et al. (1968, 1970).

These programmers accepted the need to respond to crises whether at midnight or on Christmas Day. For many programmers, these were the good old days and the excitement has gone from the field since.

Once contagion has built a critical mass and a number of projects have been successfully installed, there is a need for *consolidation.* The decentralized mode of operation needed to get things off the ground is unsatisfactory when one tries to bring the resulting chaos under some control. The EDP manager, in the mid-1960s, was thus put under great pressure to "run a tight shop." Myriads of new forms were created to provide much needed project control; whereas users would formerly go directly to the programmer to ask for a program modification, they would now go through the EDP manager, in quintriplicate.

The difficulty with this necessary emphasis on control and efficient allocation of resources became apparent during the *institutionalization* stage. By then, users were accustomed to computers, a second or even fourth generation of projects was being undertaken, and there were well-established procedures for transfer pricing and charging out the costs of the computer resource. Control and efficiency were tending to stifle innovation; the high-risk, basically R & D project (such as the early laundry equipment DSS) did not fit into the centralized mode of operation that had been effective in bringing order to the original chaos. Some organizations seem to have gotten stuck at this stage; users frequently complain that they can no longer get the EDP group to be responsive; for example, if marketing wants a simple report for year-end planning they generally have to wait 6 months, by which time it is of no use to them.

At least a few organizations have moved into a fourth stage that combines the first and third stages; it can perhaps be described as *diffusion of innovation.* Here, a two-tiered structure emerges. The established operational systems are handled as a separate area, where control and formality of procedures are stressed. New developments in these systems must be cost-justified and careful standards maintained for costs, time, and procedures. The emphasis here is on efficiency. Innovation is encouraged by having specialized application groups who interact very closely with users and clients. These groups operate with much more of a research approach; their job is to get something new done and to be very responsive to the user. Generally, they view themselves as a unit which is distinct from the standard EDP or MIS group. Their focus is on effectiveness as opposed to efficiency. It is to be expected that once their innovation has been linked into the organization, the process will repeat itself with the next step being one of consolidation, establishing procedures for efficiently running the system, appointing a system manager, and so forth. Once it is institutionalized, the system can drop to the second of the two tiers, the operational, procedural level.

The implications of this life cycle are immense. Firstly, DSS, as a natural evolution within the wider MIS and management science fields, have grown out of the third stage, institutionalization, as part of the diffusion stage. None of the DSS with which we are familiar have been built within the main EDP department. In fact, in several of the systems, the organization's EDP group was seen as the "enemy." [S. A. Alter's survey of 56 systems (1975) reaches the same conclusion.[2]]

---

[2]Nolan (1973) comments on the "Plight of the EDP Manager" who is locked into an organizational role where the data processing unit is overcentralized, overcontrolled, and lacking in resources for experimentation. One implication of Alter's study, which

The procedures necessary in institutionalization hinder exploratory, innovative, high-risk ventures such as DSS. However, and this point cannot be stressed too strongly, institutionalization provides the technical and organizational bases essential before the DSS can be developed.

Secondly, the life cycle effect suggests that the type of systems that can and should be built and the organizational procedures to support them are contingent. If the organization is in the missionary stage, developers can undertake virtually any type of system they wish (although they must make sure of the necessary backing and power base to have any effect on the organization; this will be discussed later). This freedom gives substantial discretion. However, they cannot at the same time expect to be able to set up "efficient" procedures. Any effort to get project management techniques or charge-out procedures is likely to be ineffectual. The project involves more exceptions than standard features and there is a lack of experience and precedent. By contrast, in the later stages of the life cycle, innovation can be very difficult to develop. The earlier informal relationships between the computer group and their clients will be replaced by the impersonality of control and budgeting systems. The organization will be less adaptive and flexible and justifications for new developments must focus on hard cost/benefit figures.

The basic dilemma that the life cycle reflects is common in many technical fields; it is again one of effectiveness versus efficiency. Implicit in our arguments about the types of tasks a DSS should support and the design and implementation process is the assumption that the organization has achieved a level of efficiency in its information systems usage. Our contrasting of DSS with standard EDP systems for operational tasks reflects this. The following brief description of the development of the computer function in a major bank (one of the top 20 in the United States) is reasonably typical of many large organizations. It highlights this dilemma of effectiveness versus efficiency, and the concurrent similar problems of decentralization versus centralization and personalized versus impersonal authority:

Alpha Bank was an early leader in the use of computers. At one point, it had machines from three different manufacturers spanning three generations (generation 1 was finally removed in 1974). Expenditures in 1964 for EDP were more than $20 million. Like many corporations, Alpha took on far more than it could accomplish and it also had much too much hardware (when new capacity was needed, Alpha generally bought another midsize machine, usually another IBM 360/40). Alpha's programmers were almost all college graduates and turnover was 40 percent per annum since experienced, well-trained COBOL programmers were at a premium. The head of EDP was a senior executive who had originally been assistant comptroller. He was a majestic, somewhat intimidating figure, known for political skill and empire building.

In the late sixties, Alpha's expenditures on computers grew almost exponentially. Many systems were in trouble and several major ventures had to

---

found that not one of the 56 systems studied was developed within the corporate data processing group, is that innovations in the use of computers are increasingly initiated by line departments, drawing on outside consultants. This trend must surely be reinforced by the availability of "decentralized" technological building blocks such as minicomputers and networks—and DSS.

be abandoned at a loss of several million dollars. At one stage, the decision was made to allow no more systems development. New groups were formed within EDP: a software support staff, a small unit to define standards for programming, and, more importantly, a large program maintenance group composted mostly of nongraduates.

When Moses, the original head of EDP, retired there was a sequence of new vice-presidents, most of whom lasted less than a year. The problem of getting EDP under control was attracting a lot of attention from top management. Early in 1972, David was appointed head of EDP, with a detailed charter. He was ordered to hold development expenditures and to cut operating costs substantially.

David is still (1977) in this position and is seen by top management as very successful. Alpha built a large computer operations center, several miles away from the bank's main offices. David is less happy than his superiors, mainly because he feels that the bank must commit itself heavily to new systems in the areas of telecommunications, Electronic Funds Transfer, and on-line branch operations. He has been unable to get top management's commitment to the substantial investment and expansion of staff that this will require.

Alpha is still a leader in systems development. However, most of the innovative systems in progress are being done by outside consulting groups, working directly with the line department that initiates the venture. The management science group has similarly carried through some major projects, mostly in the area of strategic planning. The head of this unit is now a senior vice-president who plays a central role in top management decision-making; he reports that he rarely has any contact with EDP and that he generally bypasses them when he needs special reports or data files.

Some of the implications of the Alpha experience are obvious. The key one is that Alpha *had* to bring its operations under control and that this stifled the EDP group's ability to innovate and respond to new needs. As EDP became more centralized, there was a countereffect with the information systems effort being decentralized and diffused into other areas within Alpha. Alpha now has a number of fragmented units, mostly using outside consultants. Some of these groups have had to build up separate operations to run their now institutionalized internally developed systems. The bank's bills for outside time-sharing are huge and it currently has contracts with almost a dozen vendors at a cost that could be substantially reduced by consolidation. Alpha has built several DSS. The most successful of these, the Magic System, encountered many problems in implementation. However, the line department involved viewed the project explicitly as part of their own R & D portfolio and were thus willing to support it over several years because they felt it had long-term value even with its high short-term risk.

R. M. Cyert and J. G. March (1963), two theorists from the Carnegie school of thought headed by H. A. Simon, introduced the useful concept of "organizational slack." Slack is spare resources that the organization uses to oil squeaking wheels, buy time, and resolve conflict.[3] For instance, production and marketing generally

---

[3]In many ways, R & D is infeasible without slack, which provides funds that are not needed to maintain efficiency and can therefore be invested for future effectiveness.

have many conflicts; as we pointed out in the description of the laundry equipment DSS, the production unit prefers to produce one run of white appliances while marketing wants every combination of color and model. An "optimal" solution could, perhaps, be arrived at, but in practice the organization spends slack to resolve the conflicting interests, either in the form of additional inventory levels or the use of overtime. A more personal example of slack can be seen in the lengths that most organizations will go to avoid the unpleasant task of firing an amiable but ineffective employee; he or she will usually be given a series of hints such as no salary increases and then, over a period of time, be squeezed out. Another tactic is to promote the employee sideways. All these actions are obviously inefficient and expensive but the saving in stress and embarrassment is seen as worthwhile. In the 1973–1975 recession, however, the spare resources that could be used as slack disappeared and managers had to learn the painful skills of firing people.

Alpha's EDP department has been squeezing out slack. The demand for efficiency and control removed excess resources that could be allocated as the department saw fit. By contrast, the unit that implemented the Magic System had enough slack for innovation. Their R & D portfolio used funds that were in some sense surplus and that could thus be put into a venture whose payoff was uncertain. Similarly, the laundry equipment project drew on slack resources. One of the main reasons that so many fiascos occurred in the 1960s in systems development was simply that there was plenty of slack available; funds could be spent on projects whose main aim was prestige for the company as technological innovators, or whose real purpose was to keep the company's hot-shot programming whiz kids happy.

Organizational slack as large as that of the mid-1960s is unlikely to reoccur in the next decade. However, any complex DSS needs some element of slack; if the system has to pass precise tests for cost/benefit analysis and be budgeted in terms of well-defined project management techniques, it will either not be authorized or will face immense problems during implementation.[4] In the Alpha situation, no DSS is likely to be generated through the EDP group because of this problem. At a strategic level, it seems clear that the development of the DSS can only come when the organization or the client is ready to risk the necessary resources and give the implementation team substantial discretion. If the organization is rigidly structured in terms of its control procedures, then there will not be any slack available; a manager who wishes to undertake a DSS in the Alpha environment may have to generate the resources within his or her own unit.

The final aspect of the life cycle that is of substantial relevance in developing information systems concerns personnel and leadership. The missionary stage requires a loose, decentralized unit with a very personalized style of leadership. The personnel who can be most effective here will be those who are good at selling, in every sense of the word, and who have built strong links with user departments. By

---

[4]It is important to stress that an innovative computer system is an invention involving some degree of risk and uncertainty in costs and benefits. While it is clearly essential to quantify these uncertain estimates as precisely as possible, it is also important to recognize the R & D nature of the venture—it is part of the organization's portfolio of investments for its future development. See Keen, "Managing Organizational Change: The Role of MIS" (1975), for more details.

contrast, the institutionalization stage requires strong centralization and the leadership role is one of control and formalization of procedures. In the Alpha situation, people who had been very effective project leaders in the missionary stage and who were promoted to fill the top position within EDP immediately after Moses retired, turned out to be ineffectual in the new context of efficiency and centralization. This was a common pattern in the mid-1960s.

The leadership and personnel required for DSS development seem closer to the missionary type than to institutionalization, although we would argue that as diffusers of innovation they can and should combine characteristics of both—or at least be able to recognize where effectiveness takes priority over efficiency and vice versa. It should be noted that the frequent debates on centralization versus decentralization of the computer resource ignore this situational factor and tend to argue that centralization is good or bad in and of itself. As the Alpha situation suggests, centralization is necessary at some stages and for some purposes, and damaging at others; as with most aspects of organizational life, there are few absolutes.

The individual manager or system designer clearly has little influence over the organizational variables implicit in this life cycle. He or she needs to be aware of them, of course. At certain stages in the cycle, innovations such as DSS are likely to be infeasible unless kept very small and informal. At other stages, they are the natural and desirable next step; a computer specialist can help prepare the stage for a DSS by making sure that the necessary slack and freedom from standardized control procedures is provided; at the same time she or he must make sure that the project is not allowed to float along with no direction and organization—one of the major weaknesses of the missionary stage in EDP was that there were virtually no guidelines or criteria for managing projects and they could drift in serious trouble for, literally, years before anyone finally faced up to the situation. The strategy for implementation that we presented in Chapter 7 suggests that at the entry stage, the system implementor must make sure that the parties involved face the question of mutual commitment and allocation of resources. A grave mistake in developing a DSS is to get locked into either extreme of the efficiency/effectiveness spectrum.

A FORMAL CHARTER FOR THE OR/MS/MIS GROUP

At the missionary stage, the computer group is generally a small free-floating unit whose contacts and activities are informal and improvised. By contrast, the institutionalization stage emphasizes well-structured routines for communication between the computer unit and the other departments. Radnor and his co-workers (1968, 1970) have found that in mature organizations, which have worked their way through the process of getting OR/MS embedded in the company's day-to-day activities, there is a strong correlation between the effectiveness of the OR/MS group and their having a formal charter. This charter is generally expressed in terms of budgets, responsibilities, reporting relationships, and the assignment of a senior-level job title to the head of the group. Again, this reinforces the movement toward control and efficiency. However, one of the difficulties that DSS sometimes encounter is that this charter is both an impetus and a hindrance; it creates the necessary credibility and power base for action, but it also can generate substantial political inertia. If the system is evolutionary and basically an experiment (in the sense that the laundry equipment system and PMS were experimental), it can become the plaything of political units each of which has its own wider interests.

The system really needs much of the missionary approach with the system designer from the EDP or operations research departments working closely with people in the client unit—we have recommended as part of the implementation strategy for DSS that the developer encourage from the outset this personal involvement and commitment. The dilemma that well-intentioned DSS developers often face is that they need the clout provided by their boss's strong position within the organization and by the group's formal charter, but this can stifle their flexibility and adaptiveness. However, no major DSS can hope to be successful if the developers do not have a power base. We have found a number of examples of DSS that simply lost impetus and faded because they were initiated by a line manager who was unwilling to commit prestige and influence to the project; at the same time, the MIS group lacked a strong enough position to either demand that commitment (or refuse to take on the project) or to substitute for it. The missionary is in a very weak situation in this respect. He or she is trying to sell a system with little centralized backing and badly needs the goodwill of the client and can be easily caught in the middle, trying to keep the client happy and the MIS group reasonably in control at the same time. This dilemma was common in the early 1960s. EDP was often regarded as a service unit whose job was to carry out the wishes of its main user groups. It thus often found that it could not turn down project requests or assign its own priorities; the value of such control procedures as charge-out methods was partly to strengthen its position in allocating resources efficiently.

ADJUSTING TO THE ORGANIZATIONAL REALITY

So far in this chapter, we have presented problems with few hints at a solution. In some situations, there *are* only problems (sensible managers or system developers will, of course, make very sure that they at least diagnose where things stand). The life cycle we have described highlights a constant dialectic:

Efficiency versus effectiveness

Control versus flexibility

Formality versus informality

Structure versus process.

In undertaking any major DSS, assessing roughly where along these spectra the project really needs to be is very worthwhile. For example, the laundry equipment project had to be positioned toward the right-hand side; it involved *ad hoc* groups whose contacts were intermittent and not very formalized, over a period of time that could not be easily predicted and scheduled. Alpha's Magic System similarly needed to be toward the right; the client for the system could not implement it within the current organization structure and thus brought in an outside consultant. Clearly, these considerations explain why virtually all the successful systems Alter identified in his survey were implemented outside the EDP group. There does not, for instance, seem to have been a lack of technical competence in Alpha's EDP department but there was an absence of the necessary organizational flexibility. David, the prescient and suffering head of EDP, recognized that what was needed was a two-tier structure, where he could allocate slack resources to DSS and similar developments; the small groups assigned to these would work on different terms from the lower-tier operations and, in effect, be a consulting group. Interestingly, one department in Alpha has, over a 15-year period, been a major innovator in information systems development because it included a very capable manager who had worked in EDP for several years and was able to build around himself temporary project teams that, due to his prestige and record, were able to operate fairly independently. Recently, a major New York bank moved toward the structure that we would recommend for the diffusion stage: a centralized MIS group who define broad guidelines for system development and who have direct responsibility for technical areas; user departments are encouraged to initiate and, if they wish, manage their own innovations within these guidelines. This seems to combine centralized efficiency and decentralized effectiveness.

The manager of a line department who wishes to introduce a DSS can usually bring in an outside consultant. We would argue that managers ought to do so in such contexts as Alpha's current structure. If they wish to draw on the central MIS group's economies of scale or expertise, one of the other choices is to position the project within their *own* unit and bring in the MIS staff; but to do this, they will generally have to foot the bills. Even in the Alpha situation, the system developer can alleviate the problems of a project needing a different climate and positioning by consciously trying to get it identified as a venture sponsored and in effect owned by the client.

The effective DSS implementor needs to be an integrator. He should thus work very hard indeed at building credibility within both the computer group and the client unit. A simple and direct analogy is with industrial salesmen, the best of whom occupy a shadowy area between their clients and home office—they are both the company's representative *and* their customers'. The long-term reward every technician can gain by sympathetic listening and well-timed assistance is additional flexibility.

In the examples given so far in this section, we have concentrated on situations where flexibility needs to be created in a relatively rigid organizational climate. However, there are many situations where the opposite approach is needed. It is often very easy—as a missionary—to get a project started, particularly a DSS, by working closely over some period of time with a manager and staff, identifying the right problem to work on, and designing the system on the basis of a decision-centered approach, all the virtuous actions we have recommended throughout this book. But centralization and efficiency also have distinctive values. In many cases the project needs to be positioned toward the left-hand side— efficiency, control, formality, and structure. For example, any follow-up DSS evolving from the laundry equipment experience can be much more clearly predefined. Such a system now builds on an existing base and has precedents and a coherent body of expertise to draw on. It would also be expected to make a solid impact on existing organizational procedures. In that situation, it makes sense to exploit the available strengths of the line units and the MIS group. Improvisation, informality, and temporary project groups have substantial side costs. They reinvent the wheel biweekly and are tangential to the ongoing activities of the organization. They lack economies of scale and do not draw on specialized capabilities and procedures.

The key issue here is that system developers, whether they are managers of the client unit or computer professionals, must recognize that they have some choices as to where and how they position the project. Above all, they must refuse to take on a system development effort if the climate is either too structured or too loose for the implementation to be effective. No manager in Alpha, for instance, should be foolish enough to believe that its EDP group can deliver an on-line DSS written in APL for commodity trading.

THE IDEAL CLIMATE FOR DSS

The senior manager *does* have the ability to alter her or his organization's structure and procedures. We can outline the organizational climate best suited to developing DSS. It is one that we have found in a number of companies that have made a broad-based commitment to OR, MIS, and DSS.

The ideal climate is one where the computer resource is both centralized *and* decentralized. It has a lower tier of well-controlled, well-structured procedures. These include charge-out systems so that user groups recognize that there is a direct cost to them for any development. It also has sufficient slack, in terms of dollars and personnel, so that it can maintain an R & D focus; if, for instance, the head of the information function (a much more important role than just EDP or MIS) feels that data-base management techniques or distributed processing offer potential benefits, he or she can assign people to explore them. The contacts with line units are flexible enough to allow communication on an ongoing basis with them about such potential opportunities. They, in turn, have sufficient confidence and expertise to provide constant impetus for new systems and, in general, prefer that the formal management of the project be handled by themselves. The computer group includes several people who have either come out of line departments or have substantial background in a discipline such as finance, marketing, or accounting.[5] Frequently, there is cross-fertilization between the information function and line units when a major DSS is assigned to a system *manager* in a line department who has direct responsibility not just for design and implementation, but for ongoing operationalization and evolution as well. It is accepted that computer personnel may choose to remain with the centralized group as technical specialists or focus on application areas where they will be much like the industrial salesmen, representing the customer and home office at the same time.

In the ideal climate, education is not something tacked onto the computer group's functions, with annual seminars on time-sharing, APL, and the wonders of interactive graphics. There are mechanisms, personal and formalized, for building "mutual understanding," the lack of which has again and again been picked out as one of the main impediments to progress in the computer field. A joint design effort is the best mechanism for such education.

The ideal climate is reasonably attainable and some companies have achieved it by natural evolution, balancing the twin demands of efficiency and effectiveness,

---

[5]Such individuals were obviously hard to find until fairly recently. Computer specialists were trained in a difficult and still evolving field and had little exposure to (or interest in) business or administrative applications. One of the main values of an M.B.A. degree from any of the leading business schools is that it provides experienced technicians with such an exposure (and also gives future general managers a reasonable overview of computers). This hybridization seems to us an important development in management education and should be complemented by further cross-fertilization between technical and user departments. (This issue is discussed later in the chapter; see also Hammond, 1971.)

of a product and a service focus. An important aspect of this climate is that it requires a very definite type of computer professional and also a special kind of client-customer. Our ideal organization builds this capability in-house; while there are no ideological reasons for not using outside consultants, this is a poor long-term strategy that would reflect inadequacies in the company's own operations.

THE EFFECTIVE CONSULTANT
AND THE EFFECTIVE CLIENT

In the process of building a DSS, the relationship between the technical professional and the group for whom the system is designed is directly analogous to that of consultant and client. The consultant is an outsider brought in on a project basis. He or she is hired as a professional and is expected to contribute a known expertise; the relationship that results may be ongoing and mutually comfortable or one of arm's length bargaining. In our chapter on implementation (Chapter 7), we defined the role of the effective consultant as being that of a facilitator and a change agent, and outlined a fairly specific approach to the development of any particular DSS. In this final chapter, we build on that definition, which is in some sense short term, and the input to a longer process of personal and professional development.

We mentioned earlier that, little by little, some operations research and management science personnel are attaining senior positions in organizations where they have substantial impact on how top management plans and makes major decisions. This group is too small for many commonalities in personality or experience to be apparent. Nonetheless, several things stand out. The first is that, although they are all excellent technicians, they strongly view their function as that of *helping* managers. They are well aware of the weaknesses in the way those managers operate and can dissect their inadequacies with surgical detachment. However, they uniformly agree that those limitations are countered by many other skills and that the reality with which the manager has to deal is a difficult one that requires a variety of approaches. They are just as critical of the technicians in the organization for their lack of the managers' wider sense of events. This management focus seems to be the key single feature of their behavior that has led to their seniority and effectiveness. (They are *not* managers; in fact, their whole career path will remain that of a staff specialist.)

Their progress was sometimes painful. A pseudonymous case developed by J. S. Hammond III (1971) provides a useful example of this. Bud Mathaisal went to a technical university and graduated armed with visionary aims and mathematical techniques. He got a job with an airline with a strong mandate (he believed) to develop some "real" strategic planning methods. He was able to identify major opportunities for savings and for better coordination in such areas as aircraft maintenance and investment. With his boss's approval, he arranged conferences with senior representatives of the relevant departments; plans were made and promises given that data would be provided and personnel assigned. Neither ever happened, although each meeting brought fresh assertions of interest and commitment. (Had Mathaisal read Chapter 7 of this book, he would have recognized a prototypical frozen stage that he was icing up even more.) He began to suffer from active sabotage; his reports based on line units' information proved entirely wrong because some key (and, to anyone who knew anything about the airline business, obvious) fact had been withheld from him. Mathaisal felt he was right and that the organization was packed with ignorant hacks.

His nadir came some time after a manager had given him, after much delay and evasion, "direct" cost figures that were, in fact, full allocation costs. He was demoted to handling odd jobs such as running a desk calculator to help the same individual. Mathaisal retorted that he could write a time-shared program in less than an hour that would cut the time needed by a huge factor. His offer was ignored and the manager refused to believe that the output from the program could be correct. However, he checked it by hand and Mathaisal's rehabilitation began. His dedicated opponent became an ardent supporter and, chastened and a little less impetuous, Mathaisal went on to a very effective and influential career. In retrospect, he saw that most of the fault was his; he had radiated a confidence that bordered on disdain and simply never *listened*. He came with answers for problems as he defined them and was seen by the organization as a nuisance; they sideswiped him by a process of passive indifference.

There were many Mathaisals. Some of them learn from their early failures and make the important adjustment to the organizational world that, in the end, allow them to change that world. Others become reinforced in their ineffectual behavior. Mathaisal himself at one point saw the problem as being caused by the misguided stupidity and lack of ability of others; by resisting his offer of the "truth," they confirmed these feelings. Mathaisal's mistakes, for such they were, are commonplace. It seems unnecessary for capable people like him to have to learn the hard way. To an extent, the fault is partly in the education system that trained him. It prepared him explicitly for a technical world with virtually no exploration of the context of techniques or of technique as means, not ends.

The computer field will always need a supply of outstanding technicians; in many DSS, no matter how well conceived, there are a variety of complex problems of software, hardware, and analytic methods that require technical specialists. However, most technically trained staff personnel who choose to work in industrial organizations are not hired as technical specialists but, like Mathaisal, as implementors whose function is to support managers or staff in business activities. The skills that they thus require may be thought of in matrix terms. The columns are technical skills and the rows are disciplinary or functional ones. For example, PMS required in its design a matrix such as that shown in Figure 9-1.

The fusion of technical and functional skills is critical in DSS—and makes them difficult to build. Sometimes the matrix of skills can be filled only by close interaction and cooperation between consultant and client. Obviously, technically trained designers are far more likely to be stronger in technical skills; the point is that they *must* acquire credibility and insight into the relevant *functional* fields.[6] If they do not do so, their careers will parallel Mathaisal's. Much of this insight can be obtained by empathy and by listening. A manager who comes into contact with an intelligent technician who makes an obvious effort to understand his or her viewpoint will generally be actively eager to help and inform. Similarly, a manager who

---

[6]"Insight" is not equivalent to "in-depth knowledge." The issue is one of credibility and ability to understand and to communicate with managers. Much of the designer's role is integrative; he or she is also a translator, taking the manager's reality and interpreting it in technical terms and vice versa. On the whole, this role requires less detailed knowledge of business functions than a broad overview (especially of accounting and finance—the Esperanto of the business world) backed by a willingness to listen to and absorb from the managers.

FIGURE 9-1   A Matrix of Skills for DSS Development

Technical Skills

Functional Skills	Time-Shared Programs	Data-Base Techniques	Interactive Graphics	Human-Machine Interface
Finance	X		X	
Accounting	X	X		
Organizational Psychology			X	X

Note: Each X indicates areas where integration of functional and technical knowledge was critical for development of PMS.

wishes to exploit the immense potential of computer-based decision aids can build the necessary insight into the technician's world by listening and questioning without in any way having to learn how to program or differentiate. This point is, in our view, absolutely critical. The future of the computer in many organizations depends on building this matrix. Far too often, managers reject the need to supplement their knowledge and experience with even elementary insights into technical areas and technicians have equally disdained the grubbiness of the nonanalytic. There is strong evidence that senior management is becoming very aware of this problem in hiring senior OR and MIS personnel and will select the capable technician who shows a two-dimensional approach to problems rather than the supremely able technician who views the world from the column down.

The computer field has always had an academic flavor. This is one of its strengths; management scientists and MIS personnel in organizations continue to lead the development of new methods and to keep up to date in their field through ongoing study, professional journals, and conferences. However, there is both a *technical* state of the art that requires mainly intellect and reading time to keep up with, and a more elusive management and *applications* state of the art that many technicians do not even try to follow. Moreover, many technicians have viewed the real world projects as really academic pieces of research. They saw them in terms of art-for-art's sake, and their management conversely felt that they showed a casual indifference to the needs of the organization. Now that managers are more knowledgeable about what the computer cannot do and have been sold (at least twice) the simulation equivalent of the Brooklyn Bridge, there is a degree of informed pragmatism that is likely to be a major factor in the next 5 years. *Managers*—not technicians—are now making the main strategic decisions about information systems development.

One of the strengths of the DSS approach is that it is firmly rooted in the management reality. Technique is subordinated to application; in many ways most DSS are comparatively trivial on a technical level, but in terms of management and applications state of the art they are dramatic innovations.

The degree of change in attitude that is becoming evident in organizations can be seen in the following panel discussion from the 1971 national TIMS (the Institute for Management Science) meeting, which later appeared under the title "Through the Glass Darkly" in *Interfaces* (August 1972). It contains brief presentations by six practitioners, all of whom are well-known and active participants in management science and MIS societies and who have been true believers in and missionaries for the analytic method.[7] Their arguments are uniform in tone; the following extracts are representative of the discussion:

> *H. Halbrecht* (Chairman, Halbrecht Associates, management recruiting company with substantial experience in recruiting senior OR and MIS personnel):   The obvious fact that many people have not been willing to face (is) that the management science profession is in trouble. (All quotes are from Halbrecht, 1972, pp. 10–22.)
>
> *E. S. Savas* (First Deputy City Administrator, Mayor's Office, New York City):   We have been reluctant to hire people with Ph.D.'s in OR on the grounds that they have acquired "a trained incapacity to think" (Herman Kahn), a rigidity brought on by some forms of higher education. (From "How to Make OR Fail Without Really Trying.")
>
> *G. Hoffman* (Manager of OR, Standard Oil of Indiana):   The graduates of OR curricula are not adequately trained in OR. I now make a more damning assertion; usually these graduates are not educated at all. (From "The Missing 90 Percent of Management Science.")
>
> *H. Ayres* (Vice-President for OR, Morgan Guaranty):   We've really made very few job offers (to OR graduates). What stands out in my mind is that I don't think many of them realize what OR/MS really is. Who is to blame for this? Let's try blaming the academicians who train these people. They do not train them in OR/MS; they train them in applied mathematics, and that's all. (From "Skills for Effective Management Science.")

Many of the panel's strictures may be less true now than in 1971; certainly most management schools are now sensitive to these issues, and there has been a tremendous growth in *applied* research and training. Nonetheless, the points have much force and the attack focuses on the same issues we have emphasized throughout this book:

1.   The need for understanding of how decisions are really made.

2.   The need to gain insight into and to identify with managers.

---

[7]In fact, several of the speakers have been president of either TIMS or the Society for Management Information Systems. Over the past few years there seems to have been a growing concern, especially among management scientists, that the theorems and techniques of the field do not seem particularly effective in the real world. In the optimistic, expansive period of the 1960s it was assumed that once managers were educated in the "one true faith," rationality and optimization would carry the day; that self-confidence has largely evaporated. Much of the argument in this book reflects the viewpoint that only by starting from a *decisionmaking* perspective and regarding analytic techniques as means and not ends can we really expect to realize the immense potential of MIS and OR/MS. Obviously, from this perspective, implementation is the central concern, rather than formal design.

3.   The importance of relating technique to context.

4.   The central need to *support* the management process.

It would be flaying a dead horse to add further comments on these issues. The last point to make though is that the decision support approach consciously meets the panel's implicit requirements. We suggest that managers who follow that approach can really at last begin to embed computer aids in their activities without the customary risks and disappointments and that computer professionals similarly can both enhance their immediate effectiveness and carve out very attractive and worthwhile career paths.

Much of what we have touched on in this section relates to education. The matrix schema we presented (Figure 9-1) amounts to a general definition of the body of knowledge a DSS developer ought to acquire. In some ways, organizations have placed too much faith in formal education. The panel's enthusiastic excoriation of the teaching profession ascribes more power to it than it probably possesses. Difficult jobs generally involve a significant and lengthy apprenticeship in which prior training and knowledge are not enough. We strongly suggest here that education has to be viewed as ongoing and as an integral part of one's career. Managers who think that they do not need to "know" anything about computer applications, or that when they do they will sign up for a two-day seminar, are doomed to be victims of their own experts. As business becomes more complex and draws on more and more professional staff skills, one of the main topics for managers will be how to manage expertise—how to be able to talk with, for example, the developer of a DSS and ask the necessary questions to decide whether or not they are being sold a bill of goods and to evaluate the quality of the expert. There is no reason for managers to keep up with computer technology or to learn how to write programs but, equally, they cannot view the technical world as self-contained and isolated from their own concerns. The best education for them is the building of a relationship with an effective DSS developer and, most importantly—the insistence on being committed and involved in the design and implementation process. A skilled manager who has flexibility of mind can and almost certainly should play a major role in the design of any DSS that she or he sponsors.

In a similar way, a DSS developer who does not relate to managers in their terms should find another line of work. This may sound dogmatic but it seems justified when we look at the mayhem caused by system designers who operate with blinders on. One of the reasons for the increasing antiacademic and antitechnical backlash is clearly the "have-technique-will-travel" approach of so many systems and model builders who tried to impose their own powerful but incomplete view of the world onto an organization at great and unnecessary cost in dollars, morale, and lost opportunity.

CONCLUSION

This book, *as a whole*, says many things that are new; nonetheless, just about every single point it makes has been made elsewhere. We present no powerful new algorithms and the systems we describe are, we hope, simple to follow—the laundry equipment system, for instance, is a fairly uncomplicated approach to a problem that is important in many organizations, and the solution that the DSS provides is sensible and easy to understand. A management scientist could plausibly propose a more powerful model to optimize production schedules, for example; however, the less technically complex DSS provides far more immediate payoff. Similarly, many of the points we make about the organizational reality are common sense to any experienced manager. The starting premise of this book is that most of the trouble we have encountered in getting computers used in decisionmaking comes from too much emphasis on the bits and pieces and minimal attention to their synthesis. A management scientist who argues in favor of an optimization model for the laundry equipment situation is proposing a solution that is organizationally infeasible. But a manager who instantly rejects any use of a computer system as unrealistic and impractical is almost certainly ignoring the tremendous potential efficiencies and extensions of his or her abilities that can be obtained from such a perspective. Managers have generally been unable to combine the two insights and approaches and are often getting the worst of both worlds.

DSS offer an opportunity that is both trivial and immense—immense in that they can embed the computer in decisionmaking activities where they provide large payoffs and trivial in that they represent no major advance in technique. We have tried to present a specific and practical approach to the development of information systems that will actually be used, that are buildable now, and that exploit the joint but different capabilities of the manager and the computer professional. We choose to end on a downbeat; we do not have great new truths to offer and what we propose can be absorbed and acted on by both a manager and a system designer very quickly. Building innovative systems will be a difficult and risky venture for some time to come; the DSS approach makes success and payoff a little more likely. Neither the management state of the art nor the technical state of the art seems likely to be as effective as the combination of close to the state of the art of both professions. The adjustments that each group needs to make to accomplish this are relatively small ones, mainly attitudinal, and require little new knowledge. But the opportunities for action are after all substantial, and the personal and organizational rewards high.

BIBLIOGRAPHY

Ackoff, R. L. "Unsuccessful Case Studies and Why." *Operations Research*, vol. 8, no. 4, pp. 259–263, March-April, 1960.

———. "Management Misinformation Systems." *Management Science*, vol. 14, no. 4, pp. B 147–156, Dec. 1967.

———, and M. W. Sasieni. *Fundamentals of Operations Research*. New York: Wiley, 1968.

Allison, G. T. *Essence of Decision*. Boston: Little, Brown, 1971.

Alter, S. A. "A Study of Computer-aided Decision Making in Organizations." Ph.D. dissertation, Sloan School, M.I.T., 1975.

Amstutz, A. E. "The Marketing Executive and Management Information Systems." In R. M. Haas (ed.), *Science, Technology and Marketing*, pp. 69–86. Chicago: American Marketing Association, 1966.

Andreoli, P., and J. Steadman. "Management Decision Support Systems: Impact on the Decision Process." Master's thesis, M.I.T., 1975.

Andrus, R. R. "Approaches to Information Evaluation." *Michigan State University Business Topics*, vol. 19, no. 3, pp. 40–46, 1971.

Ansoff, B. H. I. (ed.) *Business Strategy*. London: Penguin, 1968.

Anthony, R. N. *Planning and Control Systems: A Framework for Analysis*. Cambridge, Mass.: Harvard University Graduate School of Business Administration, Studies in Management Control, 1965.

Argyris, C. "Resistance to Rational Management Systems." *Innovation*, no. 10, pp. 28–34, Nov. 1970.

———. "Management Information Systems: The Challenge to Rationality and Emotionality." *Management Science*, vol. 17, no. 6, pp. B275–292, 1971.

Babad, J. M. "The Monetary System—Implementation and Experience: A Case Study." In P. G. W. Keen (ed.), *The Implementation of Computer-Based Decision Aids*. Cambridge, Mass.: Proceedings of a Conference Sponsored by the Center for Information Systems Research, M.I.T., April 3–5, 1975.

Bardach, E. *The Implementation Game: What Happens When a Bill Becomes Law*. Cambridge, Mass.: M.I.T., 1977.

Bariff, M. L., and E. J. Lusk. "Cognitive and Personality Tests for the Design of Management Information Systems." *Management Science*, vol. 23, no. 8, pp. 820–829, April 1977.

Bean, A. S., et al. "Structural and Behavioral Correlates of the Implementation of Formal OR/MS Projects: Success and Failure in U.S. Business Organizations." Paper presented at the Research Conference on the Implementation of OR/MS Models, University of Pittsburgh, Pittsburgh, Penn., November 15–17, 1973.

Beer, S. *Platform for Change.* New York: Wiley, 1975.

Bello, F. "The Information Theory." *Fortune*, pp. 136–140, Dec. 1953.

Bennett, J. "Integrating Users and Decision Support Systems." In J. D. White (ed.), *Proceedings of the Sixth and Seventh Annual Conferences of the Society for Management Information Systems*, pp. 77–86. Ann Arbor: University of Michigan, July 1976.

Bennis, W. G. "Commentary of 'The Researcher and the Manager: A Dialectic of Implementation.' " *Management Science*, vol. 12, no. 2, pp. B13–16, Oct. 1965.

Berry, P. "The Democratization of Computing." Paper presented at Eleventh Symposium Nacional de Systemas Computacionales, Monterrey, Mexico, March 15–18, 1977.

Blasis, J-P de, and T. H. Johnson. "Data Base Administration—Classical Pattern, Some Experiences and Trends." *American Federation of Information Processing Societies Conference Proceedings*, 1977 National Computer Conference, vol. 46, pp. 1–7, 1977.

Botkin, J. W. "An Intuitive Computer System: A Cognitive Approach to the Management Learning Process." Ph.D. dissertation, Harvard Graduate School of Business Administration, 1973.

Bowman, E. H. "Consistency and Optimality in Managerial Decision Making." *Management Science*, vol. 9, no. 2, pp. 310–321, Jan. 1963.

Braybrooke, D., and C. E. Lindblom. *A Strategy for Decision.* New York: Free Press, 1970.

Briggs-Myer, I. *The Myers-Briggs Type Indicator.* Palo Alto, Calif.: Consulting Psychologists Press, 1962.

Brooks, F. P. *The Mythical Man-Month.* Reading, Mass.: Addison-Wesley, 1975.

Carlisle, J. "Cognitive Factors in Interactive Decision Systems." Ph.D. dissertation, Yale University, 1974.

Carlson, E. D., et al. "The Design and Evaluation of an Interactive Geodata Analysis and Display System." Paper presented at the International Federation for Information Processing Congress, Stockholm, Sweden, August 1974.

———, and J. A. Sutton. *A Case Study of Non-Programmer Interactive Problem-solving.* San Jose, Calif.: IBM Research Report RJ 1382, 1974.

Carter, N. "The Executive and the Terminal." In J. D. White (ed.), *Proceedings, Sixth and Seventh Annual Conferences of the Society for Management Information Systems*, pp. 87–89. Ann Arbor: University of Michigan, Management Information Systems Research Center, July 1976.

Cartwright, D. "Achieving Change in People: Some Applications of Group Dynamics Theory." *Human Relations*, vol. 14, no. 4, pp. 381–392, 1951.

Chen, P. P-S. "The Entity-Relationship Model—A Basis for the Enterprise View of Data." *American Federation of Information Processing Societies Conference Proceedings*, 1977 National Computer Conference, vol. 46, pp. 77–84, 1977.

Cherry, C. *On Human Communication.* New York: Wiley, 1957.

Chomsky, N. *Problems of Knowledge and Freedom.* New York: Pantheon, 1971.

Churchman, C. W. *Prediction and Optimal Decision.* Englewood Cliffs, N. J.: Prentice-Hall, 1961.

———. "Managerial Acceptance of Scientific Recommendations." *California Management Review,* vol. 7, no. 1, pp. 31–38, Fall 1964.

———. *Challenge to Reason.* New York: McGraw-Hill, 1968.

———. *The Systems Approach.* New York: Dell, 1968.

———. *The Design of Inquiring Systems.* New York: Basic Books, 1971.

———, and A. H. Schainblatt. "The Researcher and the Manager: A Dialectic of Implementation." *Management Science,* vol. 11, no. 4, pp. B69–87, Feb. 1965.

Clarkson, G. P. E. *Portfolio Selection: A Simulation of Trust Investment.* Englewood Cliffs, N.J.: Prentice-Hall, 1962.

Claycamp, J., and A. E. Amstutz. "Simulation Techniques in the Analysis of Marketing Strategy." In F. M. Bass et al. (eds.), *Applications of the Sciences in Marketing Management,* pp. 113–150. New York: Wiley, 1968.

Cochrane, J. L., and M. Zeleny (eds.). *Multicriteria Decision Making.* Columbia, S.C.: University of South Carolina Press, 1973.

Codd, E. F. "A Relational Model of Data for Large Shared Data Banks." *Communications of the Association for Computing Machinery,* vol. 13, no. 6, pp. 377–387, June 1970.

———. "Relational Completeness of Data Base Sublanguages." In R. Rustin, *Data Base Systems,* pp. 65–98. Englewood Cliffs, N.J.: Prentice-Hall, 1972.

Colby, K. M., J. B. Watt, and J. P. Gilbert. "A Computer Method of Psychotherapy: Preliminary Communication." *Journal of Nervous and Mental Diseases,* vol. 142, no. 2, pp. 148–152, 1966.

Cotton, I. W. "Microeconomics and the Market for Computer Services." *Computing Surveys,* vol. 7, no. 2, pp. 95–111, June 1975.

Couger, J. D., et al. "curriculum Recommendations for Undergraduate Programs in Information Systems." *Communications of the Association for Computing Machinery,* vol. 16, no. 12, pp. 727–749, Dec. 1973.

Cyert, R. M., and J. G. March. *A Behavioral Theory of the Firm.* Englewood Cliffs, N.J.: Prentice-Hall, 1963.

———, H. A. Simon, and D. B. Trow. "Observation of a Business Decision." *Journal of Business,* vol. 29, no. 4, pp. 237–248, Oct. 1956.

Dantzig, G. B. *Operations Research in the World of Today and Tomorrow.* Berkeley: Institute of Engineering Research, University of California at Berkeley, Report ORC 65-7, 1965.

Davis, G. B. *Management Information Systems: Conceptual Foundations, Structure, and Development.* New York: McGraw-Hill, 1973.

Dearborn, D. C., and H. A. Simon. "The Identification of Executives." In H. A. Simon, *Administrative Behavior* (3rd ed.), pp. 309–314. New York: Free Press, 1976.

Dearden, J. "Myth of Real-Time Management Information." *Harvard Business Review,* vol. 44, no. 3, pp. 123–132, 1966.

———. "MIS Is a Mirage." *Harvard Business Review,* vol. 50, no. 1, pp. 90–99, 1972.

Demski, J. S. *Information Analysis.* Reading, Mass.: Addison-Wesley, 1972.

Diebold, J. "Bad Decisions on Computer Use." *Harvard Business Review*, vol. 47, no. 1, pp. 14–28, 1969.

Doktor, R. H. "Development and Mapping of Certain Cognitive Styles of Problem-solving." Ph.D. dissertation, Stanford University, 1969.

———. "Cognitive Characteristics in the Design of Implementation Facilitation Subsystems." Paper presented at the Implementation II Conference, University of Pittsburgh, Pittsburgh, Penn., February 18–20, 1976.

———, and W. F. Hamilton. "Cognitive Style and the Acceptance of Management Science Recommendations." *Management Science*, vol. 19, no. 8, pp. 884–894. April 1973.

Donovan, J. J. *Database System Approach to Management Decision Support*. Cambridge, Mass.: Center for Information Systems Research, M.I.T., Report CISR-25, 1976.

———, et al. "An Application of a Generalized Management Information System to Energy Policy and Decision Making—The User's View." *American Federation of Information Processing Societies Conference Proceedings*, 1975 National Computer Conference, pp. 681–686, May 1975.

———, and S. E. Madnick. "Hierarchial Approach to Computer System Integrity." *IBM Systems Journal*, vol. 14, no. 2, pp. 188–202, 1975.

——— and ———. *Institutional and Ad hoc Decision Support Systems and Their Effective Use*. Cambridge, Mass.: Center for Information Systems Research, M.I.T., Report CISR-27, Nov. 1976.

——— and ———. "Virtual Machine Advantages in Security, Integrity, and Decision Support Systems." *IBM Systems Journal*, vol. 15, no. 3, pp. 270–278, 1976.

Dutton, J. M., and W. H. Starbuck. *Computer Simulation of Human Behavior*. New York: Wiley, 1971.

Dyer, J. S. "An Empirical Investigation of a Man-Machine Interactive Approach to the Solution of a Multiple Criteria Problem." In J. L. Cochrane and M. Zeleny (eds.), *Multicriteria Decision Making*, pp. 202–216. Columbia, S.C.: University of South Carolina Press, 1973.

Edelman, F. "Art and Science of Competitive Bidding." *Harvard Business Review*, vol. 43, no. 4, pp. 53–66, July-August, 1965.

EDP Analyzer. "APL and Decision Support Systems." *EDP Analyzer*, vol. 14, no. 5, May 1976.

Eilon, S. "Goals and Constraints in Decision Making." *Operational Research Quarterly*, vol. 23, no. 1, pp. 3–15, March 1972.

Emery, J. C. "The Economics of Information." *Wharton Quarterly*, vol. 2, no. 1, pp. 2–7, Fall 1967.

Emshoff, J. R., and R. L. Sisson. *Design and Use of Computer Simulation Models*. New York: Macmillan, 1970.

Erikson, E. *Young Man Luther*. New York: Norton, 1958.

Feigenbaum, E. A., and J. Feldman (eds.). *Computers and Thought*. New York: McGraw-Hill, 1963.

Fine, R. *The Psychology of the Chess Player*. New York: Dover, 1967.

Forrester, J. W. *Urban Dynamics*. Cambridge, Mass.: M.I.T., 1969.

Geoffrion, A. M., J. S. Dyer, and A. Feinberg. "An Interactive Approach for Multicriterion Optimization with an Application to the Operation of an Academic Department." *Management Science,* vol. 19, no. 4, pt. 1, pp. 357–368, Dec. 1972.

Gerrity, T. P., Jr. "The Design of Man-Machine Decision Systems." Ph.D. dissertation, M.I.T., 1970.

———. "The Design of Man-Machine Decision Systems: An Application to Portfolio Management." *Sloan Management Review,* vol. 12, no. 2, pp. 59–75, Winter 1971.

Gershefski, G. Q. "Building a Corporate Financial Model." *Harvard Business Review,* vol. 47, no. 4, pp. 61–72, July-August 1969.

———. "Corporate Models—The State of the Art." *Management Science,* vol. 16, no. 6, pp. B303–321, Feb. 1970.

Gerson, E. M. "Rationalization and Varieties of Technical Work." Unpublished paper. San Francisco: Pragmatica Systems, Inc., 1977.

Gibson, C. F. "A Methodology for Implementation Research." In R. L. Schultz and D. P. Slevin (eds.), *Implementing Operations Research/Management Science,* part II, pp. 53–73. New York: American Elsevier, 1975.

———. "A Contingency Theory of Implementation: Implications for Research and Practice." Paper presented at the Implementation II Conference, University of Pittsburgh, Pittsburgh, Penn., February 18–20, 1976.

———, and J. S. Hammond. "Contrasting Approaches for Facilitating the Implementation of Management Science." Paper presented at the Operations Research Society of America/The Institute of Management Sciences Joint National Meeting, Boston, April 22–24, 1974.

Ginzberg, M. J. "A Process Approach to Management Science Implementation." Ph.D. dissertation, M.I.T., 1975.

Gore, E. J. *Administrative Decision Making.* New York: Wiley, 1964.

Gorry, G. A., and M. S. Scott Morton. "A Framework for Management Information Systems." *Sloan Management Review,* vol. 13, no. 1, pp. 55–70, Fall 1971.

Grace, B. F. *A Case Study of Man/Computer Problem-Solving.* San Jose, Calif.: IBM Research Report RJ 1483, 1975.

———. *Training Users of Decision Support Systems.* San Jose, Calif.: IBM Research Report RJ 1790, May 1976.

Grayson, C. J. "Management Science and Business Practice." *Harvard Business Review,* vol. 51, no. 4, pp. 41–48, July 1973.

Halbrecht, H. Z. "Through a Glass Darkly." *Interfaces,* vol. 2, no. 4, pp. 1–22, 1972.

———. "Great Ferrets Are Hard to Find (How to Hire the Compleat OR/MS Professional)." Paper presented at a Conference on the Implementation of Computer-based Decision Aids, Cambridge, Mass., Center for Information Systems Research, M.I.T., April 3–5, 1975.

Hall, W. K. "Strategic Planning Models: Are Top Managers Really Finding Them Useful?" *Journal of Business Policy,* vol. 3, no. 2, pp. 33–42, Winter 1972/1973.

Hammond, J. S., III. *Bud Mathaisal.* Boston: Intercollegiate Case Clearing House, no. 9371251, 1971.

———. "The Roles of the Manager and Management Scientist in Successful Implementation." *Sloan Management Review,* vol. 15, no. 2, pp. 1–24, Winter 1974.

Heany, D. F. "Is TIMS Talking to Itself?" *Management Science,* vol. 12, no. 4, pp. B146–155, Dec. 1965.

———. "Education—The Critical Link in Getting Managers to Use Management Systems." *Interfaces,* vol. 2, no. 3, pp. 1–7, May 1972.

Herzberg, F. *The Motivation to Work.* New York: Wiley, 1959.

Hirschman, A. O., and C. E. Lindblom. "Economic Development, Research and Development, Policy Making: Some Converging Views." *Behavioral Science,* vol. 7, no. 2, pp. 211–222, April 1962.

Holloway, C. A., and P. E. Mantey. *Implementation of an Interactive Graphics Model for Design of School Boundaries.* Stanford, Calif.: Stanford University Graduate School of Business, Research Paper 299, 1976.

———, et al. "An Interactive Procedure for the School Boundary Problem with Declining Enrollments." *Operations Research,* vol. 23, no. 2, pp. 191–206, March-April 1975.

Hoos, I. R. *Systems Analysis in Public Policy.* Berkeley: University of California Press, 1972.

Howard, R. A. "The Foundations of Decision Analysis." *Institute of Electrical and Electronics Engineers Transactions on Systems Science and Cybernetics,* Systems Science and Cybernetics Group, no. 4, 1968.

———, J. E. Matheson, and D. W. North. "The Decision to Seed Hurricanes." *Science,* vol. 176, no. 4040, pp. 1191–1202, June 16, 1972.

Hunt, J. G., and P. F. Newell. "Management in the 1980's Revisited." *Personnel Journal,* vol. 50, no. 1, pp. 35–43, Jan. 1971.

Huysmans, J. H. B. M. "The Effectiveness of the Cognitive Style Constraint in Implementing Operations Research Proposals." *Management Science,* vol. 17, no. 1, pp. 92–104, Sept. 1970.

———. *The Implementation of Operations Research: An Approach to the Joint Consideration of Social and Technological Aspects.* New York: Wiley, 1970.

———. "Operations Research Implementation and the Practice of Management." Paper presented at the Research Conference on the Implementation of OR/MS Models, University of Pittsburgh, Pittsburgh, Penn., November 15–17, 1973.

Kanter, J. *Management-oriented Management Information Systems,* 2nd ed. Englewood Cliffs, N.J.: Prentice-Hall, 1977.

Katz, D., and R. L. Kahn. "Organizations and the System Concept." In D. Katz and R. L. Kahn, *The Social Psychology of Organizations,* chap. 2. New York: Wiley, 1966.

Keen, P. G. W. "Cognitive Style and the Problem-solving Process: An Experiment." Cambridge, Mass.: Sloan School of Management, M.I.T., Working Paper 700-74, March 1974a.

————. "Decision Support Systems: An Overview." Paper presented at the Sixth Annual Conference of the Society for Management Information Systems Conference, San Francisco, September 11–13, 1974b.

————. "Towards a Behavioral Methodology for Study of OR/MS/MIS Implementation." Cambridge, Mass.: Sloan School of Management, M.I.T., Working Paper 701-74, 1974c.

————. "A Clinical Approach to Implementation." Cambridge, Mass.: Sloan School of Management, M.I.T., Working Paper 730-75, 1975a.

————. "Computer-Based Decision Aids: The Evaluation Problem." *Sloan Management Review*, vol. 16, no. 3, pp. 17–29, Spring 1975b.

———— (ed.). *The Implementation of Computer-Based Decision Aids.* Cambridge, Mass.: Proceedings of a Conference Sponsored by the Center for Information Systems Research, M.I.T., April 3–5, 1975c.

————. "Computer Systems for Top Managers: A Modest Proposal." *Sloan Management Review*, vol. 18, no. 1, pp. 1–17, Fall 1976a.

————. "Managing Organizational Change: The Role of MIS." In J. D. White (ed.), *Proceedings of the Sixth and Seventh Annual Conferences of the Society for Management Information Systems*, pp. 129–134. Ann Arbor: University of Michigan, July 1976b.

————. "The Evolving Concept of Optimality." In M. K. Starr and M. Zeleny (eds.), *Multi-Criteria Decision Making*, pp. 31–57. The Institute of Management Sciences (TIMS) Studies in the Management Sciences, vol. 6, 1977a.

————. *Implementation Research in MIS and OR/MS: Description versus Prescription.* Stanford, Calif.: Stanford Business School Research Paper no. 390, 1977b.

————. "The Intelligence Cycle: A Differentiated Perspective on Information Processing." *American Federation of Information Processing Societies Proceedings*, 1977 National Computer Conference, vol. 46, pp. 317–320, 1977c.

————, and E. M. Gerson. "The Politics of Software Engineering." *Datamation*, pp. 80–86, Nov. 1977.

Keeney, R. L., and H. Raiffa. *Decision with Multiple Objectives: Preferences and Value Tradeoffs.* New York: Wiley, 1976.

Keim, R. T., and R. H. Kilmann. "A Longitudinal Investigation of Alternative Implementation Processes: Traditional versus Behavioral Model Building with the MAPS Design Technology." In P. G. W. Keen (ed.), *The Implementation of Computer-Based Decision Aids.* Cambridge, Mass.: Proceedings of a Conference Sponsored by the Center for Information Systems Research, M.I.T., April 3–5, 1975.

Kelly, G. A. *The Psychology of Personal Constructs.* New York: Norton, 1955.

Kilmann, R. H., and W. W. McKelvey. "The MAPS Route to Better Organization Design." *California Management Review*, vol. 17, no. 3, pp. 23–31, Spring 1975.

————, and the MAPS Group. "MAPS as a Design Technology to Effectively Mobilize Resources for Social and Organizational Problem Solving." In R. H.

Kilmann, L. R. Pondy, and D. P. Slevin (eds.), *The Management of Organization Design: Strategies and Implementation,* vol. 1, pp. 251–294. New York: American Elsevier, 1976.

Klein, B., and W. Meckling. "Applications of Operations Research to Development Decisions." *Operations Research,* vol. 6, no. 3, pp. 352–363, May-June, 1958.

Knight, K. E. "A Study of Technological Innovation—The Evolution of Digital Computers." Ph.D. dissertation, Carnegie Institute of Technology, 1963.

Knuth, D. E. *The Art of Computer Programming.* Reading, Mass.: Addison-Wesley, 1968.

Kolb, D. A., and A. L. Frohman. "An Organization Development Approach to Consulting." *Sloan Management Review,* vol. 12, no. 1, pp. 51–65, Fall 1970.

Kriebel, C. H. "MIS Technology—A View of the Future." Paper presented at the Spring Joint Computer Conference, Atlantic City, N.J., May 16–18, 1972.

Larreché, J-C. "Managers and Marketing Models: A Search for a Better Match." Ph.D. dissertation, Stanford Business School, 1974.

———, and D. B. Montgomery. *A Framework for the Comparison of Marketing Models: A Delphi Study.* Cambridge, Mass.: Marketing Institute Technical Report 77-102, 1977.

Laudon, K. *Computers and Bureaucratic Reform.* New York: Wiley-Interscience, 1974.

Lave, C. A., and J. G. March. *An Introduction to Models in the Social Sciences.* New York: Harper & Row, 1975.

Lawrence, P. R., and J. W. Lorsch. *Organization and Environment.* Cambridge, Mass.: Division of Research, Harvard Business School, 1967.

Leavitt, H. J. "Applied Organizational Change in Industry: Structural, Technological and Humanistic Approaches." In J. G. March (ed.), *Handbook of Organizations.* Chicago: Rand McNally, 1965.

———. "Beyond the Analytic Manager." *California Management Review,* vol. 17, no. 3, pp. 5–12, Spring 1976; vol. 17, no. 4, pp. 11–21, Summer 1976.

———, and T. L. Whisler. "Management in the 1980's." *Harvard Business Review,* vol. 36, no. 6, pp. 41–48, Nov.-Dec. 1958.

Lewin, K. "Group Decision and Social Change." In T. M. Newcomb and E. L. Hartley (eds.), *Readings in Social Psychology,* pp. 330–344. New York: Holt, 1947.

Lindblom, C. W. "The Science of Muddling Through." *Public Administration Review,* vol. 19, no. 2, pp. 79–88, Spring 1959.

Little, J. D. C. "Models and Managers: The Concept of a Decision Calculus." *Management Science,* vol. 16, no. 8, pp. B466-485, April 1970.

———. "Brandaid." *Operations Research,* vol. 23, no. 4, pp. 628–673, May 1975.

Lucas, H. C., Jr., and R. B. Plimpton. "Technological Consulting in a Grass Roots, Action Oriented Organization." *Sloan Management Review,* vol. 14, no. 1, pp. 17–36, Fall 1972.

Luce, R. D., and H. Raiffa. *Games and Decisions.* New York: Wiley, 1957.

McCoubrey, C. A., and M. Sulg. "A Case Study of OR/MS Implementation in an Industrial Environment." In P. G. W. Keen (ed.), *The Implementation of*

Computer-Based Decision Aids. Cambridge, Mass : Proceedings of a Conference Sponsored by the Center for Information Systems Research, M.I.T., April 3–5, 1975.

McDonough, A. M. *Information Economics and Management Systems.* New York: McGraw-Hill, 1963.

McKenney, J. L., and P. G. W. Keen. "How Managers' Minds Work." *Harvard Business Review,* vol. 52, no. 3, pp. 79–90, May-June 1974.

McKinsey Corporation. *Unlocking the Computer's Profit Potential.* New York: McKinsey Corp., 1968.

Malhotra, A. *On Problem Diagnosis.* Yorktown Heights, N.Y.: IBM Thomas G. Watson Research Center Paper RC 5498, July 2, 1975.

March, J. G. "The Technology of Foolishness." *Civilkonomen,* vol. 18, no. 4, pp. 7–12, May 1971.

——, and H. A. Simon. *Organizations.* New York: Wiley, 1958.

Markowitz, H. M. *Portfolio Selection: Efficient Diversification of Investments.* New York: Wiley, 1959.

Mason, R. O., and I. I. Mitroff. "A Program for Research on Management Information Systems." *Management Science,* vol. 19, no. 5, pp. 475–487, Jan. 1973.

Meador, C. L., and D. N. Ness. "Decision Support Systems: An Application to Corporate Planning." *Sloan Management Review,* vol. 15, no. 2, pp. 51–68, Winter 1974.

Meadows, D. H., et al. *The Limits to Growth.* New York: Signet, 1972.

Meldman, J. "Decision Support Systems for Legal Research." Paper presented at the II Symposium Nacional de Systemas Computacionales, Monterrey, Mexico, March 15–18, 1977.

Miller, R. D. "Multidimensional Processes of Implementing Computer Based Models." D.B.A. thesis, Harvard Business School, 1974.

Minsky, M. *Computation, Finite and Infinite Machines.* Englewood Cliffs, N.J.: Prentice-Hall, 1967.

—— (ed.). *Semantic Information Processing.* Cambridge, Mass.: M.I.T., 1968.

Mintzberg, H. *The Nature of Managerial Work.* New York: Harper & Row, 1973.

Mitroff, I. I. *The Subjective Side of Science: A Philosophical Enquiry into the Psychology of the Apollo Moon Scientists.* New York: Elsevier, 1975.

Montgomery, D. B., and G. L. Urban. *Management Science in Marketing.* Englewood Cliffs, N.J.: Prentice-Hall, 1969.

—— and ——. "Marketing Decision-Information Systems: An Emerging View." *Journal of Marketing Research,* vol. 7, no. 2, pp. 226–234, May 1970.

Morgan, H. L., and J. V. Soden. "Understanding MIS Failures." *Data Base,* vol. 5, nos. 2, 3, 4, pp. 157–167, Winter 1973.

Morton, M. S. Scott. *Management Decision Systems: Computer Based Support for Decision Making.* Cambridge, Mass.: Division of Research, Harvard, 1971.

——. "Decision Support Systems: Some Lessons from an On-going Application." Paper presented at the International Federation for Information Processing Congress, Stockholm, Sweden, August 1974.

Moshowitz, A. *The Conquest of Will.* Reading, Mass.: Addison-Wesley, 1976.

Mumford, E. *Job Satisfaction: A Study of Computer Specialists.* London: Longmans, 1972.

———, and T. B. Ward. *Computers: Planning for People.* London: Batsford, 1968.

Neal, R. D., and M. Radnor. "Relation between Formal Procedures for Pursuing OR/MS Activities and OR/MS Group Success." *Operations Research,* vol. 21, no. 2, pp. 451–474, March-April 1973.

Ness, D. N. "Decision Support Systems: Theories of Design." Paper presented at the Wharton Office of Naval Research Conference on Decision Support Systems, University of Pennsylvania, Philadelphia, Penn., November 4–7, 1975.

Newell, A., J. C. Shaw, and H. A. Simon. "Empirical Explorations of the Logic Theory Machine: A Case Study in Heuristics." *Proceedings of the 1957 Western Joint Computer Conference,* pp. 218–230, February 26–28, 1957.

———, ———, and ———. "Elements of a Theory of Human Problem Solving." *Psychological Review,* vol. 65, pp. 151–166, 1958.

———, ———, and ———. "The Processes of Creative Thinking." In H. E. Gruber and M. Wertheimer (eds.), *Contemporary Approaches to Creative Thinking.* New York: Atherton, 1962.

———, and H. A. Simon. *Human Problem Solving.* Englewood Cliffs, N.J.: Prentice-Hall, 1972.

Nolan, R. L. "Plight of the EDP Manager." *Harvard Business Review,* vol. 51, no. 3, pp. 143–152, May-June 1973a.

———. "Managing the Computer Resource: A Stage Hypothesis." *Communications of the Association for Computing Machinery,* vol. 16, no. 7, pp. 399–405, July 1973b.

———, and C. F. Gibson. "Managing the Four Stages of EDP Growth." *Harvard Business Review,* vol. 52, no. 1, pp. 76–88, Jan.-Feb. 1974.

Pettigrew, A. *The Politics of Organizational Decision Making.* London: Tavistock, 1976.

Pounds, W. F. "The Process of Problem Finding." *Industrial Management Review,* vol. 11, no. 1, pp. 1–19, Fall 1969.

Pressman, J. L., and A. Wildavsky. *Implementation.* Berkeley: University of California Press, 1973.

Quade, E. S., and W. I. Boucher (eds.). *Systems Analysis and Policy Planning: Applications in Defense.* New York: Elsevier, 1968.

Radnor, M., et al. "Integration and Utilization of Management Science Activities in Organizations." *Operational Research Quarterly,* vol. 19, no. 2, pp. 117–141, June 1968.

———, et al. "Implementation in Operations Research and R & D in Government and Business Organization." *Operations Research,* vol. 18, no. 6, pp. 967–991, Nov.-Dec. 1970.

Rubenstein, A. H., et al. "Some Organizational Factors Relating to the Effectiveness of Management Science Groups in Industry." *Management Science,* vol. 13, no. 8, pp. B508–518, 1967.

Sammet, J. *Programming Languages: History and Fundamentals.* Englewood Cliffs, N.J.: Prentice-Hall, 1969.

Samuels, A. L. "Some Studies in Machine Learning Using the Game of Checkers." *IBM Journal of Research and Development*, vol. 3, no. 3, pp. 210–229, July 1959.

Schein, E. H. "Management Development as a Process of Influence." *Industrial Management Review*, vol. 2, no. 2, pp. 59–77, Spring 1961.

———. *Brainwashing*. Cambridge, Mass.: Center for International Studies, M.I.T., 1961.

Schelling, T. C. *The Strategy of Conflict*. Oxford: Oxford University Press, 1963.

Schroder, H. M., M. J. Driver, and S. Steufert. *Human Information Processing*. New York: Holt, 1967.

Schultz, G. P., and T. L. Whisler (eds.). *Management Organization and the Computer*. Glencoe, Ill: Free Press, 1960.

Shannon, C. E., and W. Weaver. *A Mathematical Theory of Communication*. Urbana, Ill.: University of Illinois Press, 1949.

Shannon, R. E. *Systems Simulation: The Art and Science*. Englewood Cliffs, N.J.: Prentice-Hall, 1975.

Sharpe, W. F. "A Simplified Model for Portfolio Analysis." *Management Science*, vol. 9, no. 10, pp. 277–293, Jan. 1963.

Shortliffe, E. H. *Computer-Based Medical Consultations: MYCIN*. New York: Elsevier, 1976.

Simon, H. A. "A Behavioral Model of Rational Choice." In H. A. Simon, *Models of Man*, pp. 241–260. New York: Wiley, 1957.

———. *The New Science of Management Decision*. New York: Harper & Row, 1960.

———. *The Shape of Automation for Men and Management*. New York: Harper & Row, 1965.

———. *Sciences of the Artificial*. Cambridge, Mass.: M.I.T., 1969.

———. *Administrative Behavior*, 3rd ed. New York: Macmillan, 1976.

———, and A. Newell. "Heuristic Problem Solving: The Next Advance in Operations Research." *Operations Research*, vol. 6, no. 1, pp. 1–10, Jan.-Feb. 1958.

Sorensen, R. E., and D. E. Zand. "Improving the Implementation of OR/MS Models by Applying the Lewis/Schein Theory of Change." Paper presented at the Research Conference on the Implementation of OR/MS Models, University of Pittsburgh, Pittsburgh, Penn., November 15–17, 1973.

Souder, W. E. "Analytical Effectiveness of Mathematical Models for R & D Project Selection." *Management Science*, vol. 19, no. 8, pp. 907–923, April 1973.

Stabell, C. B. "Individual Differences in Managerial Decision Making Processes: A Study of Conversational Computer Usage." Ph.D. dissertation, M.I.T., 1974a.

———. "On the Development of the Decision Support Systems as a Marketing Problem." Paper presented at the International Federation for Information Processing Congress, Stockholm, Sweden, August 1974b.

———. "Design and Implementation of Decision Support Systems: Some Implications of a Recent Study." In P. G. W. Keen (ed.), *The Implementation of Computer-Based Decision Aids*. Cambridge, Mass.: Proceedings of a Conference Sponsored by the Center for Information Systems Research, M.I.T., April 3–5, 1975.

——. "Decision Research: Description and Diagnosis of Decision Making in Organizations." In D. Heradstreit and O. Narvesen (eds.), *Decision Making Research: Some Developments.* Oslo, Norway: Norsk Utenriks politisck Institute, 1977.

Starr, M. K. "The Politics of Management Science." *Interfaces,* vol. 1, no. 4, pp. 31–37, June 1971.

——, and M. Zeleny (eds.). *Multi-criteria Decision Making.* The Institute of Management Sciences Studies in the Management Sciences, vol. 6, 1977.

Steinbruner, J. D. *The Cybernetic Theory of Decision.* Princeton, N.J.: Princeton University Press, 1974.

Sterling, T. D. "Humanized Computer Systems." *Science,* vol. 190, no. 4220, pp. 1168–1172, Dec. 19, 1975.

Takatsuki, T., et al. "Packet Switched Network in Japan." *American Federation of Information Processing Societies Conference Proceedings,* 1977 National Computer Conference, vol. 46, pp. 615–621, 1977.

Terrell, D. "Neighborhood Computer Stores—The Answers to Microcomputer Marketing." *American Federation of Information Processing Societies Conference Proceedings,* 1977 National Computer Conference, vol. 46, pp. 999–1004, 1977.

Tesler, L. "Computer Networks." *People's Computers,* vol. 6, no. 2, pp. 15–17, 1977.

Urban, G. L. "A Model for the Management of a Family Planning System." *Operations Research,* vol. 22, no. 2, pp. 205–233, March-April 1974a.

——. "Building Models for Decision Makers." *Interfaces,* vol. 4, no. 3, pp. 1–11, May 1974b.

Vertinsky, I., R. T. Barth, and V. F. Mitchell. "A Study of OR/MS Implementation as a Social Change Process." In R. L. Schultz and D. P. Slevin, *Implementing Operations Research/Management Science,* pp. 253–272. New York: American Elsevier, 1975.

Wagner, H. M. "The ABC's of OR." *Operations Research,* vol. 19, no. 6, pp. 1259–1281, Oct. 1971.

——. "A Managerial Focus on Systems Implementation." In P. G. W. Keen (ed.), *The Implementation of Computer-Based Decision Aids.* Cambridge, Mass.: Proceedings of a Conference Sponsored by the Center for Information Systems Research, M.I.T., April 3–5, 1975a.

——. *Principles of Operations Research.* Englewood Cliffs, N.J.: Prentice-Hall, 1975b.

Weizenbaum, J. *Computer Power and Human Reason.* San Francisco: Freeman, 1976.

Whisler, T. I. *Information Technology and Organizational Change.* Belmont, Calif.: Wadsworth, 1970.

Wiener, N. *Cybernetics or Control and Communication in the Animal and the Machine.* Cambridge, Mass.: M.I.T., 1948.

Wiest, J. D. "Heuristic Programs for Decision Making." *Harvard Business Review,* vol. 44, no. 5, pp. 129–143, Sept.-Oct. 1966.

Wildavsky, A. *The Politics of the Budgetary Process.* Boston: Little, Brown, 1964.

Wilensky, H. L. *Organizational Intelligence.* New York: Basic Books, 1967.

Winograd, T. *Understanding Natural Language.* New York: Academic, 1972.

Winston, P. H. *Artificial Intelligence.* Reading, Mass.: Addison-Wesley, 1977.

Withington, F. G. "Five Generations of Computer Use." *Harvard Business Review,* vol. 52, no. 4, pp. 99–108, July-August 1974.

Woolsey, R. E. D. "Operations Research and Management Science Today, or, Does an Education in Checkers Really Prepare One for a Life of Chess?" *Operations Research,* vol. 20, no. 3, pp. 729–737, May-June 1972.

———. "The Measure of MS/OR Applications or Let's Hear It for the Bean Counters." *Interfaces,* vol. 5, no. 4, pp. 66–69, August 1975.

Zand, D. E., and R. E. Sorensen. "Theory of Change and the Effective Use of Management Science." *Administrative Science Quarterly,* vol. 20, no. 4, pp. 532–545, Dec. 1975.

Zeleny, M. *Linear Multiobjective Programming.* Berlin: Springer-Verlag, 1974.

Zionts, S., and J. Wallenius. "An Interactive Programming Method for Solving the Multiple Criteria Problem." *Management Science,* vol. 22, no. 6, pp. 652–663, Feb. 1976.

INDEX